Between Pit and Pedestal

Women in the Middle Ages

Manesse Manuscript
Munich, ca. 1300

Dedication

With gratitude to my parents Walter Keith and Louise Newman, my aunt Myra Boone, and my husband Craig. And to my daughters Lisa and Melody, in the hope that no men will ever be misguided enough to expect them to stay put either on a pedestal or in a pit.

Marty Newman Williams

To my husband Russ, my children Melissa and Jarrett, and my parents Patricia and Frederick Schmidt.

Anne Echols

BETWEEN PIT AND PEDESTAL

Women in the Middle Ages

by
MARTY NEWMAN WILLIAMS
and
ANNE ECHOLS

Markus Wiener Publishers
Princeton

For information write to:
Markus Wiener Publishers
231 Nassau Street, Princeton, NJ 08542

LIBRARY OF CONGRESS CATALOGING-IN-PUBLICATION DATA

BETWEEN PIT AND PEDESTAL: WOMEN IN THE MIDDLE AGES
BY MARTY NEWMAN WILLIAMS AND ANNE ECHOLS

INCLUDES BIBLIOGRAPHICAL REFERENCES AND INDEX.
ISBN 0-910129-33-9 (HC) ISBN 0-910129-34-7 (PB)
1. WOMEN—HISTORY—MIDDLE AGES, 500–1500.
I. ECHOLS, ANNE. II. TITLE.
HQ1143.W55 1993
305.4'09'02—DC20 93-11298
CIP

THE ILLUSTRATIONS IN THE TEXT ARE REPRODUCED COURTESY OF THE FOLLOWING SOURCES: Österreichische Nationalbibliothek, Vienna; Würtenbergische Landesbibliothek, Stuttgart; Bayerische Staatsbibliothek, Munich; British Library, London; The Governing Body of Christ Church, Oxford; Bibliothèque Nationale, Paris; Pierpont Morgan Library, New York City; Beinecke Library, New Haven.

Cover Design: Cheryl Mirkin

This book has been composed in Palatino by Charles A. Cordes, Winona, MN.

Printed on acid-free paper by Princeton Academic Press, Lawrenceville, NJ

CONTENTS

Scribe presenting *Consolations of Philosophy* to Margaret of York.
Flemish, ca. 1476; *Universitätsbibliothek, Jena*

INTRODUCTION

Despite a plethora of recent books on the subject, most people still seem to think that medieval women did little other than sew, pray, and have babies. As any medieval scholar can attest, however, this is not an accurate portrayal of all women's roles during the Middle Ages. In fact, to keep this book at a reasonable length for general readers, we had to leave out numerous examples of medieval women who managed huge estates, ruled countries, became spies, played tennis, went to war, composed poetry, took the veil, practiced medicine, presided as judges, cast evil spells on their neighbors, offered pleasure at a price, or were an economic force to be reckoned with in a number of crafts and trades. Although it would be misleading to assert that women were as powerful, active, or important as men, the other side of the coin, totally ignoring medieval women, is equally inaccurate.

We should also mention, however, that many sources tend to encourage misconceptions about medieval women and their roles. During the Middle Ages, male authors often portrayed women as creatures from the pit of hell, sisters of Eve—weak, lusty, and generally corrupt. Other contemporary writers placed females on a pedestal at the opposite end of the spectrum, claiming they were potentially more like the Virgin Mary—beautiful, kind, sweet, pure, chaste, and obedient. Neither of these perceptions is very helpful to modern historians searching for a picture of the real medieval women who had to cope with life between the theoretical pits and pedestals.

Since the fifteenth century, writers have generally either ignored medieval women or romanticized them (as Victorian authors and scholars were especially apt to do). Recent historians have begun remedying this situation by doing a vast amount of research on women's work, family patterns, the lower classes, feminine roles, infanticide, and so on. Since much of this impressive body of work is very specialized, it has largely remained within the scholarly community. Rather than new research or an examination of a single topic, this book is a synthesis of current findings—an overview that presents an introduction to the wide diversity of feminine roles and experiences from approximately the years A.D. 1000 through A.D. 1500. Though Italy was in "mid-Renaissance" by this time, we include a few fifteenth-century Italian women to establish a broad spectrum of feminine activities and experiences during all these years across the face of much of the known world. Naturally, there are no universal answers about what their lives were like, but looking at a variety of women from different times and regions enables the reader to see certain patterns emerging for women who lived between the eleventh and sixteenth centuries.

We cover England and France most fully, but also frequently mention Germany, Italy, and Spain. We have even included some women from such areas as the Baltic lands, Scandinavia, and Byzantium. Few of our stories constitute mini-biographies, though we use an anecdotal approach and occasionally offer different views of a particular woman. For instance, Joan of Arc's story opens a window onto medieval superstitions, political machinery, and ecclesiastical laws and trials. Similarly, the redoubtable Eleanor of Aquitaine appears in the guise of an ambitious politician, a jealous wife, an efficient administrator, a manipulative parent, and a patroness of new literary genres. Since these remarkable women were not always representative of feminine society as a whole, many of "our" women—lay medical practitioners, clothworkers, prostitutes, and peasant housewives, for example—led much more conventional lives.

We begin with a very brief discussion of the literary framework that designated woman's theoretical position. This includes a few of the ideas male authors expressed about feminine nature, and some of the women writers who offered similar theories or rebuttals. The first chapter deals with words, but the body of the book illustrates some one thousand medieval women in action. Chapters Two through Four are concerned with basic necessities such as health, homes, food, and jobs, while the following two chapters discuss women's personal ties with friends, lovers, husbands, children, and parents. Since their relationship with God and His church was equally important, Chapters Seven through Ten examine women's spiritual roles, including those of pious laywomen, saints, nuns, anchoresses, Beguines, heretics, and even "witches."

Chapters Eleven through Thirteen cover more temporal subjects—women under numerous legal jurisdictions, their position in feudalism, and their roles as rulers, consorts, and regents. The final three chapters are devoted to feminine cultural activities in such fields as entertainment, education, literature, and art. For readers who may be unfamiliar with medieval history and terms, we have included several brief guides at the end of the book. Appendix I describes socio-economic class lines, Appendix II explains money and the cost of living, Appendix III discusses women's life expectancies, and the Glossary defines some unfamiliar terms.

The authors would like to thank everyone who helped us while this work was in progress. In particular, Dr. Mary Flowers Braswell of the University of Alabama at Birmingham offered valuable editorial suggestions, Sara Berman read several drafts of the manuscript with an eye to clarity and diction, and Lisa Cutler edited the final draft. The talents, patience, and support of various librarians at both Emory University and the main branch of the Spartanburg County Library are equally appreciated. We are also indebted to Susan Hollingshead and Robert Gordon for technical advice on making our computers "user friendlier." Finally, John Paul Schmidt deserves credit for his help in translating Spanish sources.

Adam and Eve; the snake with the head of a woman.
Österreichische Nationalbibliothek, Vienna

Between Pit and Pedestal

The Virgin reads while Joseph tends the Baby Jesus.
Northern French. Early fifteenth century.
Walters Art Gallery, Baltimore, Maryland

Chapter One

WRITTEN WITH YOUR OWN HAND

Medieval Writers on Women's Nature and Roles

No man was as evil as Eve, but no entirely human man was as nearly perfect as the Virgin Mary. Throughout the Middle Ages this basic statement was so popular that it was expressed in a variety of ways and a number of languages. It is also an excellent synopsis of the dual nature of woman's position in medieval theory. In philosophy and literature, womankind occupied either the pit of hell with Eve or the pedestal of heaven with Mary. Woman's literary presence in between those two extremes was rare, but neither stereotype was especially helpful to the majority of real women—those *between pit and pedestal.*

Male authors continuously tried to define feminine nature because they so often used women as symbols of good and evil. Among secular writers, courtly poets were particularly fond of employing female characters to illustrate two opposing aspects of men's psyches. These troubadour poets used good women to represent a noble kind of love that could awaken man to a new awareness of himself and to higher aspirations. The same poets used baser women to represent temporal desires—a lusty type of love that could lure men away from their duties.[1] As set down by the twelfth-century poet Andreas Capellanus, chivalric behavior, courtly love, and troubadour poetry were applicable only to the noble classes. Another rule was that marriage and love were incompatible, especially since marriages were almost always arranged by parents or guardians. Though the adored lady could not be her lover's wife, someone else's wife was acceptable. The woman's superiority to her lover was another essential ingredient, so he was required to serve her with humility.

Love poems written in this courtly tradition heaped praise on women. The twelfth-century French poet Peire Vidal said of his love, "she is the finest and gentlest lady the world has ever seen." Bertran de Born, another twelfth-century French troubadour, wrote that no woman was "so lovely and worthy" as the noble lady he admired. He extolled her "rich, joyous body," her gaiety, and her "rich, true merit."[2] Nor did lavish admiration end with troubadours. The most famous Italian poet, Dante Alighieri (1265–1321), used equally extravagant language in praise of Beatrice, who was "as high as Nature's skill can soar." In fourteenth-century Italy, Francesco Petrarch claimed his Laura:

> Did not walk in any mortal way,
> But with angelic progress; when she spoke,
> Unearthly voices sang in unison.
> She seemed divine among the dreary folk
> Of earth.[3]

At first glance, all this poetry appeared to elevate the status of womankind by extolling feminine perfection. In the long run, however, such high-flown praise merely set noblewomen atop a pedestal. It was very difficult for them to descend from those dizzying heights in order to compete with men in the real world.

Several other genres satirized the ideals of the courtly tradition. Comic stories in verse called *fabliaux* sometimes ridiculed the typical adulterous lovers of troubadour poetry by depicting them as women whose amorous knights were their own husbands. In some French *fabliaux*, the heroines cleverly outwit the male characters, and occasionally women are even the more sympathetic characters. On the other hand, these tales may strike modern readers as anti-feminine because the women are usually cunning and sly, rather than honest and assertive.[4]

A more blatantly anti-feminist French satire, *The Fifteen Joys of Marriage,* illustrates a common male view that women are treacherous and unscrupulous. In this poem, one heroine/villain is a mother who deceives an unsuspecting suitor in order to marry off her pregnant daughter. The mother even teaches the girl: "How she right maidenly shall her demean,/As though she were a holy virgin clean."[5] The poet not only condemned the mother's treachery, but also belittled the foolish young girl who had lost her virginity—

a highly prized commodity. The Italian poet Lodovico Ariosto (1474–1533) expressed this sentiment: "A virgin is like unto a rose." As soon as she lost her virginity, however, he claimed that: "Her favor, grace, and beauty, all are lost."[6]

Medieval writers frequently denigrated women for their moral inferiority, especially their sexual insatiability. They traditionally depicted old women as nefarious hags, portrayed wives as betrayers of their husbands, and pictured girls as coquettes or fools. Jean de Meung's portion of the *Romance of the Rose* contained particularly virulent abuse of women. Around the year 1230, Guillaume de Lorris started this poem as an allegory of love based on a garden motif. When Jean de Meung finished the popular work some fifty years later, however, he characterized females as avaricious, lusty, tyrannical deceivers. His portion of the romance abounded in anti-feminine tirades, such as "women are nearly all eager to take and greedy to ravish and devour," and they always "wish to torment and despoil [their] sweetheart[s]." In a lengthy speech, de Meung's character Old Woman advises: "Any woman who [loves only one man] is a fool; she should have several friends, and, if possible, act so as to delight them [all]."[7]

An elderly female, often a very lusty one, was extremely common as a stereotypical "bad woman" in men's writings. A verse written by the Scottish poet William Dunbar (c.1500) includes such an older woman who has just buried her second husband. Although she wears the proper mourning cloak, the new widow casts kind looks on all the presentable men who pass by. She even keeps a sponge under her cloak to wet her eyes so she can appear to be crying. She sagely tells her friends that truth may have "a fair name, but falsehood fares better." Dunbar had probably been influenced by the works of Geoffrey Chaucer, the most important poet of fourteenth-century England and author of *The Canterbury Tales.* At her fourth husband's funeral, Chaucer's Alisoun, the *Wife of Bath,* covers her face with a kerchief so she can appear properly grief-stricken while still noticing all the eligible men around her.[8]

Written mainly by celibate males, religious didactic treatises also tended to exaggerate good and bad feminine qualities, placing women either in a pit of degradation or atop a pedestal of virtue. Female characters often personified two male images of women—as the source and symbol of man's Fall from Grace, or as the source and symbol of his salvation. Of these, the negative view was the more common. Scriptural exegesis (explanation or interpretation) was one of the most anti-feminine forms of medieval literature, and theologians were among the most zealous detractors of women. Marbode, an eleventh-century bishop of Rennes, warned men:

> Of the numberless snares that the crafty enemy spreads for us . . . the worst is woman, sad stem, evil root, vicious fount . . . honey and poison.

Similarly, the famed theologian and scientist Albertus Magnus (d.1280) cautioned, "Woman is a stranger to fidelity . . . beware of every woman as one would of a poisoned serpent."[9]

Even more often than secular authors, theologians reviled women for yielding to their sinful sexual appetites. In the symbolism of religious writings, whores represented heresies since those false doctrines were strongly identified with sexual activity.[10] Virgins and martyrs, on the other hand, were the most highly esteemed women. The majority of early saints' legends (hagiography) concerned celibate men and women who opted for death rather than engage in sexual intimacy. Because saintly women's stories were expected to adhere to an approved pattern, biographers sometimes even changed the facts about women whose actual lives fell short of the mark to make their *vitae* (lives) conform to the stereotypes. For this reason, hagiographical literature is not always the best source for reliable biographical data. Hemmed in by monastic traditions, these works often reveal less about the pious women they extol than about the expectations of the men who wrote the *vitae*.

Much of the ecclesiastical writing about woman and her nature depended a great deal on varying interpretations of the figure of Eve. Tertullian, an early Christian theologian (c.160–c.230), had written:

> And do you not know that you are Eve?
>
> God's sentence hangs still over all your sex and His punishment weighs down upon you. You are the devil's gateway; you are she who first violated the forbidden tree and broke the law of God.[11]

Medieval philosophers continued this tradition, using the biblical character of Eve as the basis on which to create a framework for understanding and controlling females. They discussed such questions as "How did Eve's sin affect her position in God's kingdom after the Fall?" Theologians believed the answer to this inquiry should determine the status of all subsequent generations of women.

In the twelfth century, a famed canonist named Gratian stated that Eve's punishment barred all women from exercising authority, teaching, serving as legal witnesses, or ruling estates or countries. A contemporary philosopher, Alan of Lille, equated feminine weakness with a lack of mental as well as physical capacity. Several thirteenth-century thinkers enlarged upon this topic. For instance, Saint Thomas Aquinas characterized women as "naturally of less strength and dignity than [men]." Adam of Courlandon agreed, asserting that the Devil chose to tempt Eve first because Adam's superior male intellect would have enabled him to repulse Satan's advances.[12]

Another thirteenth-century writer, Thomas of Chobham, took a kinder stance, claiming that feminine qualities such as sweetness, gentleness, and concern for the needy were positive benefits that could help save men. He advised wives to persuade their husbands to be more charitable and better Christians, stating "no priest can soften the heart of a man like his wife can."[13] His argument followed the lines of another traditional ecclesiastical belief: gentle feminine qualities, in chaste and pious women, could have a beneficial effect on hard-hearted, violent, and avaricious men. Saint Bernardino of Siena (b.1380) claimed:

> the most beautiful and useful thing . . . is to have a . . . wife who is good, modest, honest, temperate. . . . If she is full of charity, faith, humility, rectitude and patience . . . how great should be your mutual friendship![14]

The preceding writers illustrate that opinions about the position of women in relation to men varied a great deal. Even theologians who believed the Virgin had redeemed womankind were unable to reconcile her perfection with what they viewed as the truly deplorable nature of Eve. Moreover, their emphasis on Mary's virginity and rigidly pure spirit makes the adored Virgin seem as incomplete a woman as the despised Eve. Like secular male authors, ecclesiastical writers continued to deny women's individuality and humanity.

While some women writers approved male ideals, others refuted men's stereotypes of femininity. Only a few relegated their sex to hellish pits, but many designed their own pedestals—possibly hoping women could improve themselves and thereby disprove male perceptions about evil femininity. Whatever their theme or genre, most female writers presented more personal and realistic depictions of their gender. They often portrayed themselves, and other real women, as living in between the two extremes.

Female troubadours used the same courtly conventions as their male counterparts, but generally infused their works with a greater sense of personal involvement. Countess Beatrice de Dia (c.1130s–1160s), for example, described the intense pleasure a woman could experience in a satisfying sexual relationship. She urged women to give themselves to the men of their choice and dare to love "face-to-face." She admitted being excessively fond of her own amorous knight. Unashamed of her desires, Beatrice longed "to hold him pressed naked in my arms . . . I am giving my heart, my love, my mind, my life, my eyes."[15]

Among female romance writers, Marie de France (c.1150s–1180s) made the greatest break away from male conventions into the realm of feminine perception. In her *lais* (verse novelettes that she claimed were based on ancient Celtic legends), Marie gave women a right to their own emotional existence rather than depicting them as mere projections of men's images or wishes. Moreover, in contrast to male lyricists, she focused on the power of love itself. Love thereby gained a life of its own as an independent, redemptive force for both sexes. In a *lai* entitled *Yonec,* Marie's heroine imagines an ideal lover, and then wills him to materialize. The lady has great power in this relationship, and her lover claims he could never have "left my own land had you not asked for me." Love eventually frees the heroine from her unhappy marriage, and at the end of the story, the populace honors her for fulfilling her quest.

Rather than emphasizing love, Christine de Pisan—the first woman known to have been a successful professional writer—focused on feminine abilities. Around the turn of the fifteenth century in France, she openly criticized courtly conventions that encouraged men to view women merely as sexual objects. Christine countered this perception by citing numerous praiseworthy feminine qualities, such as devotion and generosity. She also advised men to esteem women for their abilities and usefulness—as partners to their husbands, as protectors and educators of the young, and as examples to others.[16] In *Le Livre de la Mutaçion de Fortune* (*The Book of Changing Fortunes*), Christine contrasted womanly traits with masculine brutality. She rejoiced that "nature de femme est debonnaire"—woman has a noble nature.[17] She also refuted male stereotypes of feminine mental deficiencies. Christine instead claimed "God . . . has granted that the mind of an intelligent woman can conceive, know, and retain all perceptible things."[18] Given this premise, it was only natural for her to envision a time when women would be valued helpers in the management of town, court, and rural systems.

Christine also eloquently disproved Jean de Meung's faulty logic in the *Romance of the Rose*. Denying that women seduce and deceive males, she questioned men: "Don't you allow yourselves to be made fools of? Do [women] go to your houses to seek you out, beg, or take you by force?" Christine insisted,

> there have . . . been, are now, and will always be women more valiant, more honest, better bred, and even wiser . . . than [men]. And some are even more versed in the affairs of state and have more virtuous habits, some have been responsible for reconciling their husbands with their enemies, and have borne their affairs and their secrets and their passions gently and confidentially, even when their husbands have been disagreeable and unfaithful.[19]

Christine claimed that unfair portrayals of women by male writers like Jean de Meung persuaded her to write what we might call her most "feminist" work, *The Book of the City of Ladies*. She protested that male authors concurred in one conclusion: "the behavior of women is inclined to and full of every vice." She urged her female audience,

> see how these men accuse you of so many vices in everything. Make liars of them all by showing forth your virtue, and prove their attacks false by acting well.[20]

In *The Book of the City of Ladies,* Christine transcended medieval society by envisioning an imaginary world where feminine traits were more than equal to masculine ones. She not only presented roseate dreams of feminine powers, but also extolled the virtues of many real women. She praised Valentine Visconti, duchess of Orléans, for her prudence, loyalty, piety, and virtue. Applauding the thirteenth-century French queen and regent, Blanche of Castile, Christine called the late queen "most wise and in every instance virtuous and noble." She noted that Blanche had administered the realm "so prudently that it was never better ruled by any man."[21]

Christine de Pisan was not the only woman author who acknowledged the existence of peculiarly feminine problems and qualities. Religious writers often addressed the issue of "otherness"—being female in a male-dominated society. Despite the prevalence of stereotypes about evil and promiscuous femininity, the female religious often saw herself and other women in a more favorable light. Some even adopted a superior tone and claimed a spiritual purity linked women with God. A thirteenth-century Flemish mystic named Hadewijch did not believe Christ despised her gender. In one of her visionary conversations with Jesus, He confirmed her self-confidence:

> Since you are so heroic and since you never yield, you are called the greatest heroine. It is right, therefore, that you should know me perfectly.[22]

The famed mystic and writer known as Saint Gertrude *the Great* (1256–1301) composed a prayer listing excellent female qualities, including goodness, tenderness, faithfulness, concern for others, and a great ability to love one's neighbor. Another thirteenth-century visionary, Mechtild of Magdeburg (1212–1283), even foreshadowed Christine de Pisan's feminine utopia by imagining a convent peopled by womanly virtues. In her nunnery of the spirit, "The abbess is true love . . . the schoolmistress is wisdom . . . the portress is watchfulness."[23]

Abbess Hildegarde of Bingen (1098–1179) particularly admired Saint Ursula, an early martyr who preferred to die rather than lose her virginity. Hildegarde believed women like Ursula were important examples of holiness because less saintly females could emulate them. Julian of Norwich (c.1343–1420s), an English recluse and mystic, also accepted female saints and feminine qualities as spiritually important images for women. In addition, she pointed out that God Himself was endowed with many traditionally "feminine" qualities. Through visions, God revealed to Julian that "God the Father" is also "God the Mother." Though these ideas were not unique to Julian, she was particularly eloquent in her descriptions of a God who was all-enfolding like clothing, and who exhibited tender, maternal love for His creatures.[24]

Despite the emotional realism often expressed by female writers, to a certain extent these women merely indicated agreement with male ideals. Moreover, these shining examples of literary theory were of little more assistance to real women than were the symbols of pit and pedestal found in male writings. The literary framework created by men not only designated women's theoretical position, but affected their opportunities in the real world. Men had only to point to the Bible or the writings of famous theologians in order to justify their subjugation of real women. Nor was literature the only roadblock for females. In a recently published essay about Christine de Pisan, Renate Blumenfeld-Kosinski stated that medieval society:

> valued nurturing, piety, and passivity in women above all else. This type of misogyny is more subtle than . . . [anti-feminist] tirades, but it is nonetheless present and powerful.[25]

Christine used her literary talents to surmount the limitations on her sex. Some other women also endeavored to overcome this pervasive misogyny. They attempted to carve out a niche for themselves, showing a range of ambitions, needs, abilities, and failings similar to those exhibited by men.

In common with many men, however, medieval women's options were often extremely limited. They also had the added burden of being female in a man's world where the ecclesiastical hierarchy, judicial systems, secular governments, educational institutions, medical establishment, and business community all discriminated against women. In both public and private life, the official position of females was always lower than that of their male counterparts. Even Christine de Pisan realized women could not live in her literary vision of a feminine utopia. Understanding the restrictions on women, she knew many of their most important contributions were made within their own homes and families. In the *Livre des Trois Vertus* (*Book of Three Virtues*), Christine included specific information about home management to assist females of various socio-economic classes. For instance, she advised the woman who ran a rural estate:

> [learn about] the rights of domain or fiefs . . . , contributions, the lord's rights of harvest, shared crops, and all such things . . . so that [you] won't be misled.[26]

By concentrating on everyday details, Christine brought her writing out of the theoretical realm and offered down-to-earth assistance to real medieval women.

The following fifteen chapters deal with those real women and the society in which they lived. Because women were the mothers, daughters, wives, lovers, partners, and victims of men, every aspect of life that had an impact on medieval males was of some importance to females. As the reader will discover, females played a variety of roles in the real world—the realm between the theoretical "ideals" of pit and pedestal.

Hard-working peasants at home.

Pierpont Morgan Library, New York City

EVERYDAY LIFE

Home of a burgher: Father calculating, son improving his writing skills, mother and daughter weaving.

Würtenbergische Landesbibliothek, Stuttgart

Chapter Two

Be It Ever So Humble

Women at Home—Household Management, Houses, Food, and Clothing

Saint Bernardino of Siena described a bachelor's home as a dirty, depressing establishment where the floor was filthy and possessions were rarely washed or mended. Saint Bernardino claimed the married man's home situation was entirely different. His wife not only made, mended, and washed linens and clothes, but also took care of the fire, water, lamp oil, food, and house cleaning. Moreover, she tended the sick, aided the poor, and brought up the children.[1]

Though Saint Bernardino exaggerated, a medieval home did provide a woman with more than a roof over her head, since it was also the primary realm of feminine work and influence. Men allowed this because they believed a woman's divinely appointed function was to serve as keeper of hearth and home. Man's usual symbol in marginalia was the plow, while woman's emblem was the distaff. This indicated their different areas of authority. Men were supposed to do active, outside work, while women undertook more passive occupations inside the home. No less an authority than Saint Thomas Aquinas justified this view of woman's natural realm. He opined that women existed for only two reasons: to assist procreation and to provide food and drink for men.[2]

The Nobility

Noblewomen usually supervised workers rather than performing most tasks themselves, but they were far from idle. The typical household included the noble's nuclear family and a large number of servants. When Richard Beauchamp, earl of Warwick, visited his first wife, Elizabeth Berkeley, at Berkeley castle in 1421, he brought more than sixty retainers with him to join the fifty-six people—including damsels, yeomen, and a laundress—already in residence at the castle.[3] Especially during the husband's frequent absences from home, the wife of a *magnate* (the most high-ranking and wealthiest of landholders) directed the officials who ran the large staff of servants, entertained a variety of people, controlled estate finances, provided for adequate supplies, and commanded the defenses of her home. In the spring and summer of 1265, Eleanor de Montfort, countess of Leicester, competently performed all those tasks. In addition, she kept in constant touch with her husband and sons while moving her household from castle to castle in preparation for war[4]—another common duty for a nobleman's wife.

Lesser nobles usually ran their estates along the same lines as those of the upper nobility, but these women did more jobs themselves. Dame Alice de Bryene's household accounts for the year 1413 revealed that a large number of guests and servants had to be fed, and a wide variety of goods were produced on and bought for her estates. Her steward acquired some of the supplies, but Alice herself was responsible for many expenditures, including the food she purchased and the wages she paid to her household servants.[5]

Most of Dame Alice's servants would have been men. Treatises on household management usually advised lords against hiring women lest flirting, jealousy, and immoral behavior disturb the home's peace and prosperity. As long as the family contained women and young children, however, some female servants were necessary. A very few of these women were of the lower classes. Among the women who served Eleanor de Montfort, countess of Leicester, were a resident laundress named Petronella who earned one *penny* a day, and an anonymous alewife who came in by the day to brew, a service for which she received five *shillings*.[6] Other servants were highborn ladies. The most important and highest ranking position was that of lady-in-waiting to the royal family. Edward IV's queen, Elizabeth Woodville, had two chief ladies-in-waiting—Anne, lady Bourchier, and Elizabeth, lady Scales. The queen's lesser ladies, like Alice Fogge and Joanna Norreis, were also gentlewomen.[7] Socially prominent women vied with one another to secure the few available positions with the royal families because this type of service was considered a personal honor, as well as a lucrative job.

Gently born women also filled some childcare positions. Katherine Swynford, daughter of one knight and widow of another, was the governess in charge of Elizabeth and Philippa, the daughters of Blanche of Lancaster and John of Gaunt. Other childcare providers were lower born. After Philippa of Hainault and Edward III of England had their first son, Edward (later known as the *Black Prince*), they hired Maud de Plympton to be his *bersatrix*, or cradle-rocker. Because wet nurses were so important, women who occupied this position for the greatest families were usually well compensated. Many also gained the respect and gratitude of their former charges. After Henry Tudor became King Henry VII of England, he called on his former nurse, a Welsh woman named Jane ap Hywel, to oversee the nursery he set up in the year 1491 for his own son, the future King Henry VIII.[8]

Highborn women, including those who served their queen, often followed the same basic pattern of service within their own households. In 1265, Isabella de Fortibus, one of the wealthiest heiresses in England, named Agnes de Monceaux, as her chief lady-in-waiting. Agnes held this post for twenty-eight quite profitable years. Among the rewards she collected for her services were manors in Dorset worth £80 per year, and later Isabella gave her a large annuity.

Home to titled, wealthy women like Isabella de Fortibus was usually a castle, especially in the early Middle Ages. Many tenth- and eleventh-century French and English castles were *motte and bailey* structures surrounded by fortifications like moats and walls. A tower, or *keep*, stood on a mound, or *motte*, above the *bailey*, a large flat space containing stables, barns, workshops, dormitories, and other buildings. This style was later superseded by a design employing several towers built into a thick curtain wall. Its defensive features included slits for archers and a walkway on top from which to drop stones and pour boiling water or tar on enemy soldiers below.

Such fortresses were nearly impenetrable, but were not particularly comfortable by present-day standards. Most castle activity—eating, sleeping, and conducting business—centered around a long, sparsely furnished hall warmed by a central fireplace. Women slept in a different room or a separate part of the hall, and the lord and his wife attained some privacy by retiring to their own relatively small room, or solar. This chamber usually had brightly colored walls, and might contain a few luxuries such as a heavy chair, chests, a cabinet for storing valuables, wall hangings, and cushions. In England, rugs became popular after Eleanor of Castile, wife of King Edward I, insisted on following the Spanish style of her former home by covering her floors with carpets.

At mealtime, everyone gathered in the great hall. Because candles were expensive and inefficient, most people rose with the sun and went to bed when it set. They ate breakfast around daybreak; served the largest meal, called dinner, at ten or eleven in the morning; and had supper in the late afternoon. Tables were usually covered by tablecloths and then set with spoons, and with cups made of silver, wood, or even imported coconuts with silver rims and feet. Both men and women carried their own knives in sheaths hanging from belts or girdles, and forks were not widely used for some centuries to come. In much of Western Europe, communal cups were passed around a group of several people, and the food itself was served on *trenchers*—most often hard, thick slices of bread. Diners simply threw the refuse and bones onto the rush-strewn floor, a practice highly appreciated by the household dogs. Housewives generally tried to alleviate this smelly situation by laying down clean rushes mixed with sweet woodruff to deodorize and freshen the room.[9] Around the year 1499 the learned visitor Erasmus noted that English nobles had beautifully decorated houses, but their floors often displayed some twenty years of accumulated refuse.

Floors may not have improved much, but homes and furnishings had changed a great deal. By the fifteenth century, many wealthy people lived in great houses that offered less protection but more comfort. This new type of residence usually had real windows and chimneys, and consisted of several stories with storage cellars, a great hall, a large chamber for the lord, separate sleeping quarters for children and servants, and a huge kitchen.

By then, urban centers with increased commercial interests had also made luxurious household accessories more available. Some furnishings were made by local artisans, while others were imported from distant areas. Innovations in cabinet-making produced higher quality furniture, and many pieces were works of art.

Leonardo da Vinci designed and decorated the cupboards that Beatrice d'Este used at the Castello of Milan in the late fifteenth century. New, more comfortable beds featured soft mattresses, *testers* (canopies), curtains, and frames of carved wooden panels. Around the year 1380, Joan, *the Fair Maid of Kent*, gave a *four-poster* (a bed enclosed by hanging curtains) to her son, King Richard II of England, which included ornate red velvet coverings adorned with gold, silver, and ostrich feathers.[10] A greater quantity and variety of kitchen and table utensils were also available. In his last testament (1388), Ralph, lord Neville, bequeathed his many personal possessions, including twenty-six beds and approximately eighteen dozen dishes, to numerous relatives. For instance, his daughter Eleanor de Lumley received two beds with canopies and curtains, eighteen dishes, four pots, and two basins.[11]

The noble's diet also improved over the years. The eleventh-century lord's food differed little, except in quantity, from that eaten by his *villeins* (unfree peasants). Both classes dined on cheese, fruit, soups or stews, fish—the only meat allowed on the many fasting days, like Fridays and all of Lent—and bread, the mainstay of nearly everyone's diet. White bread was a status symbol reserved for the wealthy, and sharing bread at a feast symbolized security, allowing guests to relax. Its biblical importance also made bread a favorite charitable offering from the nobility. Ale and wine were also dietary staples since everyone drank weakened versions of one or the other with meals. Most often the beverages were combined with other ingredients, so both were usually more nutritious than their present-day counterparts. A typical recipe for *cawdelle de almaunde,* for instance, contained almonds, ale, water, saffron, sugar, and salt.[12]

The amount of salt necessary to preserve meat made it too costly for many people to afford. The salt also made meat unappealing in taste and texture, so it was usually pounded, honeyed, minced, spiced, or boiled before roasting. Most people had kitchen herb gardens and, by the 1200s, access to Eastern markets enlarged the number of available spices. Pepper, cloves, dill, ginger, garlic, saffron, anise, fennel, mustard, and sugar were some of the most popular ingredients in medieval kitchens. But since sugar and imported spices were costly and hard to obtain, they were probably used only in small quantities.

Wealthy households hired male chefs, so women presumably had little to do with the proliferation of recipes that were eventually compiled in cookbooks as each country developed its own distinctive cuisine during the later Middle Ages. These manuscripts also reveal how much the nobility's food changed over the centuries, becoming much more varied and elaborate than that of the peasantry. French chefs concocted dishes like *tarte Bourbonnaise,* an egg, cheese, and cream concoction baked in pastry—the forerunner of today's quiche. Italians especially enjoyed a variety of pasta dishes, such as ravioli and sweetened lasagne. *Black Forest Venison Stew,* consisting of meat marinated in red wine and spices, was a favorite among the German nobility. English chefs specialized in pork recipes like *Pyg in a Coffin,* a boiled ham covered with a paste of ground pork, sage, rosemary, and other herbs and spices. The cook wrapped this in pastry, baked it, and finally served it with mustard/wine sauce.[13]

Most of these delicacies were reserved for the wealthy, who could patronize new markets, acquire innovative cooking tools, hire experienced chefs, and afford meat and imported foodstuffs. In addition to inventing new recipes, cooks designed very elaborate and ornamental dishes for their titled employers. Since brightly colored foods were very popular, the chef might use a saffron mixture to turn a dish bright gold or parsley to make another food turn green. At formal dinners, each course often ended with a *soteltie*—a pastry or jelly dessert carved to represent a fantastic figure such as Saint George, a stag, a crown, a dragon, or a panther. Pastry-enclosed dishes were popular not only as edible foods; entertaining banquet "intermissions," known as *entremets,* might also feature "pies" with live animals or people inside. Probably four and twenty blackbirds actually flew out of some medieval king's pie.[14]

The amounts and types of foods consumed at banquets seem astounding by modern standards, though we should note that apparently huge numbers of guests were present on some occasions. At Avignon in the 1340s, Pope Clement VI gave a feast that included approximately 13,000 birds, 1,000 sheep, 50,000 fruit pies, and 200 casks of wine.[15] Dinners commonly included a greater number of separate dishes than is usual today. At their wedding banquet in 1404, Henry IV of England and his bride Joan of Navarre partook of some one hundred individual dishes. The menu on such a festive occasion would feature delicacies like heads of boars, roasted swans, pheasants, cranes, and herons. After birds like swans and peacocks were cooked, the plumage was carefully re-attached and gilded.

Less wealthy individuals rarely had such elaborate feasts or ornamental dishes, but they usually kept amply stocked larders.

On an average day—Thursday, August 17, 1413, for example—Dame Alice de Bryene served one hundred and forty-six loaves of bread, one and a half quarters of beef, a lamb, two mutton joints, three quarters of bacon, and thirty pigeons, all washed down with ale and wine.[16] Large quantities of food were necessary because even the lesser nobility rarely dined alone. Alice de Bryene's household accounts show that on most days her kitchens provided for her large household, several guests, and a number of *boon workers*—villeins engaged in performing their required days of extra work on their lord's *demesne* (the lord's portion of the manor lands).

Dame Alice de Bryene could not have afforded to feast in the lavish style of Joan of Navarre; nor could Alice have emulated the elaborate fashions worn by such a wealthy noblewoman. In the early Middle Ages, "fashion" scarcely existed; people of various ranks and both sexes wore loose tunics, gowns, and cloaks of simple patterns and homespun materials. But these utilitarian styles soon began to change, partly because women wished to make themselves more attractive. Since the primary requirements for feminine beauty were blond hair and smooth, white skin, chroniclers and poets usually extolled princesses and other highborn women as "fair," regardless of their actual coloring. Clear skin was particularly valued, but was hard to maintain because frequent smallpox epidemics left so many people with pockmarks. Courtly poets mentioned numerous other ideals of feminine pulchritude, including a slim figure, white teeth, a small mouth with red lips, a straight nose, and a long, slender neck.

A variety of techniques were available to help a woman acquire or maintain her beauty. Blonds frequently wore opal necklaces because these stones were supposed to guard their hair against fading or darkening. A fourteenth-century English book of practical medicine, the *Liber de diversis medicinis,* gave several formulas for making freckles disappear. One of these advised anointing the face with blood from a bull or a hare. Women might chew plants, such as fennel, anise, or cinnamon, to keep their breath sweet, and Henri de Mandeville counseled them to use lavender or musk to keep their bodies and clothes from smelling bad.[17]

The effort to appear beautiful and feminine also changed clothing styles. Eleanor of Aquitaine was reputedly an early fashion leader, and was one of the first women to wear a long train on her gown, despite clerical strictures about dressing modestly.[18] Some churchmen even worried that devils or evil spirits could ride on trains. By the twelfth century, returning Crusaders began bringing Eastern styles and materials home to Western Europe, and even their own military attire became fashionable. A small hat called a *coif*, normally worn under a helmet, was quickly adopted as a non-military head covering for women. Women also adapted the *surcote*, originally a fabric coat worn over armor, to wear over a fitted *cote* (dress) with a little of the undergown peeking out.

The stylish fifteenth-century noblewoman might wear a lavish gown that was practically molded to her body at the top, while the hem encompassed some fifteen yards of material.[19] She probably also sported extremely long sleeves that had to be tied in knots to prevent them from trailing on the ground. Elaborate headdresses ranged from very wide hats with double horns, to tall, conical steeples with long veils known as *hennins*. In 1417, the doors of the castle of Vincennes had to be enlarged to allow these well-dressed women to pass from room to room without stooping, or losing their hats.[20]

Less attention was paid to children's fashions. Between the ages of four and six, children donned the same basic styles as their parents, but the more extravagant fashions were rarely worn before the age of twelve. Most men, on the other hand, loved colorful, showy attire. A fashionable fifteenth-century man might be clothed in a *houppeland*, a long and extremely full circle of material with a hole for his head. Less modest men sported its opposite number, a revealing garment known as the *short tunic*, which was so brief it left little to the imagination.[21] Well-dressed men also adopted an extremely long-toed style of footwear (*crackowes*). To keep from tripping over the points, some men tied the tips to chains worn at their knees. This did not remain popular for long because it was nearly impossible to walk comfortably with the points of one's shoes chained to one's knees.

The scarcity and costliness of many textiles helped to keep the most elaborate fashions reserved for the nobility. Most households produced some cloth for their own use, but wealthy women could also purchase a number of finer imported fabrics—sheer linens, silks, cottons, taffetas, brocades, velvets, and damasks. Fur was used according to a system based more on rank than on wealth. Queens wore ermine, magnates' wives donned squirrel coats, and lesser noblewomen settled for rabbit furs.[22] Fashion accessories were nearly as important as the garments themselves. Rich English women began wearing long, linen gloves in the thirteenth century as purely decorative items.[23] Another popular item, ornamental perfume dispensers called *musk-balls*, were often made of gold and decorated with gems.

Armor was not merely an accessory to the medieval nobleman. In the eleventh century, this consisted of little more than a coat of linked mail rings with a conical helmet. Very gradually armor became more efficient, and so expensive that its cost eventually made knighthood available only to the very wealthiest of high-ranking individuals. The knight became totally encased in metal-plated garments, while his helmet was enlarged until it completely covered his head and face. A few of the women who went on Crusades appeared in the chronicles dressed in their own *cuirasses* (breast plates with back plates fastened together) and helmets.

Observers sometimes criticized both men and women for being slaves to fashion. Franco Sacchetti, a Florentine writer, decried women's fashionable sleeves that were so big and long,

> they cannot raise a glass or take a mouthful without soiling both their sleeves and the tablecloth by upsetting the glasses on the table.

Sacchetti also ridiculed men who could not walk because of their long, pointed shoes, could not sit because of excess strings and laces, and could scarcely breathe with their necks crammed into overly tight hoods.[24] Similarly, in Geoffrey Chaucer's *Canterbury Tales*, the character of the *Parson* deplored the money women wasted having their gowns furred and embroidered, and sneered that these dresses were so long they trailed in the dung and mud. The *Parson* was equally revolted by noblemen who wore their tunics so short they were obscene.[25]

Other moralists inveighed only against the extravagances of feminine dress, which impoverished husbands while allowing women to exercise their vanity. Moreover, churchmen claimed that enhancing a woman's charms actually endangered men, because they might be seduced by feminine beauty. A different view was expressed by a *demi-mondaine* in Bologna named Nicolosa Sanuti. She castigated city officials who wanted to restrict women from donning sumptuous raiment. Rather than mere manifestations of vanity, Nicolosa urged, "Ornament and apparel, because they are our [women's] insignia of worth, we cannot suffer to be taken from us."[26]

Merchants and Artisans

The *Ménagier de Paris*, a wealthy Parisian merchant, wrote a book of instruction for his young bride that included details about cooking, managing a house and servants, caring for the sick, and even six ways of ridding the bed of fleas. These were only a few of the household tasks the typical affluent merchant's wife performed or supervised. She had to be an able administrator and organizer, as well as a tactful labor negotiator. She might purchase some fabric, but she usually also had to supervise home clothmaking—carding, spinning, weaving, and sewing. If she lived on a rural estate, the huge job of seeing to the provisions for the entire household might also fall on her shoulders. Since only cities had well-stocked marketplaces, this task involved acquiring, monitoring, and storing supplies well in advance of demand. Her provisioning duties would include supervising the following tasks: caring for the livestock, smoking meats, baking, brewing, cheese- and butter-making, storing provisions for winter, and tending the kitchen garden. Some wives also marketed surplus goods, ran a school for village children, taught manners to female boarders, and supervised the training of male boarders.

Margaret Paston, a well-off fifteenth-century Englishwoman, provides a good example of how these women rose above their many difficulties. The handicaps often included living on isolated estates and being involved in wars or feuds; Margaret herself had to defend her estates more than once. Like many other females, Margaret lacked formal education, so she memorized all estate details. She was further encumbered by frequent pregnancies, and by several small children who were underfoot most of the time. Her husband, John (I), was frequently absent from their home on business, so Margaret was usually in full charge of their family and estates.

Less affluent city women also performed a large variety of household tasks, often while simultaneously plying a craft or selling their husbands' wares. A fourteenth-century manual, *Handbook of Good Customs*, listed some chores young girls should learn before they married. These included: plucking fowl, cooking, baking, doing laundry, making beds, spinning, weaving, embroidering, and darning socks.[27] The frequent shortage of domestic workers further complicated these women's lives. The problem was so acute after plague epidemics that the slave trade was revived in the late 1300s in certain areas, especially Tuscany. The most valuable slaves were young females who could serve as household servants or nursemaids. In other locales, women like Erembourc *la commanderesse* of 1292 Paris placed female domestic servants in private homes for set fees. A fourteenth-century Parisian running such an employment agency might receive two *sous* for placing a nurse with a family, but only eighteen *deniers* for filling a chambermaid's position.[28]

Urban employers typically expected their servants to straighten furniture and beds, tend the fires, cook the meals, wash the dishes, and even participate as helpers in their masters' and/or mistresses' crafts.[29] Domestic work for the merchant and artisan classes was not an especially lucrative career, but servants sometimes received additional gifts or bequests. When Margaret Asshcombe of London wrote her will in 1434, she left her servant Clemence a grey woolen gown and a matching kirtle with green sleeves. Agnes de Evre was even luckier since she received a house in 1315 London from her late employer.[30]

In early years, town houses were usually surrounded by vegetable and herb gardens, fruit trees, and livestock. Chronicler Matthew Paris described a thirteenth-century residence in London as having: "a chapel, several bedrooms, an orchard, stables, a kitchen, a courtyard, a garden, and a well."[31] As cities grew in size and population, however, houses became more closely packed together and the large yards with gardens and orchards began to disappear. Most town houses were tall, narrow, wooden buildings. They often had thatched roofs that provided excellent insulation, but were also highly susceptible to fire—an ever-present danger in medieval cities. After a fire destroyed much of Lübeck in 1276, the town ordered that all but the smallest dwellings had to be rebuilt of stone or brick rather than wood.[32]

The ground floor of the typical town house had one front room (a combination workplace and shop) and a hall (or storeroom) in back. The next level contained the solar and another bedchamber. If there was a third story, it was usually an attic where apprentices or children could sleep. These brightly painted houses were generally set at odd angles, and built so that each story jutted out farther than the one below. Most homes, whether large or small, were gloomy and poorly ventilated. In addition, the absence of indoor plumbing made walking in front of an open window hazardous.

An average fourteenth-century urban family might own two or three wooden beds, a trestle table, a few linens, an iron pot, baskets, wooden bowls and spoons, a chest, and a couple of straight chairs. Typical kitchen implements included iron cauldrons, mortars and pestles, earthenware bowls and jugs, *besins* (brooms made with bundles of twigs), cheese presses, and kneading troughs. The difference in quantity and quality of household goods can be seen by comparing the testament of Isabel Gregory of Hackney (d.1432) with Lord Neville's will (see above). Isabel took equal care in itemizing her possessions, but her list was much shorter. She owned one tablecloth, one bed, a couple of cushions, a few gowns, a buffet (cupboard), and several kitchen utensils.[33]

By Isabel's time, furnishings had generally become a little more luxurious than those available to early townswomen. Joan Buckland, a well-to-do fifteenth-century resident of Northamptonshire, proudly listed a dining table, a long table in her parlor, and two good chairs—one carved and the other imported—among her belongings. In the same century, a fairly affluent Parisian woman, Perrette la Havée, owned a large canopied and curtained bed (6 feet by 7 feet) with linen sheets, mattresses, cushions, and feather pillows. Houses themselves had also become more comfortable. Glass windows began appearing in some areas at the end of the fourteenth century, and these homes might also contain lamps, lanterns, and chandeliers made from iron or copper.[34]

The food served to the wealthiest merchants was similar to that in many castles, and they also hired servants to do much of the cooking. The Paston family's extant records give us an idea of the amounts and types of food available to the most prosperous among the English gentry and merchant classes. When her husband died in 1466, Margaret Paston supervised her servants at the brewing and cooking, which went on for several days. The funeral guests eventually ate their way through forty-one pigs, one thousand eggs, forty-nine calves, a great number of chickens and geese, and a large quantity of beer.

Among less wealthy artisans and merchants, women did at least some of the cooking for their own households, as indicated by an Italian miniature (c.1385) that depicts two townswomen preparing and cooking tripe while their husbands sit at a table in the background. Englishwomen would often serve *groats* (a hulled grain of oats or wheat that was frequently made into porridge), fish, pork, bread, cheese, spinach, cabbage, and carrots. Wives might disguise unpleasant tastes with spices such as pepper, saffron, and cinnamon. Like other cooks, prudent city housewives tried to use every part of the few available animals. A favorite English pork dish called *brawn* was made by simmering herbs, spices, and vegetables with the pig's head, feet, and ears.[35] Not only was this recipe popular for its flavor, but it also helped prevent wastefulness since any leftovers from the animal could be thrown in as well.

Just as the foods eaten by city residents were seldom unique to that class, exclusively "middle-class" clothing styles were equally rare. The most well-to-do townswomen copied the nobility's attire. A wealthy fourteenth-century merchant's wife, like Margherita Datini of Italy, might own a variety of linen undergarments, wool housedresses, and better wool or silk dresses, often trimmed in fur, for appearing in public. Similarly, when a well-off woman of Regensburg dictated her will in 1308, she listed fur-trimmed and embroidered clothes, and her jewelry included three silver belts and five gold brooches.[36]

Among German townswomen, the veil was an important piece of clothing. They usually also wore *wimples* (a cloth covering for the head and neck) with circlets of flowers, braid, or pearls. A fifteenth-century Nuremberg woman's list of clothing included: four cloaks (two were silk-lined), six skirts, five undervests, seven pairs of sleeves, and nineteen veils. She also owned seven aprons—particularly important accessories among artisans. The type of apron worn signified the person's social class and denoted the craft to which he or she belonged. Because drab, coarse clothing was a symbol of poverty, merchants strove to wear only bright, soft fabrics.[37]

In general, city dwellers wore less sumptuous clothing and owned fewer accessories than the nobility. As trade grew, however, the elaborate styles that had once been a privilege of rank increasingly appeared on lower ranking merchants and burghers. The nobility responded by encouraging legislative action (*sumptuary laws*) designed to maintain their prerogatives in the world of fashion. During the 1400s, English sumptuary legislation restricted pleated short tunics that did not cover the buttocks, shoe points longer than two feet, sable furs, and *cloth of gold* (the most sumptuous and expensive fabric) to use only by titled nobles.[38]

To prevent waste, extravagance, and bankruptcies, a 1279 French code specified that a merchant could buy only one new robe each year while his wife could have two furred robes annually.[39] The town government of Strasbourg's main concern in the year

1375 appeared to be that feminine styles had become too erotic. The town banished seductive fashions like short coats, facial cosmetics, wigs, and especially low necklines, decreeing:

> Above all, her décolleté should not be so low that her breasts can be seen. The neckline should not be lower than the armpits.[40]

Compliance and enforcement of sumptuary edicts were never fully successful. Fourteenth-century Florence attempted to circumvent these difficulties by hiring officers from other cities to exact fines from women who wore overly extravagant fashions. Even this tactic did not meet with unqualified success. One officer complained about stopping a woman for wearing a fringed peak, only to have the miscreant assure him that it was merely a wreath. A second Florentine female swore her buttons were simple "studs," and a third asserted that her ermine was actually "suckling fur."

Magnates usually exempted themselves from all such rules, and some great Italian clans actually viewed feminine attire as a reflection of family wealth and prestige. When Nannina de'Medici married Bernardo Rucellai in 1466 Florence, her trousseau included many gowns elaborately decorated with gold and gems. Her headdresses and jewelry were equally ornate—studded with rubies, pearls, and diamonds.[41] This served as visible proof of the de'Medici power, wealth, and social standing, since few merchants could outfit their female relatives with such opulence.

The Peasantry

Of all classes, peasant women probably worked the hardest. A diligent wife and mother helped her family prosper, while a lazy woman could spell disaster. An industrious wife performed a variety of domestic tasks including: keeping house, cooking for her family, making cloth and clothes, and caring for her children. She also kept the hens and pigs, sheared sheep, milked cows, and made cheese, butter, and ale. The peasant wife carried her water from wells or streams, hoed and weeded her kitchen garden, gathered kindling, and tended the home fire. She even helped the men in the fields, doing everything from planting to harvesting. Not only did she grow her own herbs and vegetables, but when her husband was working on the lord's lands, she performed many of the same backbreaking tasks on the family's acreage.

In addition to their normal household chores, the most efficient housewives frequently supplemented their families' income. Some Italian peasant women sold their hair to rich town ladies. One rural woman, known as *Cavolaja* because she sold cabbages, even became quite wealthy and famous by marketing the vegetables she grew on her farm to the townspeople of late fourteenth-century Florence. In the English countryside, peasant women sometimes earned extra money by shearing sheep, thatching roofs, mixing mortar for new buildings, or whipping dogs out of churches—an "odd job" indeed. In mid-fifteenth-century Cambridge, Katherine Rolf frequently worked as a day laborer for a convent, earning around two *pennies* a day for weeding, thatching, making candles, threshing grain, and cleaning wool.[42]

Village women who brewed ale or sold bread were especially common in England. In the village of Broughton, perhaps one out of every four women was occasionally listed as an alewife, although few had operations as large as that of Emma Roger. Her fines (or license fees) were three times higher than those paid by other village women from the years 1309 through 1340. Broughton had no taverns at this time, but in 1297, Joan Everard ran the village equivalent by selling her ale in a room she rented at John Crane's house.[43]

The dwellings of these English peasant women ranged from the homes of the more affluent villeins and freemen to the mere hovels occupied by many *cottars* (usually the poorest because they held no land). In the past fifteen years, archaeological evidence has revealed that villagers—especially in early medieval centuries—moved more often than most historians had realized. Individuals, families, and sometimes whole villages moved from one locale to another searching for more food, better land, or safer conditions (free from wars or natural disasters). In addition, recent archaeological finds refute the belief that peasant homes were almost always constructed from local materials. The new evidence indicates that peasants often experimented with a variety of building materials—even with ones that had to be transported over great distances.[44]

In both England and France, the typical peasant's house sheltered only one married couple and their children. It was most often a one-story structure of irregular dimensions that had corn cribs, mows for hay and straw, and cattle sheds at the back. A heavy door opened into the one large family room with its pressed earth floor. Walls were sooty because the smoke from the central fire had to escape by way of holes in the roof. Piglets, ducklings, and cats meandered about inside the house, while a hen might nest beside the fire. Even the larger animals were often kept inside during the winter, only slightly separated from the family's living space. Windows were extremely rare, and burning rushes soaked in resin usually provided the artificial light since candles were too expensive for daily use.

Most peasants slept in familial straw beds that were warm and fairly comfortable, but also provided ideal breeding conditions for vermin. The *board,* of the same design as that used in castles or town houses, consisted of a trestle table with benches or stools. Some peasant women had chests for valuables like clothing and cups, but only the most affluent owned any real chairs. The few kitchen utensils included kettles, pot hangers, shovels, and flesh-hooks.[45] During the winter, peasants made or restored cooking implements along with other household and farming tools.

The homes and furnishings of the peasantry did not change quickly, but there were some improvements in their living conditions by the late 1400s. Among these were houses built on raised platforms, stone floors, cobbled yards, and drainage ditches. Innovations in heating technology included hand and foot warmers, furnaces, and baths.[46] The most prosperous fourteenth- and fifteenth-century Tuscan farmers and sharecroppers often lived in relatively large stone houses with tiled roofs, sleeping lofts, larders, and halls.[47] Similar progress was evident in late fourteenth-century English and French dwellings, which began to include more rooms, and even fireplaces built into walls.

Rural peasants (and even the very poorest city residents) often had trouble finding enough food. Peasants who ate well in some years had to resort to soups made of dead leaves or acorns in other winters. Peasant women usually cooked for their own families. Prudent wives made the most of what was available by not wasting food and by learning how to keep it edible. In England and France, women stored fruit under straw and then preserved it in honey or cooked it in fruit juice. The mainstay of their diet was bread, which was usually made of coarse, dark flours such as rye, oats, barley, and even peas or acorns.

The major source of protein in much of France was cheese, though some peasants obtained a little meat from chickens, pigs, or sheep. Most families grew cabbages, leeks, onions, and turnips, and peasants also gleaned supplementary foods from nature's bounty, adding mushrooms, nuts, and snails to the menu.[48] Italian peasants ate coarse bread, cheese, raw turnips, noodles or macaroni, and garlic. Tripe was a staple by the fourteenth century, as was a dish of pureed beans with bacon. The poorer classes in Germany consumed dark bread, oatmeal porridge or gruel, boiled peas, lentils, and occasionally pork, which they particularly savored as leftovers cooked with turnip greens or cabbage. During the fall, English peasants fattened their pigs on roots and acorns in the forest before killing the animals at the end of autumn. The pork was then cooked with the same things the pig itself normally ate—wild sage, garlic, and windfall apples. Peasant women smoked or salted any leftover meat to provide bacon for the winter. The villein's diet also included beans, leeks, curds, and oatmeal cakes or porridge.[49] The nutritional content of peasants' diet improved over the centuries as more iron- and protein-rich foods were being grown.

Peasant attire, on the contrary, changed little, remaining largely utilitarian in style throughout the Middle Ages. The basic patterns were similar to the fashions of wealthier people, but peasant styles lacked the quality of materials and ornamentation that distinguished the clothes of the nobility. Male peasants wore loose tunics, shirts, britches, and hose, while their wives donned long, loose gowns with aprons and wimples. Shoes for both sexes were normally wooden clogs or simple leather slippers. Peasant women usually made their families' apparel from homespun wool that they colored with bright natural dyes. The poor had few accessories, although they frequently wore belts and girdles from which hung knives and other implements. In later years, many peasant women made their families' clothes more attractive by adding embroidery. Their patterns remained simple, but even the peasantry's clothing had become slightly more close-fitting and ornate by the end of the Middle Ages.

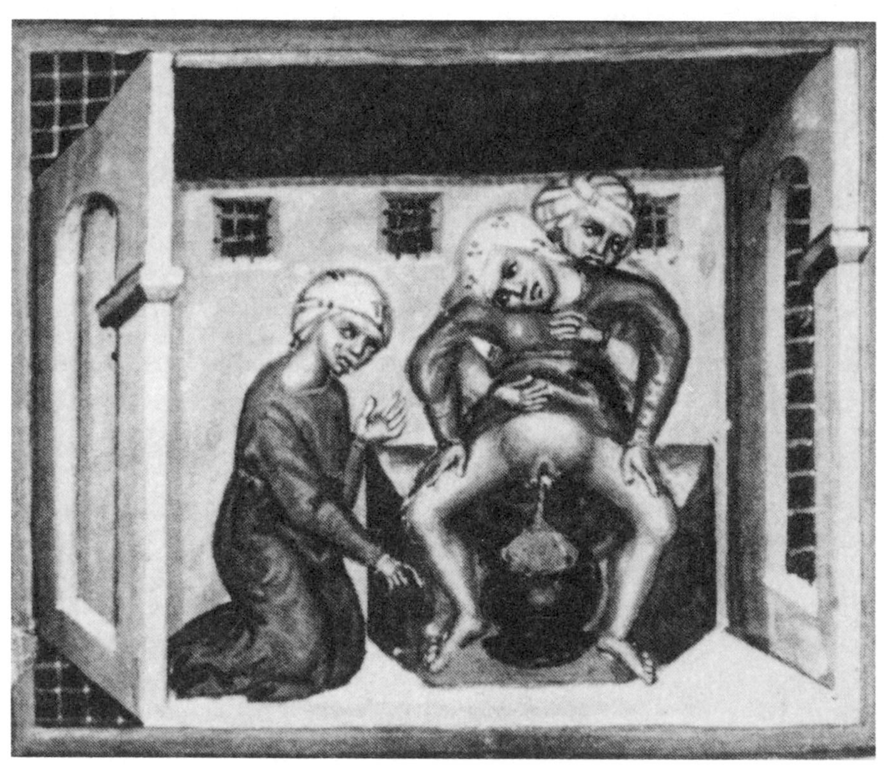

Medieval childbirth procedure.
Österreichische Nationalbibliothek, Vienna

Chapter Three

FROM A CROOKED RIB

Women as Patients and Medical Practitioners

Life was fragile in the Middle Ages. Constant wars, famines, diseases, and the clerical emphasis on the next world did nothing to alleviate the situation. A glimpse at the thirteenth-century records of London Eyres reveals a wide variety of causes of death. Among women the cases ranged from that of Lettice le Waleys who dropped dead of the "falling sickness" (probably epilepsy) in June of 1253, to that of Juliana Cordwaner who was stabbed in 1263 by her irate opponent as they were playing chess. Accidents were even more common. One year-old Amice le Soper died when she was bitten by a pig, and Beatrice de Holeborn passed away in 1256 after falling from a step in her home. Agnes de Barkyng (1253) and Isabel Paternoster (1270) were only two of the innumerable women scalded to death after falling into huge vessels of water or mash that were kept boiling on medieval hearths. Water was especially perilous because it carried pollutants and diseases, and few people could swim. Isabel Scrul drowned while attempting to draw water from the Thames in 1270, and a woman named Edith was simply trying to wash her hands when she fell into the same river in 1262.[1]

As prevalent as such accidents were, the absence of medical knowledge was the greatest health hazard. Though medieval "scientists," physicians (see below for types), and lay people paid health care a great deal of attention, a brief examination of the *Great Mortality* provides a good example of the deadly consequences of this lack of information. The *Great Mortality* was one of the names medieval people gave to the bubonic, pneumonic, and septicemic plagues that swept through Europe beginning in 1348. Apparently originating in China, plague was brought to the West by Genoese ships. The disease was particularly apt to strike the lower segments of society, but it also crossed class lines, reaching all levels of the population. Estimates of the mortality rate range between twenty and fifty percent of the total European populace. Such a death toll made the plague one of the worst medieval health crises.

Modern science has determined that fleas, which fed on diseased black rats, most likely spread the bubonic plague. Fleas infected with plague-causing bacteria had blocked digestive systems, and therefore injected contaminated blood as they tried to feed. Two to four days later, the victim of the flea bite would develop enlarged, painful lymph nodes and other symptoms.* Although a few people recovered, most died within two weeks.

The medieval scientific community postulated that plague resulted from pestilential atmospheres that entered humans through open pores. Bonfires, perfumes, and aromatic flowers were thought to prevent the spread of disease by keeping the air sweet. Doctors recommended avoiding excesses of meat and drink, bathing or sweating, and making love, because they all opened the pores to allow venomous air a ready entrance. If preventive measures failed, physicians advised ingesting herbs like detony and pimpernel, and they might also bleed the patient—on the theory that once the disease entered the body it became trapped. Equally unhelpful was the fact that nearly everyone believed the *Great Mortality* was a visitation of God's wrath, so it was entirely beyond human understanding or control. In his *Decameron,* Giovanni Boccaccio offered two explanations:

> In the year of our Lord 1348, there happened at Florence . . . a most terrible plague . . . owing to the influence of the planets, or . . . sent from God as a just punishment for our sins.

Neither possibility offered much hope for a cure. In fact, Boccaccio went on to say, "To the cure of this malady, neither medical knowledge nor the power of drugs was of any effect."[2]

The idea that it was a sin to try to alleviate such God-sent ills helped retard the discovery of desperately needed medical information. Since the deity was assumed to be an active participant in

* Septicemic plague, an extremely fast-acting variety, affected the circulatory systems, while pneumonic plague was a respiratory infection which could pass from person to person.

causing and curing sicknesses, a disease's course could presumably be influenced by one's relations with God. When Empress Matilda fell dangerously ill after the birth of her first son, she staved off the grim reaper by pleasing God with her large gifts to the poor.[3] Efforts to sway God's medical judgments were thought to be particularly efficacious when aided by a saintly intermediary, even a dead one. Hence ailing pilgrims constantly sought out saints' relics and shrines in their desperate need for heavenly cures.

Physicians joined the lay populace in appealing to God as a legitimate therapy option, but doctors did usually try to supplement His powers with their own cures. They borrowed many medical concepts from such classical authors as Hippocrates, Aristotle, and Galen of Pergamon. These ancient authorities had written about four temperaments—sanguine, phlegmatic, choleric, and melancholic—which were controlled by four humors—blood, phlegm, yellow bile, and black bile. The four elements that regulated the body were heat, moisture, cold, and dryness, and these were analogous to the four elements—fire, water, air, and earth—that composed all matter. All these factors acted in various ways on the brain, heart, and liver, which were presumed to be the three centers of life and health.

Medieval scientists also studied Islamic medical treatises. These works were often translated inaccurately, however, and some important discoveries by Arab physicians were omitted. One example is that by the eleventh century Muslim doctors knew a great deal about the circulatory system, but most Europeans did not "discover" this information until after the fifteenth century.[4] Doctors also used astrology to predict whether a patient would recover, to determine when to bleed a patient, and to make a variety of other medical decisions. Stars and planets were thought to govern various parts of the body, while the moon was understood to regulate the bodily cycles. Healers often prescribed herbal baths to alleviate many complaints, but did not recommend drinking water. Blood-letting was a major practice in the case of wounds and a number of illnesses. *Leeches* (healers and blood-letters) even performed this procedure on healthy people since it was believed to cool and restore vitality to the body, as well as letting sicknesses drain out.

Various books were available to help physicians remember all this medical advice. In the 1100s, Abella of Salerno and Rebecca Guarna wrote about childbirth procedures, while yet another woman, Mercuriade of Salerno, explained how to treat wounds and infections. Physicians might also have access to a small book called a *vade mecum*, containing a variety of information: star and planet charts, urine analyses, calendars, dates for blood-letting, and rules of diagnosis. By the thirteenth century, doctors could refer to *consilia*, or case histories, which helped them recognize new cases of such diseases as plague, leprosy, diabetes, cancer, rabies, and diphtheria.[5]

Despite these diagnostic tools, treatment remained limited. A fourteenth-century English manuscript, the *Liber de diversis medicinis* (*Book of Diverse Cures*), was probably typical of general medical works of the time. It contained charms, the Latin Mass of Exorcism, and recipes for a variety of treatments, ranging from cures for worms in the ears, eyes, and teeth, to one for a hangover. A recipe for getting rid of ringworms advised the sufferer to take turpentine and ground glass, and blend them together.[6] Once anointed with this medicine, the sore would soon heal.

Such books were sometimes available to those lay women who could read them. Physicians were a rarity, especially in rural areas, so women were often responsible for their families' health care. Beatrice of Savoy, countess of Provence, acquired her medical knowledge by commissioning Aldobrandino of Siena to produce *Régime du corps* (*Health Regimen for the Body*), including information on feminine hygiene, skin care, and gynecology. Female lay healers might also consult practical guides called *herbals*. One of the most comprehensive was Dioscorides' *De materia medica* (*About Drugs*—or *Remedies*), which contained information on some six hundred plants.

The typical medieval garden contained a number of useful herbs, spices, and flowers—like roses, violets, mint, and parsley. Gardens thereby combined the functions of providing beauty, flavorings for foods, and medical ingredients. Among the frequently recommended medicinal plants were: astrologia, which was supposed to help women in labor; ditayne, which was helpful for wounds and snake bites; and plantayne, which was not only useful for the relief of pain in the ears, eyes, and gums, but was also believed to heal dog bites. In her medical book *Causae et curae*, Abbess Hildegarde of Bingen prescribed licorice to cure eye and voice problems, and the lily to help those afflicted with leprosy.[7] Elizabeth of Poland, queen of Hungary, invented a medicinal formula of water and rosemary called *water of the queen of Hungary* as a treatment for rheumatism.[8] Lay healers also used charms and incantations, which were particularly effective if they included the mystical numbers three and nine or utilized saints' names. Amulets were perhaps the most potent devices since they not only cured diseases, but could even prevent their wearers from becoming sick, or from attracting evil spirits. Theriacs (herbal compounds) were also used to treat a variety of health problems, and were thought to be especially good antidotes to poison. One such recipe, found in the *Liber de diversis medicinis,* was made from a mixture of dried betony and wine.

Magnates who were particularly worried about poison might also wear a large diamond, since that stone was thought to serve as a charm against poisoning. A variety of other gems supposedly guarded against or cured illnesses. Used as talismans, agates cured insomnia and assured pleasant dreams. Some gems were pounded into a fine powder and then mixed with herbs to produce medicines. Other jewels were particularly effective if they were carved with certain images. Conventional wisdom held that the jacinth could protect travelers from plague and wounds, but Hildegarde of Bingen believed it was useful for warding off phantoms, magic spells, and madness. Hildegarde did agree with other experts that some stones should be soaked in a liquid to release their therapeutic properties. She recommended placing topaz in wine for seventy-two hours before rubbing it on the eyes to cure dimness of vision.[9]

Masquerading as scientific knowledge, such practices indicate that, judged by modern standards, medical sophistication in general was very low. The situation in feminine health care was even worse. The traditional belief in the four humors was one reason that little attention was paid to female medical problems. Galen, for example, had vowed that women were less perfect than men because they were cooler and moister, and because they had incomplete sexual organs. Another idea was that women were actually men turned inside out. The *Malleus Maleficarum* (known as the *Witch Hammer,* published c.1486) advanced the notion that women were crooked and imperfect because Eve was made from a bent rib.[10] On the other hand, Hildegarde of Bingen believed females were actually superior to men. She reasoned that woman was created from living flesh, but man was made of mere clay and then changed to flesh. Among her many unique ideas, this abbess also maintained that because of their composition, women did not feel the destructive passion of lust, only warm affection. Hildegarde called the womb an open space in the abdomen that allowed feminine passions to wear themselves out, thereby assuring women of weaker carnal appetites.[11] This was in direct opposition to most ecclesiastics, who claimed that women were tremendously over-sexed.

Scientists often tied feminine physiology to sexuality and advanced numerous superstitions and misconceptions about feminine health. The various theories and practices associated with the menstrual cycle are good examples. Some beliefs stemmed from the ritual significance of blood in many early societies, including that of the Old Testament Hebrews. Leviticus 20:18, for instance, termed menstruation a sickness, and classified having sex with a menstruating woman as a crime much like incest. Authorities differed, however, on the reasons for this taboo. Some believed the blood killed semen, making procreation—the only justification for sexual intercourse—impossible. Other experts claimed menstrual blood poisoned semen and thereby produced terribly handicapped offspring.[12]

It was commonly believed that menstruation was a process that started in the head and continued through the body to remove digestive wastes and purge the blood of poisonous humors. Rooted in the Bible, another widely held view was that women were unclean during the menstrual period; the blood itself was regarded either as dangerous or as having magical properties. Isidore of Seville (d.636) had claimed that the mere touch of a menstruating woman made plants die, but medieval Florentines commonly deposited menstrual blood on the soil as a fertility charm. In early fourteenth-century France, Beatrice de Planisolles of Montaillou saved her daughter's first menstrual blood for use as a love potion to entice a future suitor for the girl.[13] Some churchmen claimed witches and devil worshippers used this blood to make their magic ointments, but the most popular opinion was that menstruation was one more punishment inflicted on womankind because of Eve's sin.

Eve's opposite number, the Virgin Mary, also played a part in medical theories since she was often cited as proof that chaste young women could possess quasi-magical powers associated with their virginity. Saint Thomas Aquinas declared that women gave birth so men could be free to concentrate on more elevated tasks. Females who gave up their biological function in order to pursue the higher calling of piety thus achieved near parity with males. It is significant that extremely holy women, like (Saint) Colette of

Corbie, were often reported never to menstruate,[14] as if their piety literally turned them into men.

The emphasis on virginity also led to a number of medically approved ways to establish a woman's purity. One doctor wrote that if a sexually active woman swallowed crushed jade it would always come out in her urine. Doctors even tried to find ways to trick grooms into believing their brides were virginal. The famed eleventh-century midwife Trotula of Salerno advised the prospective bride to put a leech on her labium. An equally hazardous and painful trick involved using a pomade, described in some medical treatises as a compound of ground glass and dye.[15]

A number of misconceptions also surrounded the feminine role in the reproductive process. Some people believed the female body was only a receptacle for the fertile male seed. Under this theory the strongest man had many sons who looked like their father, while a weak man had girls who did not resemble him. Saint Thomas Aquinas (among others) asserted that females were produced by defective sperm, or some other problem—such as the presence of a moist south wind—which occurred during conception. He said that under the best conditions only boys would be produced, because:

> the male seed tends to the production of a perfect likeness in the masculine sex; while the production of women comes from defect in the active force.[16]

Doctors who considered men solely responsible for all characteristics of their children viewed sterility as a sign of extreme male weakness. More realistic experts thought it could occur in either partner. A recipe in the *Liber de diversis medicinis* instructed the couple to mix up separate pots of water and bran. The sterile party was determined by seeing which of those vessels had worms and a rancid smell after the pots had been allowed to sit for several days.[17]

Numerous other medical ideas linking health with sexuality also caused dissension in the medical ranks. For instance, the debate over the existence of female semen raged throughout classical and medieval literature. Galen recommended masturbation as a way to rid a woman's body of spoiled female semen that could corrupt her blood. His views were part of the larger question of whether the womb was stationary or wandered throughout the body. Scientists who believed the uterus was mobile thought lack of sex caused it to become too dry. They claimed that the womb of a sexually inactive woman moved around her body searching for moisture, thereby producing a variety of medical problems. If it stopped at the heart it caused vomiting, while a uterus lodged at the liver resulted in loss of voice and an ashen complexion. Physicians who disagreed with the "wandering womb" theory usually cited the fact that it would be impossible for the uterus to leap over the stomach.[18]

Hysteria, considered a feminine problem on the fringes of insanity, was thought to be one result of the physical stress caused by a wandering womb. Even physicians who disagreed with this theory usually admitted hysteria was caused by a lack of sexual intercourse. Insufficient sexual activity caused dammed up uterine secretions which poisoned the entire body. Trotula of Salerno followed Galen's lead and advocated this point of view. She wrote that spoiled female seed caused hysteria by corrupting the blood and irritating the nerves.[19] The best therapy was increased intercourse to release the dammed up secretions.

If "sex therapy" was unavailable, there was one other remedy—exorcism—which was particularly useful when the clerical emphasis on virginity had unexpected repercussions. This cure was required when a group outbreak of possession in 1491 caused all the nuns at a Cambrai convent to bark, develop great strength, and see into the future. The epidemic was said to have begun when the stress of chastity proved too great for Jeanne Potier, turning her into a "hysterical nymphomaniac." After the authorities removed Jeanne from the convent to cure her hysteria by exorcising her demons, the rest of the nuns returned to a more normal emotional state.

Other mental and/or emotional illnesses in women were also associated with reproductive organs and sexual behavior. The two true mental illnesses were thought to be *mania* (wild behavior or rage) and *melancholia* (deep depression). A particular form of the latter was love madness, an aberration of erotic love caused by dammed up sexual secretions or an unhealthy obsession with the loved one. Many females who were termed "melancholic" had cyclical disorders, so modern medicine might view them as victims of manic-depression or of pre-menstrual syndrome. The peasantry attached a great deal of fear and superstition to mental ailments, and often ousted victims from their communities to prevent them from "infecting" everyone else. Thus groups of the mentally ill wandering the forests were not uncommon, and even the *ship of fools* was a medieval reality since boats laden with mad men and women were occasionally set adrift. Many doctors, on the other hand, tried to find underlying causes for such illnesses since they realized physical problems could result in mental and emotional breakdowns. Traditional treatments included herbal remedies and prayer, but some physicians also used more experimental approaches—ones akin to modern physiotherapy, psychoanalysis, and music therapy.[20]

Less helpful than such treatment for the mentally ill, the controversy among physicians over why females had short life expectancies may have even resulted in shortening women's life spans. Scientists who wrote about this subject sought merely to explain the situation, not provide remedies for it. Since it was posited as a natural, God-ordained feature of feminine existence, few physicians saw any point in trying to alleviate the problem. Some experts believed men lived longer because they were more perfectly constructed. Cardinal Hostiensis, a thirteenth-century canonist, declared: "women are like weeds, which mature earlier than desirable plants [men] . . . but also die earlier."[21]

Women were most at risk during childbirth. Some men viewed this as God's punishment for Eve's sin, but there were actually a variety of more prosaic reasons for the high infant and mother mortality rates. One obvious problem was that girls often married and bore children at dangerously young ages. Mary de Bohun's sad fate was fairly typical. Married to the future King Henry IV of England when she was twelve, Mary died in the process of bearing her sixth child at the ripe old age of twenty-two.

Saint Augustine declared that using contraceptives made any woman, whether married or not, a whore in the sight of both man and God because procreation was the only justification for sexual intimacy. The general rule about abortion followed Augustine's dictum that after forty days the fetus had a soul of its own. Most theologians agreed that using contraceptives or aborting a fetus were grave sins, although canon law did not equate those practices with felonies. Spain was apparently the only region where women occasionally stood trial and were punished for having abortions, or for performing them on others.

For contraception, German women sometimes used beeswax or rags to block the semen. Other females believed holding their breath or performing a variety of other actions during intercourse prevented conception. The most popular contraceptives were herbal compounds of rosemary, balsam, and/or parsley. Douching and eating lead were supposed to cause abortions, and Albertus Magnus advised consuming myrrh and coriander.[22] The lack of safer, more effective contraception and abortion methods forced many women to have large numbers of babies, and to thereby put themselves at risk numerous times. Blanche of Castile married the future Louis VIII of France when she was only twelve. Over the next twenty-six years, she gave birth to twelve infants but only five survived. This high infant mortality rate was another reason that women were encouraged to give birth frequently.

Inadequate nutrition, poor hygiene, and few medical/scientific aids to handle problem pregnancies were other risk factors. Moreover, since most midwives had little training, they were often forced to resort to using magic charms, an ineffective remedy for life-threatening cases. It is significant that women who managed to survive their childbearing years tended to live at least as long as men of the same age and class. The implications of this fact apparently never fully registered on male physicians, many of whom preferred to emphasize the necessity of keeping females under control rather than keeping them healthy.

This unfortunate situation might have been ameliorated to some extent if the scientific community had helped teach women to treat members of their own sex. Instead, female practitioners were often regarded with hostility by male physicians, and were increasingly barred from the various health care fields. The growing popularity of hospitals contributed to the declining feminine role in health care. Ironically, these institutions were often founded by women, who joined men in making this a popular form of religious/charitable donation. In the mid-1300s, for instance, Marguerite de La Vent, a widowed townswoman of Lyons, willed some of her money to support all the hospitals of the town and also sponsored a bed in the hospital of Sainte-Marie.[23]

During the twelfth century, building hospitals in the Holy Land became popular because large numbers of European soldiers suddenly found themselves far from home and in need of medical treatment. People soon began building hospitals in other regions for the good of their souls, and as "pension homes" for elderly servants. A typical thirteenth-century European hospital was a large one-story building with one or two big wards, tiled floors, separate beds, plenty of light, a water supply, heating facilities, and relatively good sanitation. Some of these institutions had quarantine facilities, while others catered to specific types of patients, such as the blind, widows, pilgrims, or lepers.

With over two thousand hospitals in the early thirteenth century, the *lazar-house* was the most common type of these specialized institutions. Lepers had to be completely separated from the outside world, and hope for a cure was virtually non-existent. The evidence suggests that the lucky few who were "cured" and released had been misdiagnosed in the first place. The efficacy of treatments for leprosy can be deduced from a recipe in the *Liber de diversis medicinis*, which advised boiling a goose with virgin wax, a half-pound of frankincense, white lead, and two ounces of mercury.[24]

Although never as numerous as lazar houses, most regions also had alms-houses for the poor, and nursing homes to accommodate wealthier people. Thirteenth-century Toulouse contained fifteen hospitals and seven leper-houses to serve its population of some 25,000. Such large numbers of hospitals were common, but most institutions were very small, often housing the apostolic number twelve (or thirteen) patients.[25] The hospital staff included priests to furnish spiritual supervision, nurses and visiting doctors for physical care, and servants to perform a multitude of menial chores. Occasionally female doctors were among the practitioners called in to treat hospital patients. In 1463, Bertrande of the rue (road) Calade received payments for medicating a poor inmate at the hospital of Cor-Saint in Avignon.[26] But normally the more important staff, priests and physicians, were males, while most females were nurses or servants. Men gradually came to view those secondary roles as the proper medical "place" for women.

Medical universities also lowered the status of female healers. Medicine was originally learned through practice and apprenticeship, a method which allowed numerous women to become lay medical practitioners. Starting with the school at Salerno in the eleventh century, medical universities gradually took over the training of physicians. The general level of medical science slowly began to improve as a course of study was formalized, the profession became restricted to intelligent and literate individuals, and the status of doctors rose. These improvements paved the way for better modern medicine. Despite the long-term benefits, however, the growing prominence of universities had some detrimental side-effects—such as the exclusion of even the most intelligent, experienced, and/or skillful women.

As schooling and licensing became necessary for medical practice, women were denied access to both, except occasionally in Italy or Germany. Antonia Daniello, for instance, received a medical degree in Florence toward the end of the fourteenth century. Another Italian woman, Francesca de Romana of Salerno, passed a rigorous examination before a board of doctors and surgeons in order to earn a doctorate in surgery in 1321. A Jewish physician named Sara received a license to practice medicine in Wurzburg in 1419, upon payment of a ten *florin* tax. Sara was so successful that she was soon able to buy a house in town, which also reduced her tax rate. Marguerite of Naples also practiced in Germany. In 1394, she procured a license to work as an eye specialist in Frankfurt.

Ophthalmologists like Marguerite were lay practitioners who specialized in one field of medicine. The very existence of such specialties became another source of conflict between medieval universities and lay healers. Unschooled health care providers, such as barbers, surgeons, and druggists, often formed their own guilds (trade associations), a development that firmly segregated each field from every other medical group, and from university-trained physicians.

As universities, and the physicians who graduated from them, tried to monopolize the entire health care field, they also created a gap between theory and practice. Formally schooled doctors frequently responded to their patients' needs with scholarly theses, causing sufferers to turn to lay healers who had less theoretical knowledge but better practical treatments. Many of the most progressive discoveries were thus made by lay practitioners. Thirteenth-century ophthalmologists, for example, began to perform cataract operations using gold needles. Toward the end of that century, convex-lensed glasses also became available to remedy nearsightedness. Similarly, dentists learned to use drills or files to remove decayed portions of the teeth, and then fill the cavities with gold leaf. Great strides were also made in anesthesia research. In the twelfth century, the first attempts at anesthetizing patients utilized herbs, like the juice of mandrake roots and, later, the opium poppy. By the fifteenth century, however, doctors began to use alcohol fumes, which were much more effective.

Along with anesthesia research came improved surgical techniques. During the thirteenth century, surgery was used in England to treat cancer, and in Italy, William of Saliceto operated to remove fluid from the brain of a hydrocephalic child.[27] As impressive as such advances were, surgery had a lower status than did general medicine. It was designated as manual labor since its practitioners used their hands. Because surgery was rarely taught at universities, women were sometimes able to enter this field. In Naples, Thomasia de Matteo and Maria Incarnata, were admitted to surgical practice in the fourteenth century. Maria was even termed an "expert" in the field.[28] Similarly, a French surgeon named Leonard Pachaude obtained the right to take over her deceased husband's practice at Avignon (c.1400).[29]

As their status rose during the fourteenth century, surgeons began to relinquish a number of less delicate or important procedures to barbers. Barbers primarily cut hair and shaved their customers, but medieval practitioners also performed a variety of other chores. In fifteenth-century England, King Edward IV had a barber who regularly washed the monarch's head, legs, and feet, as well as shaving him.[30] Barbers were also medical practitioners. The 1292 Paris tax survey listed several female barbers. Judging by their taxes, most had small businesses, as did Edeline of the rue au Fuerre and Ysabiau of the rue St. Germain. However, Eudeline of the rue Saint-Christofle and Denise of the parish of Saint-Germain-l'Auxerrois apparently had larger, more prosperous practices, since both paid higher taxes. Unfortunately, the records do not indicate whether Eudeline and Denise had better locations for their shops, or were simply more skillful than Edeline and Ysabiau.

In 1372, when the French king agreed to allow barbers dominion over plasters, ointments, and surgical procedures used to treat boils, tumors, bruises, and non-critical wounds, they formed their own guilds and eventually challenged the supremacy of the surgeons.[31] France soon had to regulate the craft more stringently. Many of the new rules were designed to prevent women from practicing; by the 1400s, female barbers were extremely rare in Paris.

Another group of non-university-trained practitioners—the apothecaries, spicers, and herbalists—also formed their own guilds. Pharmacies traditionally stocked such substances as sugar, medicinal wines, olive oil, vinegar,[32] and a variety of other drugs that could not be obtained from the average herb garden. Pharmacists also acquired a good bit of latitude to prescribe and treat a variety of non-lethal ailments. This allowed an herbalist to invent his own recipes—and thereby gain fame and fortune. In 1417, Anne of Bourbon sent to Lyons to obtain a unique restorative from Raymond Dodieu, a highly-regarded *épicier apothicaire* of that city.[33] Pharmaceutics was not a university course, so many women ran apothecaries or herb shops. In 1292 Paris, Adélie l'erbière paid a fairly small tax on her business of selling kitchen and medicinal herbs. Pérronnele *l'espicière* was much more prosperous; she paid an extremely large tax of seven *livres*. She was probably also the *erbière* who went to Artois a few years later at the request of Countess Mahaut, who needed Pérronnele's herbal medicines, and her advice on using them. As was true in other fields, it gradually became harder for women to own and run apothecaries in later years.

Obstetrics was one health care field in which the overwhelming majority of practitioners were women since they naturally tended to be most concerned with the pain and risks involved in childbirth. Historian Dorothy M. Owen noted that the "common experience of pregnancy and child-rearing . . . bound together all the women in a community." She cited the case of a woman who was not a professional midwife but, having just given birth herself, was thoughtful enough to send a charm to another expectant mother to assist in her impending labor.[34]

Some women became semi-professional *medicae* (midwives). Parisian records listed several such women, like Emeline of the rue des Escoufles, who worked there in 1292, and Guibourc, who practiced in 1297. By the fifteenth-century, many French cities had begun to insist on better training for midwives. Lille had a higher standard than most, since midwives had to establish their competence in order to practice there at all. Women who proved skillful enough—like Catherine Lemensne and Agnes LeClerc—then obtained official licenses as midwives.[35]

The primary duty of these women was to help with labor and birth; this sometimes involved delivering a stillborn infant or performing a Caesarean section. The *Liber de diversis medicinis* illustrates a wide range of other duties including promoting conception, determining the gender of an unborn child, stopping excessive bleeding after delivery, and increasing the flow of breast milk. When trouble arose, the midwife could use an herbal medication, a magic charm, or perhaps a healing drink, like a popular one made of breast milk and olive oil.

In Italy the midwifery profession was highly respected, probably because a renowned group of Salernitan midwives flourished there in the eleventh century. The most famous, Trotula, is credited with having written two medical treatises, though there is much disagreement over exactly who she was. One of these books, *De passionibus mulierum ante, in et post partum* (known as *Trotula major*), discussed childbirth and its problems, as well as a number of other health topics of particular interest to women. Trotula apparently felt obligated to help others of her sex because she prefaced *Trotula major* with the words:

> Wherefore I, Trotula, pitying the calamities of women, and at the urgent request of certain ones, began to write this book on the diseases which affect [females].[36]

The sixty-three chapters of *Trotula major* reveal a familiarity with women's health problems, childbirth, and much other contemporary knowledge that may have been typical among the better trained midwives, especially in Salerno. This expertise also explains why her treatise was so widely respected throughout medieval Europe.

Nursing was another of the most common female roles in the medical profession. Many women were listed in the 1292 Parisian tax book as what we would call "private duty nurses." Anès of the rue Neuve nursed Andri l'Englais, while Jourdenette worked as a nurse for Guillaume Bourcel on the rue des Arsis. The taxes most of these women paid indicate they were not especially prosperous; perhaps, as is the case today, nurses were simply paid less than doctors. On the other hand, nurses employed by wealthy families sometimes received bequests for their work. Isabelle Despenser, countess of Warwick, gratefully acknowledged her nurse, Elysabeth Keston, when she dictated her testament in 1439. Isabelle earmarked a generous sum for Elysabeth with the poignant comment, "for the labor she hath had about me in my sickness."[37]

Nursing was also a common occupation among *Beguines* (a semi-organized group of religious lay women), and many of their early houses were located near hospitals. There were even some nursing orders, like the Cellites who cared for plague victims. Nuns in regular orders often worked as infirmary nurses—the monastic equivalent of hospital nurses. The convent infirmarian not only diagnosed and cared for patients in residence, but also grew most of her own herbs. She was responsible for all materials needed in the hospital, such as linens, food, and firewood. In addition, she frequently served as the leech (healer) to the surrounding neighborhood.

Especially in rural areas, many people relied on lay practitioners called *empirics*. Denoting any unschooled, unlicensed healer, this term applied largely to what we would call "general practitioners." It also overlapped medical specialties like obstetrics and surgery, and included most female doctors. Empirics might have access to the same remedies and possess skills equal to those of licensed physicians, but they generally had little education and formed no guilds.

An early fifteenth-century Italian physician, Anthonius Guainerius, believed some empirics were skilled practitioners, but advised "real doctors" to disassociate themselves from such lay healers. When he discussed a method for curing "suffocation of the womb," for example, Guainerius gave the same basic remedy as an empiric would use, but urged doctors to apply a slightly different substance to make the cure appear more sophisticated.[38]

Guainerius was actually fairly tolerant—doctors more often decried these lay healers as charlatans. Many physicians nevertheless trained their own daughters to be empirics. Stephanie de Montaneis, a lay healer in 1265 Lyons, had been instructed by her father, Étienne, a doctor of the same town.[39] A lay healer of the 1292 Paris survey named Sarre passed her medical knowledge on to her daughter Florian. A very few women even taught medicine to others. Sarah of Saint-Gilles, a Jewish doctor, obtained a royal decree from Marseilles in 1326 giving her the right to take an apprentice for seven months of training.

Unlike successful healers such as Sarah of Saint-Gilles, many other French empirics encountered legal difficulties. Marie de Gy, for instance, was excommunicated because one of her patients died at her house in Dijon. Authorities so frequently discriminated against women healers that it was not necessary to have a patient die—any excuse sufficed to embroil a woman doctor in legal trouble. Jacoba Felicie's great skill did not prevent her from being summoned in 1322 to a Parisian court for practicing illegally. Six patients testified Jacoba had effected their cures after male physicians had failed them. Without mentioning her success rate, the court found Jacoba guilty and fined her, because such extremely successful female healers posed a threat to formally schooled male physicians.

Fining an empiric was not always sufficient to curtail her practice, since many of these healers were so financially successful they could afford to simply absorb the court fines. Antoinette de Bellegarde was fined a total of thirty-five *sous* (a large sum in 1360), but she was prosperous enough to pay the money and continue working. In the following century, jealous doctors sometimes solved this problem by throwing women healers out of town. The physicians of Dijon banished Jeannette Camus in 1448 for practicing as a physician.[40]

Another type of female lay healer was the *sage* or *sage-femme* (wise woman), like Jehanne of Paris, who was listed as a practitioner in the 1292 tax records of Paris. Also called *old wives*, they relied heavily on superstitious remedies, such as charms, incantations, and amulets. Particularly in rural areas among the poor, old wives were often the only practitioners available. Many of these women maintained thriving businesses and gained a great deal of knowledge through experience, but they were never in very high repute as a group. Though most were ordinary housewives, *wise women* were increasingly equated with witches. Clerics claimed they could harm people and property with their magical/herbal remedies. In 1434, for instance, Henriette de Craus was condemned and then burned at the stake for supposedly using incantations and invoking demons to help cure her patients.

Attitudes against female lay healers hardened over time. University-trained physicians perceived female empirics as a threat to their own practices, while clerics viewed them as witches who healed with devilish aid and heretical incantations. In a time of widespread unrest among the peasantry, governments also began to fear female healers, who worked primarily among the poor, as potential leaders of grass-roots rebellions. In the following centuries, therefore, many lay healers were among the masses of people burned at the stake. The combination of three powerful groups—clerics, doctors, and rulers—eventually succeeded in all but eliminating female empirics, the only medical practitioners available to most women and to peasants of both genders.

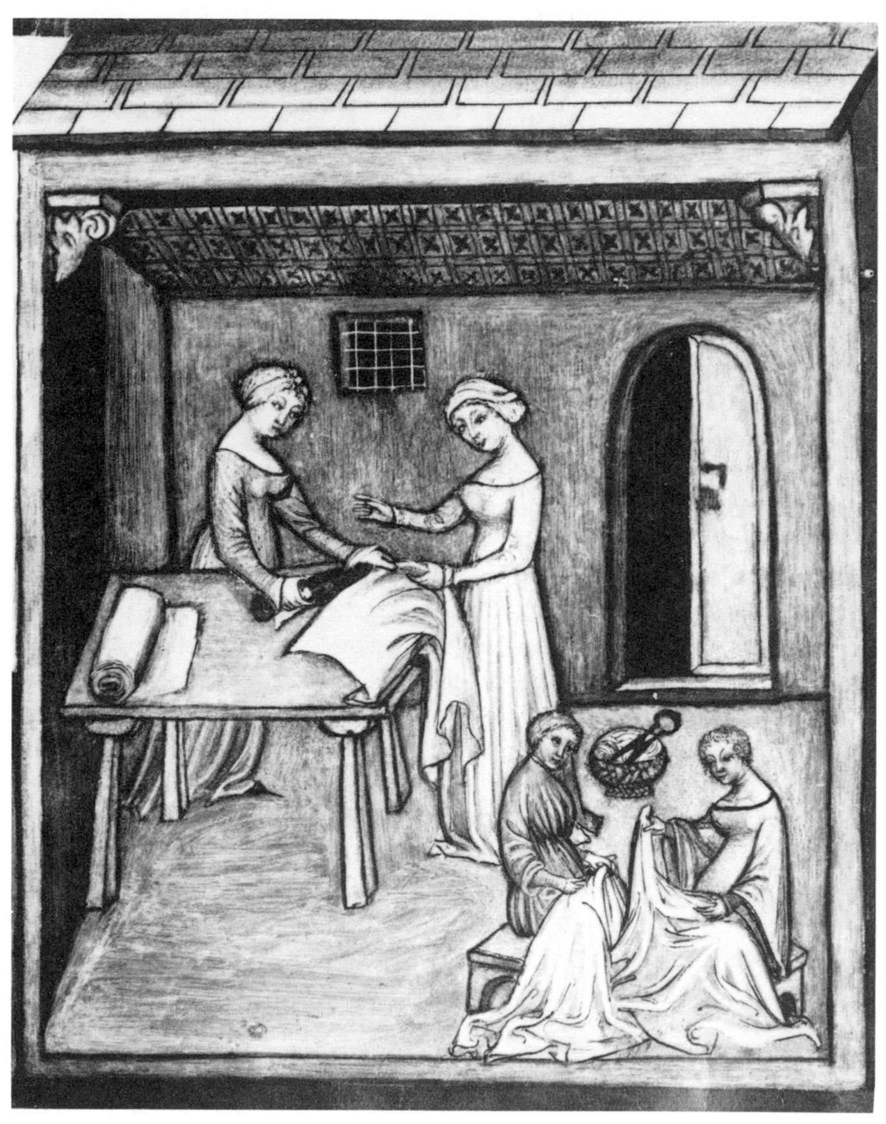

A workshop of female cloth workers.

Österreichische Nationalbibliothek, Vienna

Chapter Four

THE BUTCHER, THE BAKER, THE CANDLESTICK MAKER:

Working Women in Medieval Cities

In the rural world of the early Middle Ages there were few occupations for a woman other than farming and domestic work—whether in her own or someone else's home. Then around the 1100s, the Crusades inadvertently helped encourage a gradual shift from an agrarian civilization to a more urban one. These holy wars opened up new trade routes, while Byzantine cities revealed the importance of commerce to dazzled Europeans. Travel continued to be both difficult and dangerous, but the hazards proved no deterrent to ambitious merchants and shippers who started transporting wares such as ivory, perfume, gems, sugar, satin, damask, spinach, artichokes, dates, and citrus fruits to the West. In Europe, great fairs began offering concentrated markets for these caravans, allowing an exchange of goods from a variety of locales. Long-distance trade and shipping also established a need for new cities and ports, and provided many new careers for both men and women.

Women sometimes participated in this commercial growth as moneychangers or lenders. In 1368 Frankfurt, for example, six out of the eleven moneychangers were women. In early thirteenth-century London, Goda la Gablere became quite prosperous as a moneylender to merchants and shippers. The clerical strictures against charging interest (usury) eventually caused Goda to retire and become a religious in order to atone for her previous misconduct. Because of these Christian teachings against usury, many moneylenders were Jews. Thirteenth-century French records listed several female Jewish creditors—like Samuelis, Meliota, Durea, and

Précieuse—but they typically made only small-scale "domestic" loans to Christian women.[1]

Other women invested more directly in shipping enterprises by purchasing parts of ships. Alice Horsford was half-owner of a vessel, the *Saynte Mariebot,* which was based in London in 1370. As a "sleeping partner," she received some of the merchandise or profits after each trip. Still other women owned and ran their own shipping businesses. In the early 1200s, a Genoese shipper named Mabilia Lecavella became extremely wealthy by providing wine to the king of France.[2] Merchants' widows frequently "fell into" these trading careers when they had to close business deals their late husbands had started. In 1479 England, the newly widowed Joanna Rowley obtained sugar from Lisbon. In 1480, she shipped oil and wax from Lisbon and woad and wine from Spain. When Margery Russell, a widow from Coventry, lost one of her ships to Spanish pirates, she obtained *letters of marque* against Santander—the pirates' port of origin. *Letters of marque* were documents that essentially legalized piracy, by allowing the victim's crews to capture goods from ships licensed by the pirate's city worth the same amount as the goods originally stolen from his or her ship. Margery's wares had been valued at the large sum of £800, so she promptly seized two well-laden Spanish ships in recompense for her losses.[3]

Many long-distance traders eventually chose a city as a land base from which to conduct their marketing operations. By the thirteenth century, urban areas had also attracted many local peddlers who had once traveled around the countryside selling their wares. In a city, each trade or craft usually occupied a separate street, which was indicated by an appropriate identifying symbol—since most people could not read street signs. Shops were generally narrow and deep, so craftspeople worked in the front where the light was best. They displayed their goods hung around the doorway, or laid on a wooden trestle that acted as a shutter at night.

In urban areas, there were often at least as many women as men—and the majority of these females were "career women." Most were engaged in very small-scale marketing enterprises, but even these hucksters were an important link in the supply and demand chain. Though women did not participate in town governments or security systems, the growth of larger towns and cities gave them many new opportunities. Few trades were entirely closed to females by law, and most cities relaxed the regulations prohibiting women from participating in judicial proceedings so that businesswomen could transact legal contracts and recover just debts. The town council of Cologne even employed some women as court assessors, while others raised customs and road tolls. Though most trades had few female practitioners, there were large numbers of working women. In Frankfurt, there were approximately two hundred occupations in which women participated between the years 1320 and 1500.[4]

Some females arrived in the cities equipped with skills—such as ale-brewing or wool-carding—acquired at home on the manor. Wives, daughters, and female servants were often drafted into family businesses where they learned their trades by necessity. Unskilled workers, on the other hand, had to buy themselves apprenticeships with masters or mistresses in order to learn specific crafts. Town or craft organizations called guilds sometimes helped women find work. Each community had its own guilds, and every town's guilds had their own regulations. But all craft guilds had two main purposes: to guard the interests of the members, and to protect the consuming public by maintaining the quality of their products—functions that were not regarded as mutually exclusive. In order to accomplish both goals, guilds set standards and prices for merchandise and tried to keep membership small and select. Since this also kept prices high, it might be viewed as a "conflict of interest" today.

Unfortunately for women workers, they were often stuck in the lowest paid, unskilled types of jobs, and were thus unable to form guilds. Moreover, some guild regulations enabled men to discriminate against female members. For example, the guild of Parisian chandlers brought suit in 1379 against Guillemette Olivier to bar her from practicing that craft, contending that she was not skillful enough. The court allowed her to continue working as a candlemaker, but effectively curtailed her business by forbidding her to work in other homes, take on apprentices, or even teach a future husband the craft.[5]

Guild treatment of women varied from craft to craft. Most organizations accepted women, but had separate rules for them. The fifteenth-century guild of London saddlers on Foster Lane required the same yearly dues from both men and women. However, *sisters* of the craft only paid an entrance fee of 6*s* 8*d*, while *brothers* had to cough up 13*s* 4*d* to join.[6] A French guild of coral and shell rosary bead makers forbade women to keep apprentices if they married outside the craft. Women who worked in the gem- or glass-cutting trade could not have any apprentices because the guild masters claimed females were incapable of achieving the level of proficiency needed to teach this delicate craft to others.[7] In most of these *misteries* (guild crafts), unless a woman was a guild master's wife, she was excluded from mastery level training and was limited to performing menial tasks.

The unfavorable rules in some guilds encouraged many females to work in women's industries. Especially in France, a woman who worked alone at a trade was called a *femme sole*, regardless of her marital status. Many of these *femmes soles* worked in the predominantly female associations, which were most prevalent in the silk, embroidery, millinery, and special garment crafts. The Paris census of 1292 recorded five women's organizations, such as the ribbon-making guild. Cologne had four guilds made up almost entirely of women. Yarn spinners, gold spinners, silk spinners, and silk weavers only admitted men as infrequent exceptions. Unfortunately, many of these female crafts lent themselves to exploitation. Silkwomen, for example, were caught in a stranglehold by the contractors who supplied their raw materials, since the middlemen could cut off supplies or raise prices at any time.[8]

Another problem was that the most poorly paid jobs were the "feminine" ones, like that of laundress. London washerwomen like Beatrice le Wimplewasher and Massiota la Lauendere might receive as little as a *penny* for laundering a customer's clothes.[9] A further hardship was that women were traditionally paid less than men, even for doing the same jobs. At harvest time in France, for example, both sexes often picked grapes for extra money, but women were paid only half of what men received. In other lines of work, French women normally received three fourths of a man's wages; by the fifteenth century, this ratio had dropped to one half for most jobs. Not surprisingly, female workers, especially single women and widows, were usually the poorest members of urban society. Records from Frankfurt in 1410 indicate that 7.8 percent of the male citizens were "poor," but 33.6 percent of the female population was subsisting below the poverty level.[10]

Despite all these problems, many urban females were working women, and they held a wide variety of jobs. Mariotta Convers was a fourteenth-century pawnbroker in London, while Agnes Asser was one of thirty coopers listed in later fifteenth-century London as masters with their own trade marks. Petronilla Balle inherited a tannery from her husband in early fourteenth-century Shrewsbury.

Some two years after his death, Petronilla was still running this shop, as indicated by her inventory listing tanned skins, a vat, and tanning bark.[11] Agnes de Bury was a very prosperous London fur dealer until she was imprisoned in 1344 for buying old furs and dying them to be resold as new ones. Another London merchant, Mariot Ferars, was presumably more honest, since King Henry III paid her the large sum of £75 for several horses and accouterments. In the middle of the fifteenth century, Karyssa under Helmslegern imported a sizeable amount of copper and was responsible for more than five percent of the sheet iron exported from Cologne.[12] These women were unusual only because they achieved success in jobs normally held by men.

Candlemaking, on the other hand, was a relatively common occupation for women. In much of Germany, for instance, almost all chandlers were women. In England, Emma Hatfield became a chandler in mid-fourteenth-century London after her husband William bequeathed his shop and apprentice, Roger Gosse, to her. The contents of Emma's shop, as they were listed in 1373, were probably typical of any fourteenth-century chandler. For making the candles there were barrels of grease, lengths of cord, twenty pounds of tallow (worth 2*s* 6*d*), salt, sack-cloth, and vats. Of the finished product, Emma's inventory included 325 pounds of candles worth 55*s* 4*d*.[13]

It was much rarer for women to be involved in work like mining, which was considered too heavy for the "weaker sex." Denied access to many of the physically grueling but more lucrative jobs, women frequently worked at poorly paid tasks such as ore-washing or carting stones from quarries.[14] Like the mining industry, a variety of metal- and wood-working guilds, and related crafts, allowed women only a small role. In 1292 Paris, for instance, women were rarely listed as jewelers, and even those few were not especially prosperous. One named Anès was charged very little tax on her shop on the rue de Mau-Conseil, where she created jewelry from both real and fake gems. Similarly, only two women—Juliane and Pérronnele—were listed as potters, artisans who produced metal and clay pots, as well as a wide range of wooden kitchen utensils. Some twenty pin- and needle-makers were recorded in the 1292 survey, but Edeline was the only woman listed in the craft. She apparently prospered from the lack of feminine competition; her 16*s* tax was in the middle range.[15] Though guilds of goldsmiths—artisans who also made *cloisonné* and carved ivory pieces—restricted feminine participation, records from 1304 Arras mention a recently widowed woman named Marote de Douai, who sold three gold caskets for more than fifty *livres*. Jehanne de Brye, widow of a fifteenth-century Parisian goldsmith, even maintained her late husband Aubert's business, keeping his shop on the rue du Petit Pont open from 1424 until at least 1428.[16]

Many more women worked in bookmaking crafts. In the early Middle Ages, this trade had been almost entirely in the hands of nuns and monks, since they were usually the only people who could read and write Latin. The growth of towns made vernacular literature popular and increased educational opportunities. Bookmaking thus moved from the cloister into the commercial world, where it provided work for numerous artisans because so many different types of supplies were necessary. These included parchment, vellum, kidskin, clasps and studs, embroidery thread, leather, silk, and cowhide. Two parchmenters named Martha and Ermengard worked in the mid-thirteenth-century Parisian area of Sainte-Geneviève, and in 1292 Paris, a woman named Asceline was an *encrière*, an ink maker.[17] At the end of the fourteenth century, Philip *the Bold*, duke of Burgundy, often patronized a Parisian draper named Colette. He bought silk and ties for his books from Colette, and even commissioned her to ornament a cloth cover for one of his *Books of Hours*.[18]

Making the covers was only one of many tasks associated with bookmaking. Authors, scribes, illuminators, translators, binders, fastener makers, embroiderers, and many others might work on a single manuscript. For instance, a laywoman scribe named Maroie appeared in the expenditure records from Artois in 1312, indicating that Countess Mahaut had paid her twenty-five *sous* to copy a *Book of Hours*. Once a scribe like Maroie had finished copying a book, another woman might illustrate the manuscript—painting miniatures and/or borders throughout the work. Yet another woman might be employed to bind the books, as Alice Drax did in early fifteenth-century London for the English king.[19]

Even the bookseller was an important person in the industry since most were not mere merchants, but also made, repaired, and commissioned the production of manuscripts. Marguerite de Sanz evidently had a thriving bookshop in 1292 Paris since she paid a relatively high tax of four *livres*. An English laywoman named Elisabeth Scepens helped her mentor's widow run a bookstore in Bruges from 1476 until 1489.[20] Although Elisabeth sold finished manuscripts, most often she produced books on commission. She had to hire out some of this work, while other tasks were completed in the shop.

The rise of commercial bookmaking hurt many nuns who had supported their convents by serving as the backbone of the bookmaking industry. Nevertheless, even in the late Middle Ages, the majority of female bookmakers were still found in religious houses. The sisters at San Giacomo at Ripoli achieved such a high degree of excellence in their manuscripts that they were able to compete with lay workers and maintain a thriving scriptorium. These nuns not only copied and illustrated manuscripts but even worked a printing press, producing some seventy books during the years between 1470 and 1484.[21]

As in the bookmaking industry, women's religious foundations were frequently involved in the cloth trade. The Dominican convent at Nuremberg, for instance, developed its own recipes for making dyes and for painting cloth.[22] The nuns then used their uniquely colored threads to produce the carpets for which the convent was justly renowned. Eventually, however, the growth of cities also caused cloth work to begin evolving into a profession for the laity. It became the most female-influenced medieval industry, probably because women had always done such work. In the early Middle Ages, cloth was usually produced at home by women. In the towns of northern Europe, wives were often in charge of several workrooms in which women made silk and wool cloth. The most common type of English home workshop consisted of a few women hired to spin thread, a traditional feminine occupation. By the 1200s, women in most countries could be found performing a range of clothworking tasks from raising sheep to embroidering tapestries.

Some raw products had to be treated by carding and combing, two of the first steps in the process of producing thread. The 1292 survey listed Hodierne of la Tounelerie as a wool-comber while another Parisian named Lorence worked as a wool-carder. Other craftspeople then colored the material, as did Anees de Quinkere, a widow who joined the blue dyers craft in late fourteenth-century Ghent.[23] Once the thread was finished, the weavers took over. Though this was often considered too heavy a job for the "weaker sex," Alice de Lye wove wool cloth in the 1370s and 1380s in Shrewsbury, where she also sometimes moonlighted as a brewer. In mid-fifteenth-century Florence, a widowed silk weaver named Antonia made a moderate living producing crimson taffeta. She was forbidden to work with the much more profitable velvet brocade—a task only "suitable" for men.[24]

Wool cloth next had to be fulled, a step that consolidated and thickened the fabric as the oils were beaten and cleansed from it. Fullers (often called *cloth thickers*) were almost always men—largely because the task required a fair amount of strength. Similarly, women were rarely listed as performing the next step, the shearing of the cloth, though one woman named Isabella le Bruster was discovered shearing illicitly in mid-fourteenth-century Ghent.[25]

The 1292 Paris survey listed numerous women who produced and sold finished cloth. Aaliz de Vile-Neuve, for instance, was taxed a moderate 5*s* for making and selling linen cloth. Felt was apparently a more profitable fiber—Maheut *la feutrière* was taxed four *livres* for making and selling it. Hemp was still more expensive; a Parisian named Marguerite paid a steep tax of nearly eight *livres* for producing and selling it. Wool fabric was popular and lucrative in England. In the 1400s, Margaret Croke became so prosperous dealing in this commodity she could afford to live in a sumptuous London residence, and employ at least seven servants.[26]

All these materials had a variety of uses. In London, for example, Agnes Shepster and Margaret Swan produced sheets for the royal palace.[27] But most fabric was purchased to be made into clothing. Dressmakers and tailors were in constant demand—especially those who produced the colorful, stylish attire so loved by the very wealthy. In 1292, numerous Parisian women were listed as *couturières*, as was Ameline of the rue de Froit-Martel. Other women in that city made accessory items. Pérronnele *la chaucière* worked as a hosier in 1292, and Susane paid a large 70*s* tax on her coif-making business. In the 1420s, Guiote Sarre worked as a glover, and even produced gloves for the French king.[28]

Though these were all common occupations, in most countries the greatest feminine contribution to the textile industry was in the decorative crafts—such as producing the gold thread that was so popular in cloth decoration. Gold thread was made by wrapping a fiber thread with a thin layer of pig's gut, and then wrapping it with a very thin layer of gold. In late thirteenth-century Paris, a woman named Maheut was listed in this craft as a *fileresse d'or*. In thirteenth-century Genoa, women comprised more than half of the investors and producers of gold and finished thread in one four-week period.[29]

Female artisans also used this gold thread, along with jewels, silks, and other materials, to decorate cloth and clothing. This important craft was a major art form as well as an industry. Silkwork was yet another part of this decorative/luxury trade. It actually included three separate crafts: making thread from raw silk, weaving small silk cloths, and creating a variety of articles such as fringe, tassels, ribbons, lace, and girdles. In 1292 Paris, a woman named Pérronnele was listed as a lacemaker, and Ameline of la Grant Rue made and sold silk and leather straps, belts, and other such items.[30] In fifteenth-century Cologne, Tryngen Ime Hove was a mistress in the silk craft for some fifty years. She not only trained at least thirty-nine apprentices, but served as an officer of the guild. Tryngen bought nearly one fifth of all the raw silk purchased in Cologne in the early 1490s, which suggests that she turned out an enormous amount of finished silk.[31]

London records indicate the overwhelming presence of women in this industry in England. In the fifteenth-century, Elizabeth Stokton appeared in various London documents as an embroiderer and a silkwoman who made silk cloths for export to Italy. Some Englishwomen even became prosperous enough to dispense with middlemen and purchase their own silk. Though this could greatly increase a woman's profits, it was a complicated and expensive proposition involving several long-distance trades. Isabel Norman, for instance, bought her materials, which originated in Cyprus, from merchants who operated out of Genoa, though she herself was based in London.[32]

London eventually had so many women working in this craft they were even able to take legal action and influence legislative decisions. A group of *silkwymen* sent a bill to the mayor and aldermen of London in 1368 complaining about Nicholas Sarduche, a Lombard who was buying up silk and then raising its price in violation of the law. Not content with this action, the women also petitioned the king. Materials worth more than £1,000 were finally seized, and Nicholas was imprisoned. In 1455, silk workers again successfully petitioned the crown. This time they stopped the importation of rival foreign goods.

Though less influential than cloth workers, numerous women also worked in the food provisioning industry. Many could be found crying their wares—such as milk, green peas, pears, spinach, lettuce, eggs, parsley, and cheese—on the streets, adding to the bustle, aroma, and noise of all medieval cities. Records from late fourteenth-century Coventry indicate that forty-five percent of that city's street hawkers were women. The products available on London streets in the 1370s included the ale that Emma atte Grene sold for five *shillings* a barrel, and the salt-fish that Agnes Teukesbury hawked beside the Conduit. Around the same time, London housewives could purchase eggs from Juliana Tanner at a cost of one *penny* for seven eggs. In fifteenth-century London, Agnes Deyntee worked as a buttermonger until her customers complained about her product being spoiled. The incensed London court not only put Agnes in the pillory with the rancid butter hanging around her neck, but also ousted her from the city.[33]

The 1292 Parisian tax rolls give a particularly vivid picture of the activity on urban streets and illustrate women hawking a variety of foods throughout the city. A late thirteenth-century resident could buy tarts from Berte, pastry from Félise *la pastéere*, and kitchen herbs from Emeline. If the shopper were hungry, she could purchase cheese from Edelot at la Ferronnerie, fried fish from Phélipote on la rue de Merderel, mince pies from Pérronnele and her daughter Florie, fruit from Pentecouste, or bread from Mabile in front of the Louvre. All these delicacies could then be washed down with a drink bought from Béatriz the winemonger.[34]

In addition to street vending, women also participated as merchants in the more profitable provisioning trades, albeit in smaller numbers. Women often entered these professions as their husbands' helpers, and then inherited the businesses as widows. Jacqueline la Macherre (Machecoue) inherited a poultry shop, the *Golden Lion* at the Saunerie, from her husband in mid-fifteenth century Paris. Jacqueline continued to run the store for some years, making herself both wealthy and famous. Even fewer women were butchers because the financial and civic prosperity of this trade kept feminine participation to a minimum. However, in 1370 London, a woman named Emma Bayser was her husband's partner in a butchershop. Emma's *Skaldynghous* in Pentecostlane greatly annoyed her neighbor, who complained that hair, blood, and water from slaughtered animals flowed through her ditch into his garden.[35] This was not an unusual case since the waste products were always a problem in the butchering trade.

Numerous women made and/or sold bread and bakery products. Fines were frequently exacted in this trade, especially for giving short measure. Because bread weight was regulated by law, many bakers made a practice of giving thirteen loaves—a baker's dozen—for the price of twelve. In England, an *Assize* determined the weight of loaves to correspond to grain prices, and also limited the baker to certain amounts for overhead and profit.[36] In 1292 Paris, the women in this trade ranged from Sedile, who merely tended a public oven, to Thomasse, who baked and sold her own bread. A woman named Jehanne paid a very large tax of six *livres* on her bakery because she made a special type of bread from expensive white flours, which she cooked under the fire's ashes.[37]

Women were equally involved in the ale making and selling industry. When rural alewives moved to urban areas, they often continued brewing on a larger, more professional scale. Because competition was so fierce in this industry, many of these women simply moonlighted as alewives while continuing to practice other crafts. In fourteenth-century Coventry, for example, one woman was listed as both a tailor and a brewer. Similarly, a *brewstress* of Kings Lynn doubled as a stable keeper. Other brewers needed no such second occupation. For instance, two women listed in the 1292 Parisian survey apparently had thriving businesses. Pérronnele's 45*s* tax is evidence of her prosperity, as is the 48*s* paid by Anès of the rue St. Martin. A successful English alewife named Roysia Taillour had a relatively large brewing establishment in 1305 London. Her assets probably included a copper brewing kettle, mash-vat, coolers, wooden rudders, yeast tubs, mesh tubs, steeping cisterns, malt mills, and kiln cloth. By the next century, the number of female brewers in London had dropped. In 1420, only 20 of the 269 members of the London brewing company were women.[38]

Sometimes women even sold ale to the public in their own taverns. In the 1470s, Marguerite Turgis operated the famous *Pomme de Pin* on the rue de la Juiverie in Paris after she inherited it from her husband. Unfortunately for honest owners, taverns all over Europe tended to be associated with disorderly behavior and prostitution. Joan la Tapstere's establishment on Apcherche Lane, for instance, was a notorious refuge for bad characters in 1340 London.[39]

Women might also become innkeepers. In early years there were very few inns, but the numbers later increased, along with the number of people who traveled for business reasons. These establishments were not luxury hotels. Male guests often slept two or three to a bed, and each room contained several beds. Guests had to purchase everything separately, and most items were over-priced. The extant accounts of one English traveler listed a number of items that were charged individually. Among them were the bed, the bread, the beer, the meat he ate, and even his firewood.[40] The high cost of living at inns may explain why guests sometimes had problems with debts. In 1417, an innkeeper at Zwickau named Dorothea Storchin even had to help one of her guests arrange credit.

The gender of the owner of the inn at Zwickau was probably not unusual. Isabella de Toppesham, for instance, was listed as a *hostelere* in the court records of 1350 London. In fourteenth-century Ghent, Quintine van den Zande inherited and then ran her father's hostelry. Though she later relinquished the job to her second husband, Quintine likely continued to be in charge of food and beverages for the customers—a normal duty for wives of male innkeepers. The 1292 Paris survey also contains evidence of several *hostelières*. One named Denyse la Normande paid a 6*s* tax, while Ysabel de la Heuse paid a similarly moderate 8*s* on her inn on the rue Saint-Christofle. The Dame de Viane's establishment on the rue Auberi-le-Bouchier may have either been larger or more popular since she was charged a 20*s* tax.[41] It is also possible, of course, that she prospered because she offered some additional "services" at her inn.

There are so many records concerning women involved in such a variety of trades that we can easily conclude women did play a part in economic growth and urban development. Like immigrants from rural areas, women workers were actually needed to help cities and industries grow, so they were an asset at first. By the 1400s, however, most large cities had begun to discourage both immigration and women workers. The declining status and numbers of independent guild mistresses and female workers were rooted in the economic problems of the later Middle Ages. Once cities became well-established, their populations often increased to such an extent that resident men began to have trouble finding work. Hence cities and guilds enacted more rules toward the end of the Middle Ages to restrict immigrants and women from taking jobs away from male citizens. Less affluent urban males typically considered female workers and rural immigrants unfair competition since both would work for lower-than-average wages. Men who could not find jobs often complained about masters who preferred to hire women or newcomers, and so keep down their labor costs. In addition, since all women were supposed to be under the

A woman selling bread.

Österreichische Nationalbibliothek, Vienna

protection of men, theoretically the providers (men) had a greater need for and right to the available jobs.

The cloth industry provides a good example of the way women were pushed out of many trades. The job of spinning had always been largely in the hands of female workers until the craft was restructured late in the fifteenth century because men could not find other work. Thereafter, many spinning guilds made it illegal to hire a woman, unless she could prove that the job was her sole means of support. Similarly, the city of Bristol passed a law in 1461 that prohibited a master from enlisting the help of even his wife or daughter in the weaving trade, because so many men were seeking jobs in the industry. Clearly many female crafters and businesswomen were capable enough to hold their own in the marketplace, since the only way men could defeat their female competitors was to pass laws restricting their trade activities.

A marriage scene with a priest and witnesses.

Bayerische Staatsbibliothek, Munich

Personal Life

Bath scene.

Chapter Five

"LIKE A DOG TO HIS MASTER"

Personal Relationships in Theory and Practice

In a fourteenth-century Florentine survey, Caterina Rucellai disclosed her plan to build a new house for herself because she felt uncomfortable living with her married sons. In fifteenth-century Italy, after Contessina de'Bardi's repeated pleas failed to persuade her young son Giovanni to write home, this worried mother urged him, "I have neither had letters from you, nor anything written with your own hand . . . if I do not hear from you . . . I fear you may be ill."[1]

Twentieth-century women can easily identify with the sentiments expressed by Caterina and Contessina. The ideals regarding medieval relationships may be harder for us to understand since even the most intimate aspects of life were supposed to be firmly regulated. Women often found their personal ties strictly circumscribed by familial, societal, and clerical expectations. Moralists warned girls against developing friendships, falling in love with "unsuitable" men, or even becoming too closely attached to their children.

Friendships between women were considered to be mere distractions, since females were expected to concentrate on their homes and families. In practice, a number of factors did make friendships difficult to establish and maintain. Noblewomen, for instance, often lived on estates isolated from each other, and they were admonished to refrain from crossing class lines to become personally involved with lower-class servants or neighbors. The fact that highborn girls might be sent to distant lands to fulfill marriage treaties also made bonds between noblewomen hard to preserve. Despite these difficulties, some medieval noblewomen managed to maintain long-lasting friendships with their peers. In the mid-1300s, Mary of St. Pol, countess of Pembroke, retained close ties with Agnes de Mortimer. Mary's estate records reveal that Agnes was a frequent guest at the countess' dinner table. Mary and Agnes presumably derived a great deal of enjoyment from one another's company. Anne de Despenser, on the other hand, seemed to be motivated more by the age-old need for comfort and sympathy when she invited Lady Audele to visit her in 1402. Anne stressed that she desperately needed a friend to talk to about "my problems and the great pain I have lately suffered."[2]

Friendships among cloistered women were probably easier to maintain since nuns were usually confined together and had fewer distractions. Boredom and forced familiarity may well have led to jealousy and rivalry in some instances, however. Moreover, clerics frequently enjoined nuns and pious lay women from developing close relationships because worldly ties might impede their spiritual progress. Women did not always heed such advice. The renowned abbess Hildegarde of Bingen, for example, had a very close friend named Richardis von Stade, a sister at Rupertsberg (the convent Hildegarde had established in 1150). Richardis helped copy and correct Hildegarde's *Scivias*, and was a particularly beloved companion to the abbess.[3]

Well-off city dwellers expressed many reservations about extra-familial relationships between women. In his book of instruction the wealthy merchant of Paris, the *Ménagier de Paris*, advised his bride against such ties. In fact, he demanded that she walk through town, on those rare occasions when she went out at all, without stopping to speak to any man or woman on the road. This would presumably keep her from harm while protecting his reputation. The *Ménagier* further insisted that his bride must never allow "any ill famed women to be seen in [her] presence."[4] Again, despite the restrictions, there is evidence of friendships among prosperous gently born and urban women. The correspondence between Pippa di Tedaldi and Ginevra degli Alessandri reveals an enduring bond between these two fifteenth-century Italian women. For many years, they exchanged letters and small gifts. In a letter Pippa wrote in 1455, she "rejoiced" in her close friendship with Ginevra, saying it was a source of "great pleasure" to her.[5]

Poorer townswomen left little direct proof of friendships, but the close proximity of urban neighbors presumably initiated much of the same personal interplay—friendships, enmity, and gossip—that takes place in towns today. We can glean some indirect evidence of friendships from wills. For example, when no family member was available, close friends were usually named as executors. Isabel Dove of London died around the year 1435 while her husband Thomas was away from home. She thus needed someone she could trust to pay her debts, see to her burial, and then keep the remainder of her small property for her husband—as she poignantly stated, "unto his coming home from beyond the Sea."[6] Isabel's choice of Gertrude de Lunhx probably indicates that she was a close friend since Isabel trusted her, and because Gertrude was willing to assume such a task.

Written evidence of friendship is still rarer among rural peasants. They lived under numerous restrictions designed to protect the noble's property by tying his work force to his lands. For example, it was more expensive for a girl to marry a man from a different manor since she (or her family) had to pay her manor lord a fee to make up for his/her loss of a worker. Camaraderie and social ties for these women were almost always limited to their equals in their own villages. Nevertheless, contemporary sources often depicted peasant women talking, working, and playing together, an indirect confirmation that what we would term "friendships" probably existed among them. Saint Dominic wrote about how fond village women were of talking together. He even advised his friars that one of the best places to preach was in front of a village oven, since a group of women could always be found there, happily gossiping together while waiting in line to get their bread baked.[7]

Though such sources indicate that women did often have friends, the most important personal bonds for the majority of medieval females were their family ties. In a mid-fifteenth-century letter, the Florentine widow Alessandra Strozzi commented that her cousin Costanza frequently came to visit so the two women could enjoy a nice long gossip session.[8] A mid-thirteenth-century Englishman, Lucas de Worth, was apparently quite devoted to his sister Childlove. Though Lucas was not especially wealthy, he gave his sister the means to live as an anchoress at Faringdon, Berkshire, by purchasing a *corrody* for her[9]—paying Oseney Abbey to provide maintenance for Childlove for the rest of her life.

Though there were many important relatives, according to both ecclesiastical and secular theories, marriage should provide the primary personal/family relationship for a woman. Girls were expected to either marry or enter convents. Men believed women were simple and weak, and must be protected by "wiser and stronger" males. Theologians who thought females were oversexed added another wrinkle to this theory: women should wed as soon as possible so their sexual desires could be legitimately satisfied by their husbands.

Few young people chose their own partners, however, since marriages were usually business ventures arranged by parents or guardians to garner material advantages—political, economic, or social gains. Betrothal contracts between noble families specified dower, dowry, and property disposal if the couple remained childless, as well as a wide variety of other considerations. Marriage was originally a secular ceremony; the presence of a dowry, rather than a religious ritual, validated the union. During the course of the Middle Ages, the church became more involved in marriage ceremonies, but their legality still depended a great deal on appropriate dowry specifications. One reason for conducting the ceremony at the church door, for instance, was to let friends and neighbors bear witness to the exchange of property—and therefore to the couple's marital status. This was in the interest of both bride and groom, especially among the nobility, who had to concern themselves with the security of their estates and the rights of succession. As historian Erika Uitz stated, "The legally-acknowledged and church-sanctioned monogamous marriage" safeguarded the noble's lands and heirs, while granting "the wives of feudal lords authority in their husbands' long absences."[10]

In addition to financial gain, there were political benefits to be considered in marriage transactions. Parents or guardians frequently sacrificed brides to seal peace treaties or political/military alliances. In fact, marriage usually involved a trade-off of advantages. If the bride's relatives were already quite rich, for example, they might exchange a portion of the family wealth for a socially high-ranking groom, a political treaty, or a militarily important alliance. In 1360, John II of France sold his young daughter, Isabella, into marriage with Giangaleazzo Visconti, because the king needed money to pay off his own ransom. Visconti, on the other hand, already had money; what he wanted was royal blood and status, and the possibility of a crown for future generations of Viscontis.

The possibilities were staggering for a member of the upper nobility who was blessed with many offspring, since he or she could increase family wealth, prestige, and power by allying children across the continent. For instance, Beatrice of Savoy, countess of Provence, managed to acquire royal husbands for all four of her beautiful daughters. Matthew Paris was one of many thirteenth-century chroniclers enthralled by this brilliant success story. He said of Beatrice:

> No mother in all womanhood had so much reason to be proud and happy in fair and exalted offspring as she in her daughters.[11]

To a smaller extent, efforts to achieve the most profitable trade-off also regulated marriages for those of less exalted status. Among the gentry and wealthy urban families marrying above one's station was a primary goal, but wedding a person of lower rank was viewed with disdain. Seventeen-year-old Margery Paston discovered this fact when she fell in love with and secretly married the Pastons' estate bailiff, Richard Calle, in 1466. Her family was so irate that her parents refused to let her see anyone for three years. Her mother, Margaret, treated Margery as if she were dead. The Paston family allowed Richard to stay on as bailiff, but they never treated him as a relative. They viewed Richard's action as a legitimate method of achieving a higher status, but his young bride was censured for marrying an inferior who could bring them no social, political, or financial advantages.

To merchants, the financial aspects of marriage were frequently more important than class considerations. An entry in a Florentine merchant's diary/ledger shows a typical lack of sentimentality at the wedding altar. In 1393, Gregorio Dati needed almost a thousand gold *florins* for his business, so he married a woman named Betta. A couple of days later, Gregorio recorded his receipt of Betta's dowry—the gold *florins* he needed so badly.[12] Among less prosperous town inhabitants, the dowry was naturally smaller than it was for rich brides. In 1313, Agnes Cook of London could offer a dowry of twenty *marks* in cash, as well as a variety of household furnishings—such as a feather bed, coverlets, and table linens.[13] Although dowries were important to townspeople, the lack of extensive local family ties (especially among recent immigrants from rural areas) allowed some to pick their own marriage partners. An urban couple who chose each other sometimes viewed their marriage as a partnership, and their marital bond as more important than their former family identifications.

Peasants might also marry for personal reasons like mutual attraction, but there were many determinants of who married whom among the rural populace. To an even greater extent than in other classes, a peasant girl's marriage intimately involved her family, church, lord, and community. Peasant girls, who normally had access to fewer financial resources than men, were encouraged to wed since marriage offered a higher standard of living than they could attain alone.[14] But peasants also had some financial expectations. John Wade complained to the Belper manor court in 1312 that he had not received his wife Avis' dowry. Her father, Richard, immediately had to turn over goods and animals worth twenty-two *shillings*—a cow and calf, a surcote, and three sheep—to Avis' husband.[15] This case also demonstrates that it was John Wade, rather than his wife, who was being deprived of his rightful property.

It was unfortunate for women of all classes that the economic, social, and/or political benefits to be gained by marriage sometimes led men to attempt extraordinary ploys in their efforts to wed. In 1342, Henry de Suttone abducted Alice atte March, a London orphan. While a court case was pending over this irregular situation, Henry married the seven-year-old girl to Thomas de Staundesby.[16] The two men were apparently working together in a scheme to collect Alice's income of fifty *shillings* per year.

Despite all these practical considerations, marriage was naturally also expected to provide the most basic and important personal relationships, especially for women. Philosophies about exactly what was "ideal" in these relationships varied greatly. For instance, women of all classes frequently wished for kind, generous, loving husbands who would never beat them. Christine de Pisan advised women to look to their own behavior if they wanted such considerate husbands. She noted that women typically tried to make their husbands love them by making themselves more beautiful. But Christine claimed men would rather have "honest, virtuous, and simple" wives, so she stressed chastity, humility, and patience to her female audience.[17]

Similar sentiments were expressed by an anonymous Florentine mother who penned a letter just before her daughter's wedding, advising the girl on how to behave as an "ideal" wife. The mother cautioned her against taking her husband's money, even for charity, lest she be called a spendthrift and thereby tarnish her husband's good name. Since dishonor also resulted from spending too much time outside the home, the bride was admonished not to go into the city. She should not have close friends, or become too fond of her servants.[18] As outlined by this young girl's mother, the wife's primary duty was to guard her reputation and that of her husband by carefully attending to home and family.

Men generally approved of such advice, but most stressed an even greater desire for obedient brides. In his 1360 *Handbook of Good Customs*, Paolo da Certaldo advised Italian businessmen to return home frequently in order to keep their wives "in fear and trembling." Even though the *Ménagier de Paris* was a wealthier French merchant, he expressed a similar attitude, stating that a wife should be to her husband "like a dog to his master." According to him, when the husband came home, the ideal wife sat him down by the fire, washed his feet, fetched his slippers, and fed him a good meal. With endearing realism, however, the *Ménagier* admitted that a clean house and good food were not sufficient to make a man happy with his spouse. He suggested that a wise woman should also provide her husband with "delights, privy frolics, [and] lovings,"[19] which would make him long to return home to her.

Despite the lack of sentiment displayed in most courtships and marital negotiations, a variety of sources indicate that there were affectionate, happy medieval couples. Some men took pains to make up for the businesslike nature of betrothal arrangements. Enguerrand (VII) de Coucy did so in 1386 when he married his second wife, Isabelle of Lorraine. The middle-aged Enguerrand totally renovated and redecorated his castle—even building an indoor tennis court—in a romantic gesture that must have pleased his young bride.[20] After Richard II of England married Anne of Bohemia in 1382, they grew to be quite fond of one another. When Anne died in 1394, Richard became extremely melancholic. Outraged by the earl of Arundel's late arrival at the queen's funeral, the king actually knocked Arundel down. Richard II also demolished Anne's favorite palace because he could not bear the memories of a happier time there.

Less sensational evidence of loving couples is available in some extant correspondence from members of the Paston and Cely families. For instance, Margery Cely wrote a letter to her husband, George, in 1484 while he was transacting business in Calais. After assuring him everything was fine at home, Margery pleaded with him to return quickly to her:

> As soon as you may make an end of your business I pray you to speed you home, for I think it a long season since you departed

from me, and I know well I shall never be merry until I see you again.[21]

A variety of other documents reveal that the opposite state of affairs was equally common. Some couples were simply incompatible. This could even occur as a result of spiritual differences, such as one spouse being much more pious than the other. Dorothy of Montau's husband was very irritated by her frequent ecstatic trances. He was particularly incensed when these mystic experiences made her forget to buy groceries or scale the fish before she cooked it.[22] Another problem occurred in some towns where men traditionally married late in life, only after they had acquired status and wealth through their business or craft activities. Because young women were presumed to be most likely to bear healthy babies, these old men often wed young girls. Such marriages were frequently unsatisfactory to both spouses. However, forced unions between two children could also have unfortunate results. The parents of Elizabeth and John Bridge made them marry in the later 1400s, when both were only thirteen years old. Forced to get into bed with Elizabeth, John proceeded to turn over and go to sleep with his back to his frustrated new bride.[23] Although we know little about their later lives, the resentment expressed by both children after this night did not bode well for their future happiness together.

Among the nobility, the large amount of time men spent away from home—on their other estates, at the royal court, or fighting in wars, feuds, and Crusades—more frequently caused marital problems. While Godefroi, count of Namur, was at war in the 1080s, his wife, Sybille de Château-Porcien, apparently became extremely lonely. When her neighbor Enguerrand (I) de Coucy offered himself as a substitute for the absent Godefroi, Sybille willingly agreed. She evidently had no great feelings of love or loyalty for a husband she rarely saw.

Though some unsatisfactory marriages did end in divorce, acquiring papal approval for this drastic course could be a complicated and expensive procedure. Unhappy unions occasionally had much more disastrous consequences. In 1482, Galeotto Manfredi of Faenza married Francesca Bentivoglio in order to ally himself with her powerful family. From the first, a variety of problems beset the union between forty-two-year-old Galeotto and seventeen-year-old Francesca. She was particularly outraged by her groom's nightly visits to his mistress, Cassandra, who was living in a nearby nunnery. Galeotto and Francesca finally separated for a time, but the estranged couple were reunited in 1487. This reconciliation attempt was a spectacular failure. Francesca got so fed up, she tricked Galeotto into coming to her bedroom and then stabbed him in the back.

Such sensational endings to uncongenial marriages were relatively rare. More often people just endured their unhappy relationships or tried other ploys to escape. Men often did their duty and married for material benefits, but then kept mistresses for emotional satisfaction. The marital career of John of Gaunt, a great English magnate, ran the gamut of possibilities. His first marriage, to Blanche of Lancaster, was a happy union, though it was arranged merely to increase his wealth and power. After Blanche died in 1369, Gaunt married Constance of Castile to gain a crown for himself and his heirs while, for emotional fulfillment, he maintained Katherine Swynford as his mistress. They had four children and were lovers for more than twenty-six years, longer than most marriages lasted. Even though she had little money or status, Gaunt finally married Katherine after Constance died.

Other women were less patient than Katherine Swynford. Some who were unwilling to wait a quarter of a century for happiness even defied society and married for love. Uniting in a clandestine marriage was the most popular method of short-circuiting opposition; it dispensed with the formal ritual, calling of banns, and other public observances. Even a mutual promise to wed, if made before witnesses, generally sufficed to trick the church into confirming an unarranged match, regardless of parental anger. The church disapproved of secret unions as strongly as lay society did, but it was often forced to accept their validity—albeit reluctantly. The widowed heiress Marjorie, countess of Carrick, supposedly fell in love with handsome Robert Bruce in the 1270s. According to some chroniclers, she threw caution to the wind and kidnapped Bruce in order to wed him. Their clandestine marriage so angered King Alexander III of Scotland that he held several of Marjorie's estates for ransom.[24] Despite the unorthodox beginning of their relationship, the church upheld its validity and the couple remained together. Their son later became King Robert I (Bruce) of Scotland.

Though it involved no secret wedding, the irregular marriage of another impatient royal couple—Bertrade de Montfort and Philip I of France—caused an equal stir. Clarius of Sens and

Hugues of Flavigny were among the chroniclers who delighted in recording and embroidering this tale. The story began in the latter half of the eleventh century, when sixteen-year-old Bertrade was forced to wed Foulques *le Rechin*, count of Anjou. Foulques was not a romantic figure. Not only was he fifty years old, but he had already been married five times. According to the chroniclers, the new bride was quite unhappy until Philip I, the young king of France, came to visit and the two fell in love.

Young girls like Bertrade usually did acquiesce to arranged weddings because they had been raised to expect them, had been taught to obey their elders, and had few other options. But an unhappy bride might later seek elsewhere for the fulfillment her political union lacked. Though Bertrade was at first a dutiful pawn, she ended up fighting for her own happiness. Disguising herself as a page, Bertrade sneaked away to join Philip shortly after he left Foulques' castle. They persuaded a bishop to annul their previous marriages and wed them to one another. Unfortunately for the new royal couple, the pope excommunicated Philip because the annulments and marriage were irregular. The irate king had the case reopened, but it dragged on for more than a decade. Twelve years and three children later, the Parisian *curia* of 1104 finally ratified Bertrade's divorce, declared Philip's previous marriage null, and ruled that the couple could live together in a valid marriage.

Unlike Bertrade de Montfort, many women presumably suffered in silence through years of being tied to men they disliked. In light of such unhappiness, we might expect medieval women to fill the emotional gaps in their lives by becoming especially attached to their children. Many women probably did so, but mothers who apparently had little affection for their offspring were not uncommon. In secular literature, the emotional bonds between mother and child received little attention. These sources rarely depicted medieval women as mothers; nor did contemporary art works often show parents caring for their offspring.

Fathers were supposed to be in charge of discipline, and were often admonished to treat their offspring severely so that they would not become proud. The same moralists usually advised women to put their husbands' needs and interests above the welfare of their children. Children were supposed to be useful to their families, and parents often manipulated their offspring to obtain financial or political ends. In fifteenth-century Florence, parents expected young widows to return home with their dowries in order to be re-used on the marital chessboard (a common expectation in many regions). Women who did so thereby removed themselves, along with financial support, from their own children. The docile daughter who went home was condemned for ignoring her children's needs, but the loyal mother who refused to return was equally despised by her blood relatives for being headstrong and neglecting her own lineage.[25] Florentine society apparently spared little thought for the emotional bonds between daughters and their parents, husbands and wives, or mothers and children.

Peasant families also traditionally viewed children as assets—helpers who were much needed on the family plot of land, or babysitters for younger siblings. Although a couple might produce a child prior to marriage to prove that the partners were fertile enough to provide heirs and future workers, other peasant women killed or abandoned their babies. Infanticide was often a result of poverty; when economic conditions improved, the number of cases of suspected infanticide usually dropped. In some regions it was not uncommon for unwed mothers to dispose of their illegitimate babies—because of guilt feelings or fear of reprisals. In either case, girl babies were the most frequent victims because they were seen as expensive to raise but less valuable as adults.

"Overlaying" (suffocating the baby while he/she was in bed with an adult) was the most frequently cited cause of "accidental" infant deaths. Mothers and nurses were warned against sleeping with their babies, but it was difficult to distinguish between deliberate and accidental infant deaths. Temporal authorities tended to believe infanticide was restricted to women who gave birth out of wedlock, while the church favored the explanation that witches killed the children. Modern research suggests infanticide was probably most often committed by married couples who needed fewer mouths to feed, especially female ones.[26]

There were numerous reasons for the absence of emotional bonding between some medieval mothers and their children. One cause was the idea that reproduction was a male function, while the mother's body simply incubated the baby for nine months (see Chapter Two). Furthermore, legitimate offspring were rarely the result of love; producing heirs was a duty for both men and women. During discussions in 1477 about whom Marie of Burgundy should marry, a lady-in-waiting named Jeanne de la Clyte successfully argued that Maximilian of Austria was the best consort for Marie because he was old enough to father children.[27]

The greatest impediment to close bonding was the brevity of life expectancies for the young. Recent excavations of twelfth- and thirteenth-century cemeteries in Poland, Sweden, and Hungary revealed that forty-three percent of the skeletons were those of children under the age of fourteen.[28] Among peasants, adults could rarely provide full-time supervision because they usually had to work the land to prevent the entire family from starving. Babies might be left in the care of extremely young siblings, or even remain at home alone. Slightly older children learned adult tasks from their parents. Even at this age (four to ten), there was little close supervision. The accidental death rate for these children, who often died in mishaps associated with their "job training," was also extremely high by today's standards.[29]

Although affluent families hired nurses and other adult childcare providers, even royal children frequently died as a result of mishaps or diseases. Hence, in all classes, some mothers feared making a great emotional investment in offspring who had little better than a fifty percent chance of survival. Margaret and John Paston typified the brutally realistic attitude some parents adopted. They named both their first and second sons "John," since they wanted a "John Paston" to continue to hold the family estates. They simply assumed that at least one boy would die before their sons were old enough to inherit.[30]

This short life expectancy also made many parents feel obliged to have numerous children in order to ensure an heir for their family estates. Eleanor of Aquitaine and Henry II of England had eight children, and the realm eventually passed to their youngest son, John. The church put still more pressure on the faithful by calling procreation a duty and by forbidding contraceptive practices. Clerics even railed against couples who abstained from engaging in sexual relations solely to prevent conception. Though abstinence for spiritual purposes was highly approved, the same marital chastity practiced for contraception was perceived as an insult to God's plans. The cautionary tale of Clementia, countess of Flanders, was used to illustrate the perils of contraception. Clementia and her husband, Robert II of Flanders, had produced three sons within three years. A twelfth-century monk named Hermann de Tournai claimed that Clementia then used "feminine arts" to prevent conceiving again, because she feared the boys would have no inheritance if she kept up such a pace. Her assumption that she could arrange things better than God angered Him and He taught her a lesson by causing all three of her sons to die young.

Clerics rarely commented upon the other aspect of Clementia's sad story; she only used the prohibited contraceptives because she loved the children she already had. Presumably many mothers did feel great affection for their children. By studying English coroner's records, Barbara Hanawalt even discovered that villagers generally expected mothers to love their children, and neighbors expressed great disapproval of those who neglected or abused their offspring.[31]

Other medieval parenting concepts may be less understandable to the twentieth-century reader. One example was the notion that breast milk consisted of blood left in the womb after childbirth. In the process of traveling to the breasts, the blood turned white as it was purified. This idea encouraged many doctors and mothers to think a large variety of traits, both good and bad, could pass through breast milk into the suckling child. The story of Eustace of Boulogne typified this belief. Because he was once sullied by a servant's lower-class milk, he was never as brilliant as his brothers, both of whom became kings of Jerusalem. Though this idea lost popularity in the later Middle Ages, most prospective wet nurses were still carefully examined for correct behavior and the absence of moral or physical defects.

Another practice that may seem unusual was that some high-ranking parents sent very young children to be raised in other nobles' homes, claiming that this prevented them from becoming spoiled while giving them a better chance to learn the techniques of service, homemaking, or fighting. Children in this placing out system, those whose mothers died in childbirth, and youngsters whose widowed mothers left them in order to remarry, all grew up with little maternal nurturing. Today we might view these youngsters as deprived, though not all children were unhappy under the placing out system. Strong emotional bonds were sometimes forged within these surrogate homes. Yolande of Anjou and Sicily, who raised the future King Charles VII, was also his mother-in-law and biggest supporter. His mother, Isabeau of Bavaria, however, signed away his rights to the throne of France and, in essence, denied Charles' legitimacy. When Isabeau demanded that Charles be sent to her, Yolande's quill must have singed the page as she replied:

> A woman provided with a lover has no need of a child. I have not raised and nourished this one . . . for you to let him die . . . to send him mad . . . or to make him English . . . I keep him for my own. Come and take him if you dare.[32]

Not surprisingly, Isabeau let Charles stay with Yolande.

Among the peasantry, poverty sometimes forced parents to send their children away from home. Some desperate or greedy parents even tried to sell their children. Both temporal and ecclesiastical officials insisted that girls not be sold into prostitution, but parents or guardians could artificially stunt a child's growth and make him or her a dwarf. Knotgrass, dwarf-elder, and daisies were among the substances fed to children to prepare them for the underground dwarf trade. Dwarves were in such demand as court performers they were worth quite a lot on the black market.[33] The children themselves may have approved of this practice since dwarves were usually much better fed and more pampered than most peasant youngsters.

Even the church had no uniform policy regarding children. Many churchmen touted the popular notion that severe and frequent corporal punishment was necessary to suppress childish desires and curiosity, especially in the realm of sex. Several medieval theologians, however, contradicted the earlier belief that unbaptized infants went to hell.[34] Canon law insisted on parents supporting their illegitimate children, and the church helped some of these youngsters by legitimizing them. By the thirteenth century, another beneficial rule theoretically prohibited marriages between children who were not old enough to give their consent—twelve for girls and fourteen for boys. Since this was merely a guideline and the pope could grant a dispensation, in practice, some titled parents still united their offspring as mere toddlers.

Some mystics and theologians also helped ameliorate the harsh perception and treatment of children. Monks like Bernard of Clairvaux and Ailred of Rievaulx espoused devotion to the Baby Jesus, and simultaneously idealized youth itself. Numerous women became especially interested in this humanizing, nearly maternal trend. Future saints like Umiliana dei Cerchi (d.1246) and Agnes of Montepulciano (d.1317) reported visions in which the Christ Child visited them. In fact, Saint Agnes enjoyed holding the baby so much that she did not want to return Jesus to his mother. Female mystics sometimes even miraculously secreted breast milk to feed the Holy Infant. Saint Gertrude of Öosten lactated from

Christmas until the Feast of the Purification, presumably because she was so caught up in her visions of nursing the Christ Child.[35]

The treatment of orphans also varied considerably during the Middle Ages. Some were well cared for by relatives, guardians, or religious foundations. Other orphans had to fend for themselves, but many were helped by private or public donations. A relatively prosperous townswoman named Rose Raymond bequeathed four *livres* in 1335 to supply marriage portions for poor orphaned girls of Lyons. In the fifteenth century, the city of Frankfurt annually provided two such poor girls with small dowries so they could marry. The increase in such municipal support and in the numbers of orphanages in cities like Rome, Bologna, and Paris by the later Middle Ages may be evidence of slightly greater concern for the survival of the young. This trend would parallel the growing emphasis on Christ's childhood in the clerical community.

Rome, Florence, and other cities also established foundling homes to prevent large numbers of children from becoming victims of infanticide. In those communities, girl babies were not only more likely to be killed by their parents, but were also more at risk at the foundling institutions. Because fathers were less likely to "redeem" daughters (which required paying for their care), female infants were more apt to die of neglect than were boy babies.[36]

Not only foundlings, but female children in general were often abused or neglected. When Vincent of Beauvais advised Margaret of Provence, queen of France, about caring for daughters, he warned: "Guard their bodies and do not show a joyful face to them." A boy child was more valuable than his sister because he was the foundation and heir of his family. The girl child was merely a future childbearer for someone else's family, as well as a symbol of her father's weakness. Moreover, the family wealth had to be divided in order to provide her with a dowry. Thus the great Italian poet Dante claimed that the birth of a daughter usually "struck terror into her father's heart."[37]

Historian Dorothy M. Owen noted several cases of medieval mothers who played unsympathetic roles—such as forcing daughters to wed unwanted suitors. She then balanced that information by citing evidence of more caring mothers.[38] Significantly, the examples she unearthed of "more natural mothers" consisted of women who displayed affection for sons, not for daughters. A fifteenth-century Florentine widow, Alessandra Strozzi, also cared most about her sons. Shrewdly marrying her daughters below their social position, she was able to reduce the size of their dowry portions and save more of the family wealth for her sons. Once her daughters married, Alessandra essentially treated them as if they were no longer her children. In contrast, she kept in close touch with her sons, tried to negotiate financially and socially excellent marriages for them, gave them much advice, and struggled to keep their fortune intact.

Some mothers perhaps cared a great deal for their daughters, but believed that treating them harshly served as a "baptism by fire" which would train the girls to be extremely strong adults who could withstand childbirth, hard physical work, loneliness, husbands who beat them, and the variety of other hardships medieval women often faced. When these girls grew up, they presumably repeated the pattern of coldness and abuse with their own daughters. Margaret Paston, for example, was certainly not pampered as a child, and she in turn treated her own daughters with little affection.

Other documents indicate the existence of better relationships between some mothers and daughters. One example is a letter written in 1479 by an Italian woman named Bianca de'Medici. In her ninth month of pregnancy, Bianca yet appeared most worried about her mother, Lucrezia Tornabuoni. As the plague hovered over the vicinity, Bianca wrote:

> I am glad our family is well, for that is no small thing in these times. But I have worried about you, and still do, for you say you have to deal with so many people.[39]

There were clearly a wide variety of patterns among mothers and daughters, and obviously not all these relationships were unhappy ones. Since medieval girls and boys had lower expectations of selfless parental devotion than do some present-day children, many were probably quite satisfied with whatever affection they did receive. Furthermore, sermons and other men's writings provide indirect proof that there was frequently a huge gap between theory and practice. For example, both lay and clerical advisors constantly admonished women not to grieve and cry when a child died. The orthodox position was that such a fate was God's will, and the youngster was better off in heaven than on earth.[40] However, the mere fact that so many preachers and writers felt called upon to re-emphasize this traditional advice time after time indicates that few women actually remained calm when their children died.

Woman with child.

Bayerische Staatsbibliothek, Munich

In fact, the information available in extant wills, coroner's records, letters, and a variety of documents often contradicts the way other sources insist ideal relationships were supposed to work. Though no universal conclusions can be reached about personal relationships, these sources reveal that not all medieval mothers treated their daughters with the severity recommended by advisors like Vincent of Beauvais, nor with the coldness of women like Margaret Paston and Alessandra Strozzi.

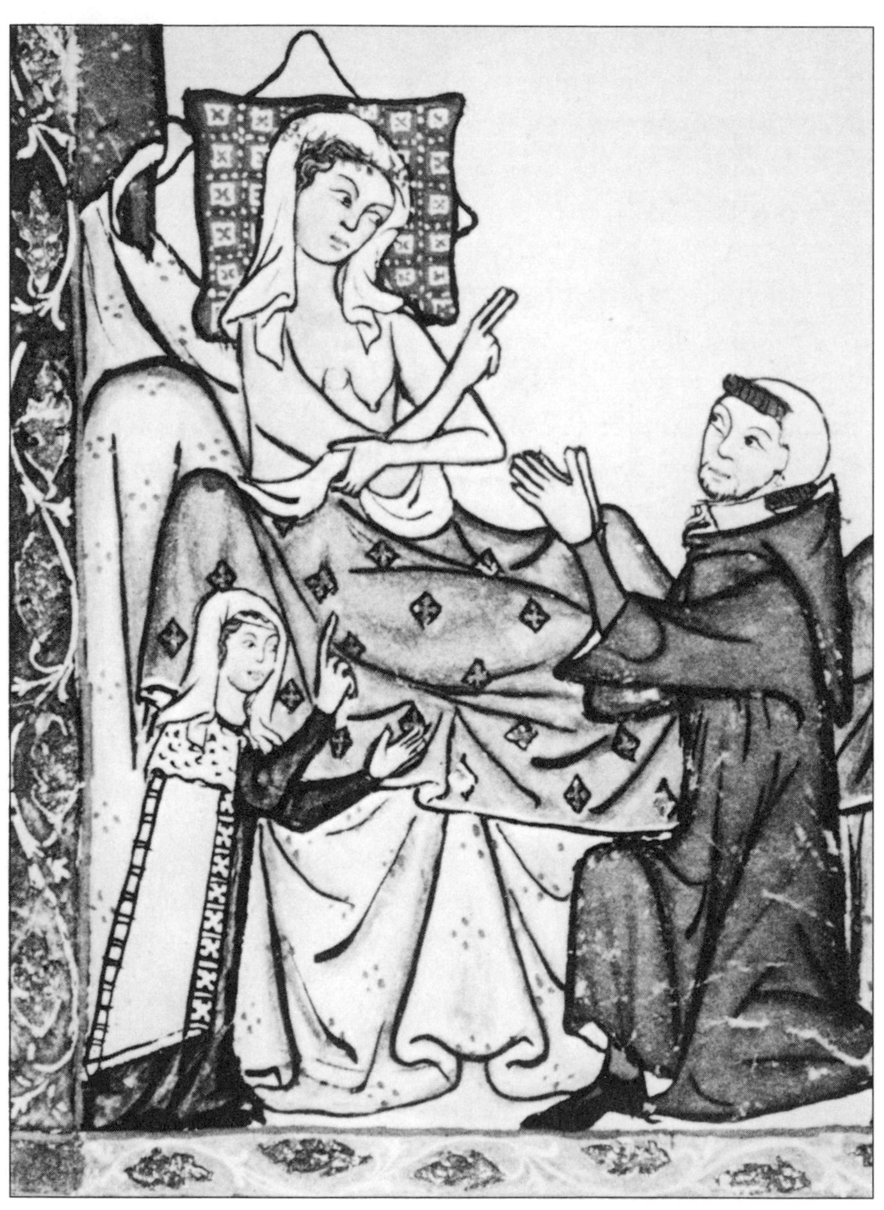

Troubadour scene, Manesse manuscript.

Chapter Six

NEVER ON SUNDAY

Sexual Mores and Behavior

Medieval literature often seems to present contradictory ideas about sexual mores and behavior. Courtly poetry, for example, traditionally embodied a conflict, or at best an unstable truce, between sexual desire and spiritual admiration. Troubadours romanticized highborn women, consigning them to a place atop a pedestal of virtue and nobility. Yet the exalted woman could never be the poet's own wife, since love was presumed to be impossible within the bonds of properly arranged and negotiated matrimony. Moreover, secular literature frequently depicted other female characters as extremely lascivious. This reflected a common male fantasy, and also helped men justify their own behavior to themselves and society. Like secular authors, religious writers placed women at two opposite sexual poles. Clerics extolled the virtues of pious women who chose to remain chaste, while simultaneously claiming that women were so lusty they constantly tried to seduce good men in order to quench their insatiable appetites.

The church tried to extend its philosophy into actual practice by strictly forbidding sexual intimacy outside of marriage, denouncing a variety of "unnatural perversions" like incest, and even scrutinizing marital sex. For instance, orthodox tenets insisted that the only acceptable position for lovemaking was face-to-face with the man on top of the woman. Among other teachings, most clerics also advised engaging in sexual intimacy only for procreative purposes, not for mere pleasure. Some theologians contended that even marital sex was sinful if the participants greatly enjoyed it.

Certain penitentials (manuals used by confessors as aids in determining suitable penances) restricted intimacy to those

Mondays, Tuesdays, and Thursdays when the community was not observing any holy day or fast. Other days were considered to be off-limits. Indulging in sexual intimacy on Wednesday, for example, was improper according to some penitentials because it was a traditional fasting day. Theologians often drew analogies between lust and gluttony. Both fasting and abstaining from sexual activity cleansed the body of worldly desires and prepared the soul to receive God. As historian Pierre Payer claimed, many theologians were completely unable "to reconcile sex and the sacred because sex was viewed as something unholy and unclean."[1] Clerics even used scare tactics to persuade the laity that these rules came directly from God. Gregory of Tours related the cautionary tale of a woman whose baby was monstrously deformed because she had conceived the infant on a Sunday. Engaging in sexual intimacy with a person who had taken holy vows also doubled the sin because both lechery and breaking a sacred oath were involved.[2]

Though the church talked a good game, its inability to keep even its own officials chaste diminished its moral authority. Celibacy had always been preferred, but originally some churchmen were allowed to marry. In the eleventh century, however, a reform campaign tried to reduce simony by prohibiting clerics from marrying. Churchmen who had children habitually bought church offices for their offspring; getting rid of married clergymen was therefore expected to be a major step toward removing this corruption from the church. But the papal edicts against clerical marriages were very unpopular, and enforcement was not immediately successful. Many village priests simply concealed their wives or mistresses by calling the women their "housekeepers."

Some priests supposedly threatened the virtue of village wives and daughters when their congregations tried to deprive them of feminine companionship. Other communities forced their priests to wed in order to safeguard village women from the danger they assumed any unmarried cleric represented.[3] In some cases the danger was all too real; extant court records are full of clerical rape cases. The vicar of Brent Eleigh, who raped Margaret Webbe in 1401, was evidently not a first-time offender since the judges called him a "common ravisher of wives and virgins"—a term the courts often employed when referring to iniquitous clerics. Churchmen also frequented brothels and bathhouses in large numbers. Records from the French town of Dijon reveal that twenty percent of the clients in these establishments were clerics—monks, friars, priests, and higher officials.[4]

Many high-ranking churchmen eschewed their vows of chastity; Rodrigo Borgia, who later became Pope Alexander VI, was one of the most famous. Escorting a beautiful courtesan named Nachine, Borgia was among the guests at a notorious christening party at the baths of Siena in the summer of 1460. This event turned into such a scandalous orgy that Pope Pius II wrote a letter to Borgia warning him against indulging in such excesses in the future. He had several children by another mistress, Vanozza Catanei. In common with some other high-ranking clerics, Borgia used his exalted position and church wealth to enrich his lover, and Vanozza thus amassed a fortune. She then wisely invested her "ill-gotten gains" in real estate, inns, and pawnshops. Borgia's last known relationship, with a young married woman named Guilia Farnese, continued after he became pope. The Romans sometimes poked fun at this, calling Guilia "the Bride of Christ."[5]

Celibacy was equally unpopular within the walls of some monasteries. In particular, homosexual relationships among medieval monks have received a great deal of attention in recent years. During the twelfth century, there was even a flourishing homosexual subculture in some monastic communities, though it disappeared in later years as attitudes hardened and punishments became harsher. This condemnation was not really new; theologians had never approved of homosexuality but, in the twelfth century, they had been concentrating most of their energies on stamping out heterosexual affairs among the clergy. It was impossible for church philosophers to condone homosexuality since the Bible denounced it. Leviticus 20:13, for example, stated that, "If a man lie with mankind . . . both of them have committed an abomination."

Saint Thomas Aquinas claimed that the act of sodomy was "unnatural" because only "the union of male and female . . . is natural to all animals." But Aquinas only condemned the act, not the person. Most theologians agreed, calling homosexuality "a habit deliberately taken up as an act of defiance and wickedness."[6] Thus homosexuals (a word not used in the Middle Ages) did not exist; they were heterosexual people who had chosen to engage in deviant sexual practices. Other churchmen were even less tolerant. In the 1230s, the Dominicans descended upon Germany after Pope Gregory IX charged them with putting a halt to what he believed was rampant homosexuality in that country. Gregory described homosexuals as "abominable" and declared they were:

> despised by the world, dreaded by the council of heaven, . . . more unclean than animals, more vicious than . . . anything alive.[7]

Though Gregory's rhetoric was harsh, he meted out few punishments. Within the next forty years, however, Castile, much of France, and parts of Italy instituted regulations against homosexuals in their law codes. By that time, lay and clerical officials alike had begun to speak out strongly against homosexuality. They sometimes linked homosexual acts and masturbation on the grounds that both led the laity away from marriage and procreation. These activities were social crimes because they led to depopulation, and were carnal sins because they were "unnatural."[8] Homosexuality was the greater sin so it required harsher penalties. By the fourteenth century, sodomy was punishable by death in many regions, although evidently this sentence was rarely carried out during the Middle Ages.

Nuns were also part of the flourishing homosexual subculture of the twelfth century, until increasingly sharp rhetoric and penalties forced lesbians to go underground with their relationships in later years. Canonists initially avoided this topic. The few early theologians who discussed the subject appeared shocked, but did not view it as a great sin or a threat to moral and social values. There were some exceptions, however, especially among clerics who condemned autoeroticism. Men who used sexual aids were subject to a forty-day period of penance, but Burchard of Worms (965–1025) decreed that females should do penance for a whole year. The term of punishment jumped to three years for women who used sexual aids as a group activity.

Popular opinion gradually hardened against lesbians, and once again the Bible was the source for condemnation. Theologians cited such passages as Romans 1:26, which stated that "vile affections" were evil and that "even . . . women did change the natural use into that which is against nature." Nor were these illicit relationships confined to cloistered women. Matthew Paris related an intriguing story of

> a good-looking noblewoman . . . [who] impregnated another woman . . . and in some weird and wonderful way became a father.

After citing biblical strictures against women who "take the active as well as the passive role in sexual intercourse," the chronicler claimed: "Such people have a deservedly abhorrent and filthy reputation."[9]

By the middle of the thirteenth century, such harsh rhetoric was typical and severe penalties were often recommended. Around the year 1270, the legal school at Orléans issued a code that called for dismemberment as punishment for a convicted lesbian. If this did not deter the woman, on conviction for a third offense, she was to be burned alive. As was the case with men, apparently there were few actual executions in the Middle Ages, though one girl in Speyer, Germany, was drowned in 1477 for being involved in a lesbian relationship.[10]

Intimacy between nuns was only one of the tempting forbidden fruits. Some religious women were no more virtuous in heterosexual matters. Girls who had no religious vocation, but had merely been enclosed in convents by their parents or guardians frequently found chastity too onerous a burden. When an early twelfth-century nun at Auxerre inscribed the mortuary roll of a recently deceased abbess, she eloquently expressed dissatisfaction with her chaste life. This anonymous nun harangued abbesses who strictly enforced the vows of chastity. According to the poet:

All Abbesses deserve to die
Who order subject nuns to lie
In dire distress and lonely bed
Only for giving love its head.
I speak who know, for I've been fed,
For loving, long on stony bread.[11]

Not all abbesses demanded strict adherence to chastity. Abbess Huguette du Hamel turned the French foundation of Port-Royal into a house of revelry in the 1450s. She and her lover, Baudes le Maître, also attempted to induce the young nuns of Port-Royal to join them in various wanton activities, such as bathing together. When ecclesiastical officials finally forced Huguette to abdicate her position, she and Baudes ran off together, absconding with many of the most valuable abbey possessions. In England during the same century, Margaret Wavere, prioress of Catesby, was charged with a variety of illicit activities. Her misbehavior ranged from pawning the convent's silver service to allowing frequent visits by her lover, a priest named William Taylour.

A double standard clearly prevailed with regard to illicit relationships. Very high-ranking clerics sometimes kept mistresses, while at the same time admonishing mere village priests and all women to remain pure and chaste. The same hypocrisy flourished among the laity. Kings and great noblemen were rarely censured for having mistresses. A fifteenth-century cleric probably spoke for most churchmen when he explained that mere adultery did not detract from a monarch's dignity or his divine right to rule.[12]

For the woman involved, such a position was presumably an honor, as well as a very lucrative career. Moreover, because females were denied official roles, some undoubtedly enjoyed having the power to influence the men who did govern. Diplomats and courtiers often petitioned the king's mistress, since some appeals were most likely to be granted when presented by the woman who shared the royal bed, had intimate access to the monarch's ear, and could put the king in the most receptive mood. Some women evidently had no qualms about selling themselves to kings and magnates, though most did take care to get a good price. Alice Perrers, for example, was quite well compensated for her lost virtue when she became the mistress of King Edward III of England. Among other gifts, she received the manor of Wendover, a large annuity, and many of the late queen's jewels from her royal lover. Alice became so wealthy that she could afford to lend a thousand pounds to Lord FitzWalter in 1375—a wise investment since she subsequently collected his castle of Egremont when he was unable to repay her.

Many noblemen happily emulated their kings by keeping mistresses. These women were also well compensated, albeit on a slightly lower scale than were royal concubines. Along with other gifts, John of Gaunt bestowed two manors (Gryngeley and Wheteley) upon Katherine Swynford, his long-time mistress. Other great nobles preferred a succession of short-term mistresses. Philip *the Good* of Burgundy had numerous lovers—including Agnes de Croy and Catherine de Tiesferies—and a great many bastards.[13] Temporary paramours were rarely compensated on the level of an Alice Perrers or even a Katherine Swynford, but they too were well-paid. As an added bonus, their children were traditionally brought up with the father's legitimate youngsters. Noblemen usually also found good marriages or jobs for their illegitimate offspring.

Few spiritual or temporal leaders condemned noblemen for straying from the marriage bed, but wives were not always so complacent. Strong-willed Beatrice d'Este insisted that her new husband Ludovic Sforza remove his mistress, Cecilia Gallerani, from court in 1491. Ludovic acquiesced to Beatrice's demands, but repaid Cecilia by marrying her to a highly placed noble and by giving the couple a palace. Though Cecilia received excellent retirement benefits from Ludovic, her story indicates that life as a mistress could be a degrading and insecure career. Women, in general, had virtually no rights, but a concubine's status was even lower. Cecilia was by no means the only paramour who was summarily ousted from court, as well as from her lover's bed, as soon as a new wife or mistress arrived. Nor was banishment the only tragedy that might befall such women. After her lover King Edward IV of England died, Jane Shore not only lost her position at court, but was accused of witchcraft by Edward's successor, Richard III (according to Thomas Moore). Her wealth gone, Jane eventually became a pauper haunting the streets and prisons of London.

Some mistresses also suffered pangs from their own guilty consciences. Rosamund Clifford, presumably the paramour of Henry II of England, retired to a nunnery (c.1170s) when she felt death near. She evidently took the veil in a last-ditch effort to atone for the sins of the flesh and be granted a place in heaven. In addition to divine retribution, townswomen often literally had to pay for their sins. A 1461 Parisian court charged Colette la Cherette of the rue des Gravilliers with committing adultery. Colette admitted she had been intimate with Noel Jolis for the past two years, so she had to pay a fine as punishment for her wanton behavior.[14]

The court records from 1397 in the English village of Ross-on-Wye reveal that peasants also condemned illicit relationships. The parish court reported that all was well, except several persons were guilty of fornication. A list of names—including Thomas Bewe and Alice Bryngwyn, and William Chiltenham and Helen Wade—followed this announcement. Typically, these fornicators and adulterers were cited by "common fame," because even activities that we think of as very private could scarcely be kept from village neighbors.

Villagers convicted of indulging in illicit sexual activity were chastised, fined, whipped, or sometimes even ousted from their communities. Adultery was deemed so serious an offense that even taking in promiscuous miscreants was illegal. A 1337 Warboys village court cited John Tymme for receiving Richard Reynold and Mabil Decoun—a couple the court termed "known adulterers."

Some women who gave birth out of wedlock were so ashamed that they killed their infants, the physical symbols of their transgressions. Little evidence exists about their partners in sin, except for those men who actively pressured their lovers to dispose of the illicit babies.[15]

As such information indicates, promiscuity was strictly forbidden for females. Eleanora of Arborea, a fourteenth-century ruler of Sardinia, commented on the fact that women were almost always more severely punished for committing adultery than were their male partners. Noblemen's mistresses notwithstanding, even women of the most exalted social status were expected to remain chaste. The chronicler Roger of Wendover expressed the traditional view about the importance of feminine virginity in his account of the wedding in 1235 uniting Isabella of England with Frederick II, Holy Roman Emperor. Roger stated:

> Much as [Isabella] had pleased [Frederick II] in outward appearance, she pleased him even more in the marriage bed, when he found the signs of her virginal purity.[16]

This attitude explains why girls of all classes were admonished to retain their virginity until marriage, especially if they hoped to achieve socially and financially "good" matches.

Because society viewed non-virginal unmarried women as "spoiled," and even a breath of scandal could ruin a girl's chances, a further hazard was that a less than morally honorable suitor could use seduction or even rape to force a marriage. John of Gaunt's daughter, Elizabeth of Lancaster, had been betrothed as a child to John Hastings, earl of Pembroke. He was an acceptable husband for the daughter of one of the richest and most powerful men in England. In the later years of the fourteenth century, however, she married John Holland in a very hasty ceremony. This medieval version of the "shotgun wedding" was performed for the sake of appearances. Gaunt had to accept the poorer, lower-ranking Holland as his son-in-law, because the young man had already bedded and "ruined" Elizabeth.[17]

Women needed to guard their purity after marriage with equal vigor. Wives who did not do so were as greatly condemned as promiscuous young girls. Adultery was usually considered just cause for the unfaithful wife to forfeit her property—dower, dowry, and all other financial holdings. Isabeau de Cambrai, a rich Parisian merchant's wife, lost her dowry and other property in 1466 because her irate husband, Guillaume Colombel, had lodged a charge of adultery against her.

Society as a whole viewed an adulterous wife's actions more as an insult to her husband's honor than as an offense against a moral code. This belief permitted the wronged husband to avenge his honor, as the celebrated story of Francesca da Rimini illustrates. Her husband, Giovanni *the Lame* Malatesta, discovered Francesca in a compromising position with his brother Paolo *the Handsome*. Giovanni took his "justified" revenge by murdering the lovers (c.1285). In Dante's *Divine Comedy* the lovers languish in hell, where Francesca contrasts their current "wretchedness" with her memories of how happy they once had been.[18] Though Dante did not envision Francesca in the lower regions of hell, he did believe her sin consigned her to eternal unhappiness. Apparently men assumed an adulterous wife could not expect much more compassion from God than she received from her husband.

Francesca's story may be the most famous example, but hers was not an isolated case. Filippo Maria Visconti's marital history is perhaps an even better illustration of the double standard in sexual behavior. Visconti, the ruler of Milan in the early fifteenth century, accused his wife, Beatrice da Tenda, of committing adultery with her lute player. Though the evidence was flimsy, if not non-existent, Visconti had Beatrice executed for sexual misconduct, while he continued his own long-standing affair with Agnes del Maino.

Despite such dangers, some women did manage to conduct and survive their own love affairs. Catherine Sforza, for instance, was never executed for her scandalous conduct. After her first husband, Girolamo Riario, died, Catherine enticed young Antonio Maria Ordelaffi, the heriditary ruler of Forli and Imola, into her bed. She hoped to persuade him to marry her, thus strengthening her position as ruler of these cities. The papacy did not want Ordelaffi back in power, however, so the pope exiled him and then confirmed Catherine's right to govern as regent for her minor son. She did not even have to remain for long without male companionship. In 1489, Catherine fell in love with her nineteen-year-old brother-in-law, Giacomo Feo. He first became her lover, and then her husband. After he was murdered, she had an affair with Giovanni de'Medici. She secretly married him after she became pregnant. Catherine's behavior was not so different from that of some noblemen, but she was an unusually strong-willed and powerful woman.

Perhaps there were other women who behaved much like Catherine Sforza, but were simply not "important" enough to have had their activities recorded. In cities, women whose sexual transgressions made their way into the written records were most often prostitutes, rather than merely "loose women." On the other hand, in regions like southeastern France, vagabonds, part-time prostitutes, mistressses, and "easy" women were legally and socially viewed as the equivalent of common whores. In many cities, common bawds were often run out of town, but this never prevented the "oldest profession" from flourishing throughout the medieval world. In several poems, François Villon mentioned Parisian prostitutes—like Marion *l'Idol* and *La Grosse* Margot, who both owned houses of ill repute. Villon could undoubtedly have disclosed other names; by the 1400s, Paris was home to some 3,000 whores among its population of about 75,000. Nor was the French capital unique. Other cities across Europe boasted similar numbers of prostitutes. By the year 1500, Rome's population of nearly 100,000 included approximately 7,000 scarlet women. At the same time, Venice reputedly contained 11,654 ladies of pleasure, to service its general population of less than 150,000. Even in smaller cities like Dijon—which contained 2,614 households in the later 1400s—there were numerous prostitutes. The records indicate that approximately one hundred whores worked in Dijon at that time.[19]

Although the church disapproved of prostitution, its views on the subject were tempered by its misconceptions. Some theologians claimed women were too promiscuous to control, while others called prostitution a necessary social evil to prevent men from turning to other males for sexual gratification. Most churchmen did advocate reforming prostitutes. They could marry if they could find husbands; in 1198, Pope Innocent III even declared wedding a whore in order to reform her "a work of charity." But the main clerical focus was on converting the women into nuns. The Parisian ecclesiastic, Fulk of Neuilly, preached vehemently on this subject and even helped found a community for reformed prostitutes in the early thirteenth century.[20]

Despite the efforts of well-meaning churchmen, houses for penitent whores probably never achieved the standards of other religious foundations. A typical establishment, the Order of the Repentant Sisters of St. Catherine founded in early fourteenth-century Montpellier, fulfilled primarily social rather than spiritual needs. It came to serve as both a refuge for reformed "hookers" and a retirement community for older, possibly less repentant ones. Religious duties were not especially rigorous at St. Catherine's; everyone simply said a few *Hail Marys* and *Our Fathers*, and went to confession once a month.[21]

Civil legislation was generally much less helpful. A lack of legal protection was one major problem. In most cities, whores could not sue for their fees, nor could they accuse anyone of theft or assault. Municipalities were especially unwilling to pursue complaints against men who raped ladies of the evening, since most people believed only chaste women could actually be raped.[22] During the later Middle Ages, however, authorities in some regions began to perceive prostitution as a valuable social service. Prostitutes protected "honest" women from unruly men, they prevented foreigners and young local men from committing more serious sins or crimes, and their ready availability decreased the number of female adulterers since men could satisfy themselves with whores rather than trying to tempt other women.[23] In these areas, town laws and even rape statutes might help protect prostitutes.

A few cities—like Bologna in 1259 and Venice in 1266—attempted to eliminate prostitution entirely.[24] Most merely tried to regulate it. Efforts to control prostitution in many regions focused on simply modifying the streetwalker's attire so she could be easily identified. Mid-thirteenth-century Parisian authorities instituted a *cloak of prostitution* specifically to identify whores. The city adopted this measure after Queen Margaret of Provence unknowingly gave the *kiss of peace* to one such woman at a city church.[25]

Many cities particularly enjoined ladies of pleasure from wearing the fashions of "honest women." In 1353, an English chronicler reported,

> it was ordained at the insistence of the people of London that no woman who was known to be a prostitute should wear a hood unless it were striped, nor should she wear furs, nor lined garments.

Each town or region used different styles or colors to set its prostitutes apart from the rest of feminine society. Several French cities adopted red knots on the shoulder; Toulouse and Parma designated white as the whore's color; Leipzig women wore yellow and blue cloaks; and Bern and Zurich both used red caps to distinguish females engaged in the oldest profession.[26]

Paris particularly forbade prostitutes to wear gold and silver buttons, buckles, belts, pearls, and furred robes. In 1427, a Parisian court publicly chastised Jeanette la Petite for overdressing, and looking like an "honest woman." The authorities tore off her linen sleeves, cut her train, and donated her silver belt to a hospital. By the middle of the fifteenth century, however, cities such as Dijon and Lyons had begun allowing whores to dress in more stylish clothes with no "sign" to indicate their profession. In Avignon, prostitutes could even wear furs and silks.[27]

Clothing regulations were one way for cities to attempt to maintain control over prostitution, but various areas tried different methods. Small villages and towns in Languedoc often tried to insure public order by passing regulations allowing whores inside municipal walls only once a week. Other communities confined prostitutes to designated streets or areas, like Cock Lane in London or Hot Street in Montpellier. Such efforts were never entirely successful; city records continued to cite resident prostitutes—such as Dulcia de Gravesend of 1266 London or Jehannetta Bardin, called "La Noire," of 1421 Paris[28]—for straying from the prescribed areas.

Municipal records also contain frequent references to problems caused by prostitution. In 1483, the London city council approved its latest in a long line of petitions designed to remove what it called "strumpettes" and "mysguyded and idil women" who walked about the city, frequenting taverns and plying their trade among righteous men.[29] Southwark, a separate municipality across the Thames, was home to many of these whores. Prostitutes who solicited business on most streets in London proper were usually banished to that community.

Women who owned or worked in brothels frequently had their own legal difficulties. In 1364 London, the court forced Joan Grene to discontinue running her bordello, apparently because it was outside the prescribed red light district.[30] Brothels could also be dangerous since they were traditionally houses of true ill-repute where fights, murders, and other criminal activities flourished. In 1271 London, Philip le Orbatour murdered Hugh the Cook during a fight at the whorehouse in Bredstrete owned by a "madam" named Richolda. Another example indicates that the practice of "rolling" drunks did not originate in the twentieth century. In 1263, Richard Valet was out for an evening's pleasure at a bawdy house in London when three residents of the place relieved him of his valuables. The women quickly discovered Richard was not as drunk as he had appeared since he pulled a knife and killed Beatrice de Wynton, one of the prostitutes.[31]

In regions like southern France, this kind of violence decreased somewhat as prostitutes and their clients became slightly more acceptable in the later Middle Ages. The fifteenth century was also the peak period for municipally owned whorehouses in this region, and many women, like Raynauda of Melius, became very successful madams. The town of Pezenas actually owned Raynauda's establishment, a typical arrangement among area bordellos of the day. She simply continued to run the house as a brothel *farmer*, or middleman between the town and the prostitutes. Brothel farmers, also called *abbesses*, usually received profits from their whorehouses in exchange for paying certain fixed sums to the town. Though many early farmers were women, by the end of the fifteenth century, there was a growing tendency to replace them with male farmers. This trend often proved detrimental to the prostitutes' welfare. The residents of a brothel farm lodged a complaint against their municipality at the royal court of Toulouse, because they resented their new male farmer's callous attitude. The prostitutes accused him of forcing them to work too many hours, and being no better than a common procurer.[32] This conflict was caused by a new view of prostitution as a very lucrative business—one that predominantly male middlemen could easily milk for its maximum profit potential.

Some women escaped from municipal problems by taking to the road. Many camp-followers who accompanied male armies were professional or semi-professional prostitutes. Generally accepted as necessary adjuncts to army life, whores not only kept troop morale high, but many also doubled as nurses, cooks, and laundresses. Arabic accounts of the Crusades frequently dwelt upon the hordes of scarlet women who accompanied the Latin warriors. One historian reported that three hundred beautiful whores sewed crosses on their bodices and sailed to Acre. He claimed they set up tents into which they enticed even celibate men and Muslims. According to writer Imad Ad-Din, Western women believed that if they had sex only with celibate men, they had committed no sin. Yet another chronicler vowed that Christian soldiers would not do battle unless they were first satisfied by women.[33] Many of these accounts were obvious exaggerations, if not outright lies. They were useful propaganda because they made the enemy seem like lecherous fools. On the other hand, both Arabic and Latin chronicles show that the Crusaders, like most armies, were accompanied by their fair share of prostitutes.

Women who did not wish to travel sometimes attempted to bypass laws against prostitution by covering up their actual profession—pretending instead to work at more legitimate crafts. This ploy allowed a madam to run her "cathouse" in a more commercial area, thereby increasing her clientele and, ideally, avoiding legal complications. But a number of trials reveal that this deception did not always work. In 1415, a Parisian court heard a case against Alison la Jourdain who was accused of using her craft membership to conceal her activity as a prostitute. The weaving guild claimed that her house on a street of textile establishments was actually a brothel, and her apprentices were really professional ladies of the evening. Alison had deserted her husband, and she owned an expensive and much-visited house full of young women—facts that lend credence to the assumption that she was indeed a medieval madam. This conclusion is not necessarily negated by some of Alison's witnesses who claimed she was no prostitute, "but just good company."[34]

Possibly the most widespread camouflage effort was that of hiding bawdy houses under the guise of bathhouses. Respectable baths were extremely popular with both genders, and commercial bathhouses also provided employment for both sexes. Shaving male customers was one of the few occupations available to male workers. Female attendants performed a variety of chores like pouring water, rubbing bathers with brushes, and providing couches for resting after the baths. Since bathhouses employed and catered to both men and women, temptations were ever-present, and in many areas, they were openly acknowledged as bordellos. In fifteenth-century Dijon, for example, it was no secret that Jeanne Saignant worked as a procuress in the bathhouse she owned. Similarly, Casotte Cristal openly ran a very profitable bathhouse/brothel in late fifteenth-century Lyons.[35]

Extant marginalia routinely caricatures female bath attendants as prostitutes, indicating they had a very low reputation.[36] Moreover, by the fourteenth century, *stewe* had become synonymous with bawdy house in London, although *estewe* had originally meant merely a hot bath. The number of laws enacted to restrict lewd activities at bathhouses also supports the conclusion that these establishments richly deserved their unsavory reputation. Spanish records indicate that courts frequently levied large fines on men we would call "peeping Toms," and on those who stole female bathers' clothing. Legislation against illicit sexual activity at bathing establishments was never a total success, and many rulers simply accepted bathhouses as thinly disguised brothels. Philip, duke of Burgundy, for example, once hired a Valencienne bathhouse and all its ladies of pleasure to entertain an English embassy.[37]

By and large, efforts to reduce and/or control prostitution merely added hardships to the lives of many poor women. A few prostitutes may have been attractive women who could make better livings as demi-mondaines than they could at more "honest" professions; in much of France, a prostitute could make as much money in one hour as a female vineyard worker earned with a full day of hard labor.[38] But most whores on city streets were not women who had chosen this life; they were impoverished females who had few other career options. The legislation enacted to curtail women's craft activities, especially in the later Middle Ages, forced many unemployed women into prostitution for survival. In late fourteenth-century Prague, for instance, a creditor named Anna Harbatova put Dorothy of Strygl to work on the streets because Dorothy could not pay off her loan in any other manner.[39]

Most cities contained orphans, "ruined" girls, and untrained women of the lowest classes who frequently had no choice but to sell their bodies. Their problems usually increased as they got older; some prostitutes went from one branch of the profession to another in a downward spiral. Simone Plateau of Dijon, for example, began her career as a mistress. She later became a prostitute in a private brothel. As she aged, her clientele apparently dropped off and she had to leave this establishment; she then entered a municipal brothel.[40] There is no record of where Simone went next, but many such women ended up destitute on the city streets by the age of thirty. A few could enter convents, find husbands, or acquire jobs as servants, but many others undoubtedly eked out a living as beggars.

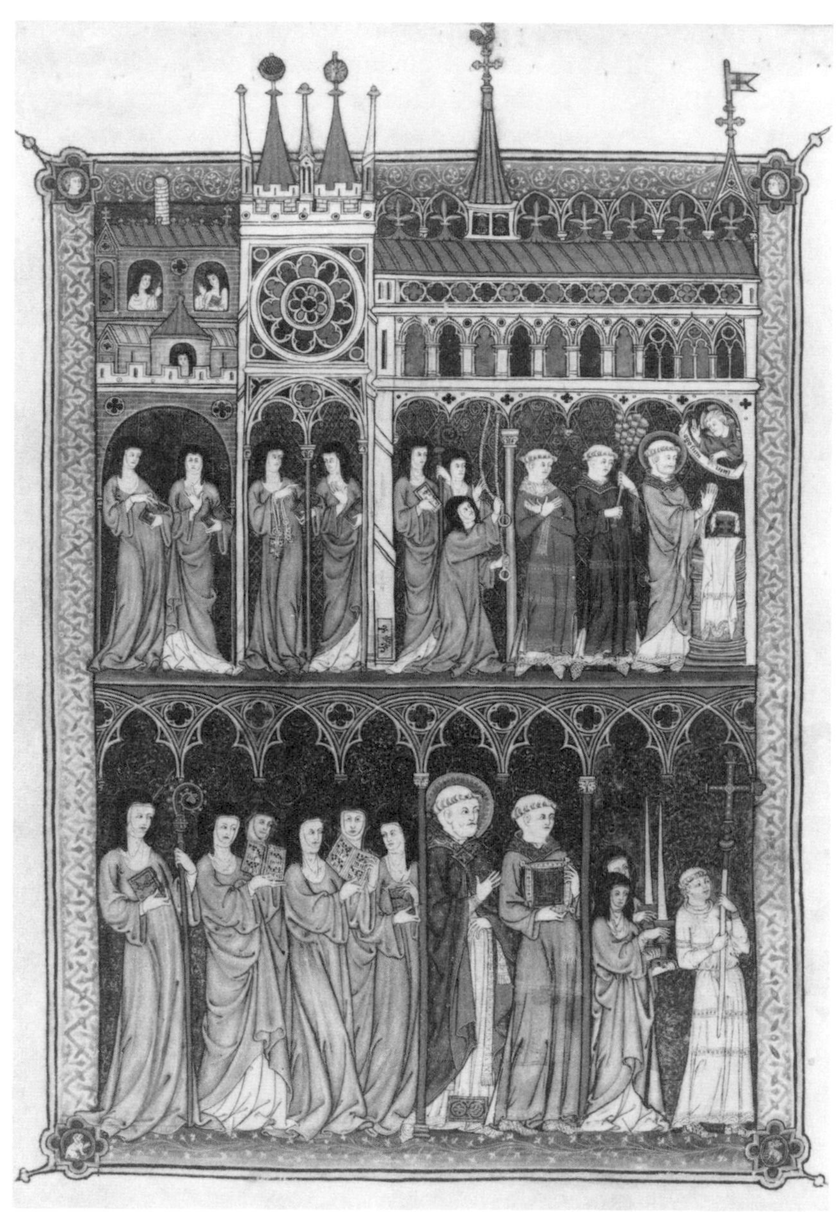

Abbess and nuns in procession.

British Library, London

SPIRITUAL LIFE

Saint Brigitta of Sweden receiving a revelation.

Pierpont Morgan Library, New York City

Chapter Seven

NAKED STATUES AND HOLY BONES

Woman's Place in the Medieval Church

To the wife suffering from a severe beating by her husband, the mother watching her children die, and the farmer breaking his back to put a loaf of brown bread on the table, Catholic doctrine offered hope for a future of happiness and ease in heaven. The Middle Ages is sometimes called *The Age of Faith*, since it is nearly impossible to overemphasize the church's importance. Regardless of gender or socio-economic class, the tenuous hold people had on life tended to make them extremely conscious of the afterlife. Moreover, when natural disasters, diseases, and wars struck, most people believed the only way to alleviate their suffering was either to appease or appeal to God.

Religious beliefs and rituals were a part of everyday life at all levels of society. In nobles' households, for instance, clerics served as almoners, secretaries, bookkeepers, clerks, scribes, messengers, and other functionaries. Some also conducted religious services, since almost every castle had its own chapel and its own resident chaplain. The entire household—masters and servants—normally attended Mass, daily worship, and other services together, helping create a closely knit community.[1] Townspeople revealed their reliance on God and His church in the large numbers of city buildings that housed various religious groups. In London, for example, a city of only some 35,000 inhabitants in the early 1300s, there were one hundred and twenty-six parish churches. This did not include other London institutions dedicated to God, such as monasteries and hospitals.[2]

The church was perhaps even more vital to rural peasants because it served so many functions in village life. The building itself doubled as a meeting place, and was frequently used as a bank or vault. A school, a hospital, and a hotel, the church served as the core of village life. The graveyard provided an area for meetings or a haven for the local populace, as well as being the only sanctified burial ground. Wakes held in the churchyard for patron saints provided food, drink, and entertainment to the peasantry. In both rural and urban areas, fleeing criminals could find forty days sanctuary in a church, and the church tower housed bells that were used for many purposes, including "ringing off" hails or thunderstorms.

Throughout Christendom the ecclesiastical hierarchy and the doctrines it espoused had some influence on every facet of medieval life—art, science, law, economics, and education. As the highest ranking churchman, the pope occupied the top of this structure. Some pontiffs were very worldly, while others were ascetics; some were apolitical, but others concentrated on the political, military, and financial bases of their position. Regardless of individual character, however, each pope believed himself to hold a divine commission to enforce papal authority by using moral ascendancy, ecclesiastical courts and armies, excommunication, and political expertise.

There were a wide variety of clerical ranks and offices beneath the pope. One basic division was that between the regular and the secular clergy. Derived from the Latin word *regula*—meaning rule—the "regular clergy" were clerics who were bound by a rule and who belonged to a religious order. The Latin word *saeculum*—meaning the world—was the basis for the term "secular clergy." These clerics were ordained but did not belong to a monastic order; parish priests, for instance, ministered to people under the jurisdiction of a bishop. High-ranking officials, such as bishops, abbots, and abbesses, were often great landlords on the same level as temporal earls. The lesser clergy included sub-deacons, priests, and still lower-ranking jobs like those of chorister, parish clerk, or lector. In general, churchmen held an exalted position in medieval society. They were the intermediaries between God and humanity, and were often the only people who could read and write. By default, they also became the transmitters of much of history and philosophy, which may affect the accuracy of extant records.

As we noted when discussing clerical celibacy, the doctrines these clerics espoused changed and evolved over time. For instance, two elements the modern reader is apt to associate most strongly with the Roman Catholic Church were not adopted until the 1215 Lateran Council in Rome. At this time the doctrine of transubstantiation was formalized. Annual auricular confessions also became compulsory, enabling the clergy to exercise greater control over the laity, who now had to make these personal confessions on a regular basis. One point did remain constant: because only the ordained clergy could perform the sacraments (special rites sanctioned by Christ) necessary for salvation—Baptism, Holy Eucharist, Penance, and Extreme Unction—the church had some authority over all its parishioners. In addition, its female members could not become too powerful, since only men could say Mass and perform most sacraments. Even the most powerful abbess had to turn to a man for the rites necessary for salvation. Of course, many male clerics—like doorkeepers, clerks, and lectors—were also obliged to turn to the ordained clergy to receive the sacraments.

Occasionally, however, women achieved a quasi-priestly role in death denied to them in life. After Mary of Oignies died, she appeared in a monk's dreams to give him the chalice of communion wine. A similar visionary glimpse of Juliana of Cornillon revealed that she was also handling this sacred cup at the heavenly altar, as Christ's assistant. By this time, the laity was not allowed to even partake of this wine—the blood of Christ—much less hold the cup, so these visions were presumed to indicate that Mary and Juliana were extremely holy and were greatly favored by God. Some living female mystics supposedly received communion directly from Christ after they had been denied it by their earthly superiors. In effect, they bypassed or controlled male priests; after God showed His approval, the church almost always allowed these pious women to receive communion as often as they wished.[3] Barred from obtaining official clerical powers, they achieved charismatic powers—to teach, heal, and even denounce immoral priests—because of their holy asceticism and mystic visions.

Pious authors frequently urged less visionary laywomen to live up to ecclesiastical images of the best feminine behavior. In her later years (c.1480s-90s), Cecily Neville, duchess of York, followed a daily routine that conformed perfectly to these clerical expectations. Every morning she got up at seven o'clock, in time to hear her chaplain say two services. She dressed before participating in two more services and three Masses. Cecily held audience for an hour after dinner, rested for fifteen minutes, and then prayed until

Evensong (she usually heard three of these services). After supper she indulged in "honest mirth" with her ladies for a short time, before saying her prayers and retiring at eight in the evening. For entertainment, at both meals she listened to a talk or a reading from some religious text.[4]

Clerics generally approved of women who behaved like Cecily Neville, but their most frequently expressed sentiment was that all females were weak and particularly apt to lapse into sin. This view helped popularize, or at least justify, a variety of harmful practices, such as wife-beating. An accepted custom in many societies, canonists sanctioned it on the grounds that physical brutality kept women in proper subjection. Far from finding sympathy in the church, abused wives were instructed to win back their husbands' favor by being more obedient. When rampant abuse finally forced clerics to scale down their acceptance of wife-abuse, some merely advised husbands to treat their wives no worse than the men treated their hens and pigs.[5]

The many theologians who displayed extreme aversion to sexual intimacy were also apt to voice negative opinions about women. Some claimed Eve's principal sin was not disobedience to God, but opening up a Pandora's box of sexual passion. As a result, theologians often projected sexual guilt onto Eve, and by extension to all women. Faced with such rabid disapproval, some women went to surprising lengths to refute these perceptions, and feminine miracle-workers' names swelled the rolls of medieval saints (Chapter Eight). The majority of women did not aspire to the heights of spirituality that marked female saints, but even many of these more moderate women proved their worth as active participants in the church.

Purgatory and its Financial Ramifications

The fear of hell and purgatory had a considerable effect on both men and women. Purgatory was where souls not totally purged of sin went after death—a place of punishment and cleansing between heaven and hell. For a price, clerics would say prayers to help sinners progress from purgatory to heaven. This belief system thereby encouraged the faithful to support holy men and women with alms, bequests, and other donations. Sinners could also speed up the journey from purgatory to paradise by earning or purchasing indulgences—papal grants that removed part of the penalty for sin. The first portion, the sin's guilt, could be removed only by the sacrament of Penance. This ritual involved repenting and confessing the error to a priest, who could absolve the sinner. The second part was the temporal penalty for sin, which required the penitent to make earthly retribution by contributing to charities or performing certain good works. It was only this second, temporal consequence of sin that could be partly or entirely removed by a papal indulgence.

Because undischarged sins caused the sinner to land in purgatory or hell, people eagerly bought indulgences in their efforts to avoid such consequences. Abuses in the granting of indulgences quickly multiplied, since overeager clerical sellers (*pardoners*) rarely explained to their desperate and naive customers that repentence, confession, and absolution were still necessary to remove guilt. Unscrupulous peddlers sometimes even persuaded the faithful that indulgences could remove both guilt and temporal penalty from any past or future misdeed—making them virtual licenses to sin. Some pardoners also charged exorbitant sums or even sold fraudulent indulgences.

Even after the sinner died, money could still ease his or her path toward heaven since the family of the deceased could buy a related grant known as posthumous absolution. When Galeazzo Maria Sforza of Milan was assassinated in 1476, his wife, Bona of Savoy, worried about his soul's destination. According to contemporary standards, her fears were probably justified since Galeazzo had not received the last sacrament, nor had he lived according to Christian tenets. Bona appealed to the pope for help, and gave him a hefty sum of money to grant Galeazzo a posthumous absolution.

This entire belief system—involving heaven, purgatory, and hell—offered numerous ways to buy or work one's way out of the consequences of sin. Though some people did give to the church solely in an effort to gain a spot in heaven, most were probably genuinely concerned with the plight of the poor or with the good to be gained from new ecclesiastical foundations. But regardless of their motives, in the race for the Pearly Gates, women became important financial backers of the medieval church and its welfare system. Females donated at least ten percent of French lands *alienated* to the church in the eleventh and twelfth centuries.[6] This popular practice, the *alienation in mortmain* of real property, simply transferred the absolute ownership of manors or lands to designated ecclesiastical institutions.

The establishment of La Trinité in Vendôme during the 1030s provides one example. Though Geoffrey Martel, count of Vendôme, was a guiding force behind this foundation, his wife, Agnes of Anjou, also personally donated two churches, and then persuaded others to help enrich the monastery. After La Trinité was established, Agnes continued to support it with gifts of lands, mills, churches, and other holdings.[7] Around the same time in England, a very pious woman named Godgyfu (better known today as Lady Godiva) began Coventry Cathedral by founding St. Mary's, a Benedictine priory. She gave her own money and property to this establishment, and even persuaded her somewhat less devout husband, the earl of Mercia, to join her in enriching the priory.[8]

It was even more common for women to make donations when they wrote their last testaments. In 1351, Katherine Estmare willed sixpence to each poor Flemish lady in the city of London, most of whom were prostitutes.[9] Perhaps to compensate for their lack of power while alive, many women also left detailed instructions designed to make sure their last wishes were respected. A Beguine known as Aleydis of Strasbourg left a pension for her sister Gertrude, but tied it up in a trust for a Cistercian abbey to administer. Aleydis further stipulated that if Gertrude lost her virginity, whether by marriage or otherwise, the abbey would receive the legacy outright.[10]

The testament (c.1414) of Elizabeth Montague, countess of Salisbury, reveals the common focus on burial arrangements. She earmarked funds to clothe a number of the poor, distribute four thousand pennies to the needy, and give another eighty sick, poor people six *shillings* and eight *denarii* each. Elizabeth also commissioned three thousand Masses to be sung immediately after her death, two daily Masses to be sung for a year, and two priests to pray perpetually by her tomb for her soul and that of her husband. The preoccupation with burial details sometimes went to surprising lengths. Isabelle Despenser, countess of Warwick, left directions for the construction of her tomb at Tewkesbury Abbey—complete with a statue of her own naked body surrounded by the figures of saints and several poor men and women.[11]

Women also gave money to a number of building funds that were church-approved charities; even road and bridge upkeep was entrusted to churches, and thus deemed a legitimate charity. In

1360, Guyette Chevrier, a member of a wealthy patrician family of Lyons, bequeathed twenty *sous* to help construct a church, and forty *sous* to repair the bridge over the Rhone. A less prosperous individual, Alice de Wylesdone of London, bequeathed three *shillings* in 1305 to aid the repair of London Bridge.[12] Other people formed confraternities to support building funds. Between the years 1374 and 1445, 530 men became members of the religious fraternity of Holy Trinity at the church of St. Botolph's Aldersgate in London, and 274 women also joined the confraternity. Such associations often traversed normal class lines. A confraternity in Lyons included members of the highest nobility, like Jeanne de Bourbon; wealthy townswomen, like Marguerite Chaponay; and artisans' wives, like Jeannette Viviers.[13] The clergy pledged to say Masses for the members' souls as a return on the investments made by these organizations of benefactors.

Women also made charitable donations to universities, even though they were not allowed to attend these schools. Devorguilla of Galloway (c.1260) not only established Sweetheart Abbey in her husband's memory, but also saw to generous endowments for Balliol College at Oxford, which he had founded. Around 1347, a dowager patroness named Mary of St. Pol founded Pembroke, the fourth college endowed at Cambridge, to accommodate thirty pupils and one master. Poor-relief was yet another branch of medieval charity. In 1360, Guyette Chevrier bequeathed a large sum to be distributed among the poor of Lyons, and earmarked another generous amount to provide marriage portions for poor girls in that city. In fifteenth-century Nuremberg, women were in charge of three charitable endowments: an orphanage for girls, a dowry establishment for young women, and an alms fund for poor pregnant women. Royal and noble households usually had a special official called an *almoner* to take care of daily giving to the poor—including money, clothing, and even leftover food. In the late thirteenth century, Joan de Munchensi, countess of Pembroke, not only fed the poor at her castle, but provided daily for many hungry people as she traveled.[14]

Relics, Shrines, and Pilgrims

Like the belief in purgatory and the welfare system it spawned, the faith in saints, miracles, and relics also allowed for substantial feminine participation. Some women played a role in this belief system by becoming saints themselves. Saint-making usually began with a cult that grew up around a holy individual's relics (various portions of the corpse, and/or certain personal possessions), or the shrine that housed them. The local clergy might even sponsor relics and shrines because they enhanced religious status and were a good source of capital for the foundation associated with the saint. Relics were so important that their authenticity and the question of who owned or controlled them sometimes caused serious quarrels. Disputes were particularly apt to occur when women possessed the holy items because men believed this situation gave women too much power. This criticism had some basis in reality since women did occasionally use relics as tools to help them get their own way in the face of male opposition.

In the middle of the thirteenth century, Abbess Hawide of Aywières even used the relics in her possession to indulge in a little benign blackmail. Thomas de Cantimpré wanted a relic of Lutgard of Aywières to display at the papal court so badly that he dedicated Lutgard's *Vita* to Hawide, hoping to soft-soap her into parting with some relics. Hawide lured Thomas on, encouraging him to press for sainthood for Lutgard. But she was too wise to actually part with any major relics—those that would be most useful to the abbey should Thomas succeed at the papal court. She resisted all Thomas' efforts to acquire Lutgard's head, and he finally had to be content with carrying off a mere finger.[15]

Proving relics genuine frequently posed a different type of problem. Exceptionally holy women could sometimes employ their mystic powers to distinguish true relics. Juliana of Cornillon possessed this useful talent, as she revealed when she miraculously spotted that the "Holy Lance" brought back by a Crusader was a fake.[16] In many cases, however, the solution involved more observable miracles: a corpse with no visible deterioration, hair and nails that continued to grow after death, and body parts that fire could not burn were among the most typical "proofs" of sanctity.

Once their authenticity was established, all true relics were believed to possess supernatural powers that could bring about miraculous cures of diseases, wounds, or birth defects. For example, Bertsenda of England had terrible pains in her legs until, around the year 1000, the relics of St. Judoc cured her.[17] Genuine relics could also accord spiritual benefits, such as the remission of sins. A fourteenth-century woman who traveled to Rome to view the *Holy Vernicle* (the handkerchief Saint Veronica used to wipe Christ's face on His walk to Calvary) thereby earned hundreds of years of indulgences.[18] It was even possible to transfer the benefits gained by visiting a shrine to another person. Margaret Paston journeyed to the shrine of the Blessed Virgin at Walsingham in a selfless effort to cure her husband's "great disease."

Especially for women, pilgrimages offered one of the few acceptable excuses to travel. Women did visit a variety of holy places, even including far-off Jerusalem, but their freedom to travel was more restricted than was men's. Out of twenty-nine pilgrims (not including the servants of pilgrims) in Chaucer's *Canterbury Tales*, only three were women. In reality, at least two-thirds of all English and French pilgrims were men. Until the fourteenth century, nearly eighty-six percent of these female pilgrims were from the lower classes, demonstrating that they had more opportunities for movement than did wealthier or titled women.[19]

A few women even profited financially from this aspect of Catholic piety. At numerous booths located near shrines, most pilgrims bought badges (the medieval version of bumper stickers) to wear as advertisements of the holy sites they had visited. The badge of the most frequented shrine, that of St. James at Compostella, was a shell. A picture of the Virgin signified the pilgrim who had journeyed to Rocamadour. Pilgrimages were so popular that badge making and selling became a lucrative business. A woman like Elisabeth Quintin of Le Puy, France, who owned the rights to a pilgrim badge concession, could become very wealthy.[20]

Relations with the Papacy

Ingeborg of Denmark was one of the many women who enlisted papal support in their quarrels with men. King Philip II *Augustus* of France married Ingeborg after his first wife, Isabella of Hainault, died around the year 1190. Taking an immediate dislike to his new wife, Philip repudiated her and later married a German woman named Agnes of Meran. Much of the ecclesiastical hierarchy supported Ingeborg, and helped her thwart Philip's plan to annul their marriage for some twenty years. He finally capitulated and acknowledged Ingeborg as the rightful queen of France. The king's defeat was reputedly caused as much by papal influence as by Ingeborg's staying power.

Women might even assume more active roles when papal and lay powers found themselves on opposite sides of the political fence. In the early twelfth century, for instance, King Henry I of England and Anselm, archbishop of Canterbury, disagreed about *investiture*—the confirmation and installation of clerical officials. Many monarchs, like Henry, felt this was the province of secular authorities because bishops were often royal vassals. The papacy, and most clerics like Anselm, asserted that investiture was a purely ecclesiastical privilege. Henry's queen, Matilda of Scotland, supported Anselm, making her useful to the pope as a potential arbiter. Around the year 1103, she wrote at least six letters to the archbishop as she attempted to heal this breach. In one of these missives, Matilda reported some success in her campaign, and informed Anselm,

> his [Henry I's] spirit is better disposed toward you than many people think. With my favorable influence and my prompting him . . . he will grow more . . . friendly toward you.[21]

The queen also wrote to Pope Paschal II suggesting a compromise. Although her efforts did not meet with total success, Paschal and Anselm had good reason to be grateful to Matilda. She softened up her husband for a resolution of the crisis; it ended with a compromise in 1107, similar to the one she had proposed.

On rare occasions, women had an impact on the papacy itself. After the papal seat was transplanted to Avignon in 1309 (the so-called "Babylonian Captivity"), succeeding popes continued to pay lip service to a desire to return to Rome. This was partly due to Avignon's many detractors. Petrarch, for instance, claimed the city was a "hideous" place where the papal court gave itself up to greed, "licentious banquets . . . unnatural and foul sloth . . . and slavish luxury."[22] Nevertheless, it was not until the year 1377 that Pope Gregory XI re-established the Roman papacy, a move recommended by Bridget of Sweden and Catherine of Siena—two women of unimpeachable moral authority. Denouncing the decline in spiritual leadership at the "French" papal court, both women beseeched the pontiff to remove himself to the more rarefied atmosphere of Rome. Saint Bridget even had a mystical vision of Avignon as a field sown with pride, envy, ambition, lust, and simony. To uproot such corruption, she claimed the "field" needed to be weeded with an iron hoe, purged by fire, and then smoothed again with a plow.[23] Though their criticism was not the only reason for his move, Bridget and Catherine did greatly strengthen the pope's resolve to return to Rome.*

The Crusades

In the long-running campaign known as the Crusades (1096–1271), various popes again found women to be among their most fervent supporters. This series of holy wars constituted one of the most important political and military interventions attempted by the medieval papacy. The popes had many reasons to support Crusades, including their desire to free the Holy Land from the "infidel," their hope to unite the Eastern and Western churches, and their attempt to prevent violent nobles from fighting each other in Europe by providing them with a distant common enemy.** The soldiers themselves also had a variety of motives for participating. Some espoused holy ideals, and others needed to do penance for their sins. But many warriors who joined Crusades did so largely in the hope of increasing or building estates by appropriating land and possessions from the infidels they killed.

Women might be similarly tempted by primarily secular thoughts; some even perceived these wars as an exceptionally good chance to amass a fortune plying "the oldest profession" among the large numbers of lusty men gathered far from home and wifely

---

* Returning to Rome actually set off more problems and resulted in what is usually called the Great Schism (1378). Attempts to alleviate the situation backfired when three separate men claimed to be pope. The Council of Constance regularized this situation and elected Martin V as pope in 1417, but the schism was not officially healed until 1429.

** One perceived "enemy" was not so far away; the Jews often bore the brunt of much pre-Crusade fervor, since they were regularly massacred shortly before Crusades. Perhaps as many as 3,000 Jewish men, women, and children died in Mainz, Cologne, and Worms as the soldiers of the First Crusade tried to annihilate the "infidel" at home before going on to massacre Eastern non-believers. See Ronald Finucane, *Soldiers of the Faith*, pp. 184–7.

comfort. Other women merely wanted to travel or wished to atone for past sins. According to the thirteenth-century chronicler Matthew Paris, Simon and Eleanor de Montfort were quick to take the cross because of their irregular marriage.[24] Eleanor had renounced a previous vow of perpetual chastity in order to marry Simon, so she may well have wished to assuage her guilty conscience. Simon and Eleanor did not actually go on Crusade; in common with many other people, they took the cross and then later bought back their pledges. This allowed them to contribute to the Crusades and gain some spiritual credits without ever leaving home.

As was true of Eleanor de Montfort, even women who stayed at home often became financial supporters. Louis IX's sister, Isabella of France (a nun at Longchamp), used her entire inheritance to send ten knights on the Seventh Crusade, one of her brother's two expeditions. Pious donors ranged across class lines from such wealthy women down to poor townswomen like Agnes le Horir of London who bequeathed three *pennies* in 1349 to help send a man on a planned Crusade, one that never became a reality.[25]

Other women actually ventured forth with the crusading armies. Many warriors and adventurers who responded in 1095 to Pope Urban II's appeal to release the Holy Land from the infidel took their wives and families along. Baudouin of Lorraine's wife, Godevere (or Godchilde) of Töeni, began the journey with her husband, but she died in 1097, before reaching Palestine. There were many such fatalities among the Crusaders long before they arrived at their destination. Matthew Paris claimed,

> There died, moreover, nobles of both sexes who, falling sick because of the changes in diet and climate usually abhorred by nature, flew like martyrs to the celestial kingdoms.[26]

Another chronicler reported that some fifty thousand women died of plague on the First Crusade alone.

The first Crusaders took Antioch and recaptured Jerusalem from the Muslims in 1099. Crusading women assisted in both victories, though their numbers were probably not significant. Females gathered weapons by filling their sleeves with stones, nursed and brought water to the wounded, and endured bleeding feet when they no longer had shoes. A chronicler reported that there were women in Godfrey of Bouillon's army when he besieged and conquered Assur. Women also helped defend Jerusalem by guarding the doors to the walls of the city.[27]

The rise of a new Islamic leadership, which conquered Edessa in 1144, undid the accomplishments of the First Crusade. Two pious women, Hildegarde of Bingen and Mechtild of Magdeburg, were among those who strongly advanced the notion of another Crusade (1147–1149).[28] Accompanying her first husband, King Louis VII of France, Eleanor of Aquitaine and some of her ladies, like Faydide of Toulouse and Sybil of Flanders, were among the many females who ventured into the East on this Second Crusade. Both this Crusade and the following one (1187–1192) were dismal failures. The situation was so bad during the third venture that one of the leaders, Richard I of England, banished women from camp, blaming them for decreasing his troops' martial spirit. The only exceptions allowed in his mandate were washerwomen; they were apparently considered either indispensable or not very seductive.

Richard's action had little lasting effect since women continued to join Crusades. Even in 1267, when Louis IX of France and his three sons left on the Eighth, and last official Crusade, they were accompanied by a number of women, including Jeanne of Toulouse, Isabel of Aragon, and Margaret, countess of Flanders. Both Jeanne and Isabel died on the Crusade. Isabel was fatally injured, not by the enemy, but by falling off her horse while crossing a river.[29]

Although the Crusades failed to establish any permanent religious or political gains, they did have a great impact on women. Many used these wars to justify an expanded view of their roles. Some women stayed at home, gaining more responsibility over their estates and wealth while their authoritarian menfolk were far away, and frequently proving themselves better managers than their male relatives. Other females joined Crusades, thereby getting a chance to see the world. Some became doctors or nurses, gaining expertise and fame by performing battlefield surgery or nursing the wounded. A few Western writers also mentioned female fighters, but most Latin men played down the feminine role in the Crusades. Thus it is difficult to determine accurately the extent to which women participated as warriors. Western records named few women, such as Richilde, countess of Flanders, who fought in the first Crusade.[30] Many others who did battle in these wars died unidentified, and therefore unhonored.

The story was different when Arab historians told it. They claimed women warriors formed part of both the Christian and Muslim armies. One writer related the story of a queen who commanded a force of five hundred knights plus their retinues.

Pious woman dispensing soup to beggars.

Bibliothèque Nationale, Paris

This queen personally led her army into battle, where her men fought bravely so long as she stood firmly in their midst. Arab historians also wrote about elderly women who galvanized Western knights into action. These old ladies played on male egos and emotions by painting a lurid picture of the fate of Christ's sepulchre in the hands of the enemy. They also reminded the men that they could win eternal salvation by sacrificing their lives.[31]

Though women were less influential than men, in the Crusades as elsewhere, they clearly did play a role in *The Age of Faith*. Moreover, as the following chapter will reveal, their participation was not limited to feisty Crusaders, confraternity members, or papal supporters. Many women became active participants in their church as anchoresses, saints, canonesses, and nuns.

Chapter Eight

FLOATING TO THE RAFTERS

Lifestyles of Saints and Religious Women

Saints were presumed to be exceptionally holy individuals who displayed miraculous signs of God's favor. Saint Bridget of Sweden (1302–1373), for example, was reputed to have prophetic visions and to be so sensitive to corruption that she could smell sulphur when in the presence of notable sinners. Since the most respected thinkers came from the cloister, the monastic ideals of asceticism and chastity also dominated philosophies about sanctity. In fact, virginity was so highly revered that especially pious, ascetic virgins like Catherine of Siena were particularly apt to be set atop the pedestal of sainthood.

Catherine was born in 1347 into a large, "middle-class" Sienese family. She steadfastly refused to marry because she had vowed to wed only Christ. Catherine chose to live alone in a small cell for about three years, learning to conquer all earthly desires and needs. She then re-entered the world to care for the sick and poor, teach others her beliefs, and attract disciples. Her popularity and forcefulness also enabled her to become a political force. Never at a loss for words, Catherine eloquently pleaded with the pope to return to Rome, sent letters admonishing rulers to behave themselves, and dictated her visions to her scribes—who recorded them in a manuscript known as *Divine Dialogues*.

Saint Catherine died at age thirty-two, presumably in large part from starving herself. Though modern readers are apt to see in her story the classic symptoms of what twentieth-century medicine calls *anorexia nervosa*, this is far too simple a label for a medieval saint. Refusing food actually provided Catherine with a useful tool for controlling her environment. Nor was she atypical; devout medieval religious women often fasted for a variety of reasons—as a way to gain power, as a way to give meaning to life, or because of an intense desire to imitate Christ. Claiming she was unable to eat, Catherine substituted the Eucharist for worldly food, as did some other ecstatic religious women. Catherine believed her suffering enabled her to achieve a physical and spiritual union with Christ, while buying heavenly blessings for her fellow humans.[1] To her contemporaries, this was a very visible and acceptable sign of her great holiness. Her ability to survive without normal nourishment was perceived as an indication of marked favor from God. It gave Catherine a moral ascendancy that aided her in her life's work—having and recording visions, advising others, teaching God's word, caring for the sick and poor, and becoming a saint.

Women like Saint Catherine went to great lengths to achieve holiness because, merely by being female, they started with a "defect" men did not have. The life stories of Saint Margaret of Scotland and Saint Elizabeth of Portugal also illustrate typical orthodox beliefs, as well as some ways that medieval women could acquire recognition for their holiness. In addition, they demonstrate that married women, while theoretically considered inferior to virgins, were not barred from sainthood. Margaret, queen of Scotland, exemplifies one traditional pattern among non-virginal female saints since she married a man who immediately recognized, appreciated, and supported her superior piety.

Margaret was probably born in Hungary around the year 1045, the daughter of the exiled Prince Edward of England and Agatha of Hungary. After her father died, the family moved to England and then on to Scotland, where she married King Malcolm III. While he fought to unite Scotland, Margaret worked to bring culture, education, and Christianity to the populace. She built up a small library of religious works, aided the poor, and ordered the reform of the Scottish church. Bishop Turgot reported that her generosity pleased her husband. Malcolm sometimes joked with Margaret about her largesse but always allowed her to continue such donations, even when she used his money to do so.

Though Saint Margaret's marriage followed a common pattern, many saintly women's marital relationships were of a different type. In these stories, a devout woman marries a very worldly man, who is at first unimpressed by his wife's piety. Over the years, however, the wife's prayers and actions persuade the husband of her holiness. This type of relationship is exemplified by Saint

Elizabeth of Portugal's story. Born in 1271 at Saragossa to Constance of Sicily and Pedro III of Aragon, Elizabeth married Diniz, king of Portugal, when she was twelve. An intensely devout woman, Elizabeth supported many charities. For one of her pet projects she founded an agricultural college to prepare young girls for marriage to farmers, and even provided the graduates with their own farms. Perhaps because her husband was continually unfaithful, Elizabeth became increasingly generous in her charitable contributions and obsessive about fasting. Diniz did not approve of these activities, especially her almsgiving. He once accused her of throwing his money away, but when he forced open her hand the silver had miraculously turned to roses—a typical sign of sanctity. After several such examples of her holiness, Diniz finally began to appreciate Elizabeth's spiritual quality.

Numerous other women's stories could be added, but these suffice to show some common elements in the literature about feminine sanctity. Each of these women was said to have felt an intense spiritual calling, to have performed miracles, and to have assisted the orthodox church in some way. In addition, each had to overcome the "defect" of feminine gender. It is also significant that only Saint Catherine was not a member of the highest classes. Especially in the early Middle Ages, a woman needed either a great family or a prominent religious community in order to attain the visibility in public life required to achieve recognition.

These saints also demonstrate that a religious calling did not necessitate taking the veil. Nevertheless, many men and women did join a variety of holy orders to save their own souls, to serve God more effectively, and for a variety of less pious reasons. Most of these women neither attained the dizzying height of sanctity nor fell into the abyss of sin; they remained between the two extremes of saintly pedestals and heretical pits. Since they often had no true vocation, it is difficult to draw conclusions about the spirituality of these religious, who were officially categorized as neither saints nor sinners.

The story of Heloise, abbess of Argentueil (1101–1164), offers a vivid illustration of a woman who claimed to have no pious vocation. She became Peter Abelard's lover, and had his baby, while he was tutoring her at her uncle's house. Unaware that the couple had secretly married, her uncle had Abelard castrated to avenge family honor. Abelard became a famous theologian and Heloise became a nun, and later abbess, at Argentueil. After some years, she presumably wrote several letters to Abelard. Angered by his reluctance to write back to her, she reminded him, "when in the past you sought me out for sinful pleasures your letters came to me thick and fast." Haunted by memories, Heloise struggled to come to terms with her cloistered life. She claimed to have taken the veil only for love of Abelard, and reminded him, "When you hurried towards God I followed you." Though she had become a respected abbess, Heloise sounded doubtful and lost when she lamented,

> I can expect no reward . . . from God, for it is certain that I have done nothing as yet for love of Him.[2]

Many women could probably have empathized with Heloise since a religious calling was not a necessity for enclosure. Some women retired from the world to find peace after their husbands died, while others were sent to convents as children by their families. To most of these women, home was a *monastery*—a place where a group of people, either male or female, lived under religious vows and a religious rule. A *convent* was the community or group—of either monks or nuns—who lived together under one superior and under the discipline of a religious order. The terms "monastery," "nunnery," and "convent" can all be used correctly as synonyms to denote a women's religious house—the set of buildings where a community of nuns lived.

Within the monastery, the religious lived under an abbot or abbess, observing a *rule* and taking vows of chastity and obedience. The primary goal was to save one's own soul by avoiding the temptations of the turbulent outside world. A secondary purpose was to serve God and the world by praying, producing religious books, and preserving ancient learning. Most monasteries for either men or women were similar in structure, purpose, and daily routine. Inside the walls, there was land for cultivation and a number of buildings grouped around the cloisters—a covered passage with one open side where the residents spent a large portion of their time. The buildings usually included: a church, a refectory, a chapter-house, a bakery, a dormitory, latrines, stables, and an infirmary. Many religious foundations also had guest houses since monasteries often took in travelers and visitors.

In the sixth century, Saint Benedict of Nursia developed a code that became one of the most widely followed rules for living in a monastery. The three main tasks under his *Benedictine rule* were the divine service, manual labor, and study. Nuns or monks observed strict silence, except for certain rest periods, and owned no personal property—everything was communal. In most houses, each day was divided by seven *offices* (services). In between these appointed times, the residents slept, ate, heard Mass, and worked—for nuns this was usually embroidery, or copying and illuminating manuscripts. Some female houses also did laundry and other housekeeping chores for neighboring priests or monks. In poor nunneries the women did their own housework, but wealthy convents hired cooks, brewers, bakers, dairymaids, and laundresses.

To maintain their wealth and prestige, convents usually required a dowry from prospective sisters—although it was rarely commensurate with the portion expected by prospective husbands. Many nunneries admitted only the highborn, another practice which helped maintain status and a secure power base. This was helpful, since respect for nunneries sometimes declined dramatically in later years, especially during wartime. Around the year 1300, a convent at Coldstream was destroyed during the fighting between England and Scotland. The unfortunate nuns were forced to disperse, and most ended up in a variety of different English houses.[3] A wealthy, powerful family of patrons, especially one that had daughters living in the establishment, was quite useful to prevent such disasters. The greatest convents might even have royal boarders, students, and sisters in residence, especially in early centuries.

Religious foundations offered these high-born women power and a professional career. In the early Middle Ages, abbesses whose families owned and operated their convents could acquire a great deal of authority. They sat on councils and participated in synods and national assemblies. English abbesses of large and important houses were almost on a par with the greatest spiritual and temporal lords of the realm. In some cases, they owed obedience only to the pope. A few German abbesses had the same rights as barons and held property directly from the king. They could also go (or send a representative) to the imperial diet. At least one early Saxon abbess was even allowed to mint coins struck with her own likeness. Even in later years, abbesses were often presumed to be above the fray, a status giving them an influential role as mediators in political or military crises. Abbess Jeanne de Valois (dowager countess of Hainault), left her convent in the 1340s to negotiate a peaceful settlement to an extremely acrimonious dispute between two of her relatives, King Edward III of England and King Philip VI of France.

Convents were also quite popular among the nobility as havens for widows, orphans, illegitimate daughters, girls with birth defects, and political prisoners. A religious calling was unnecessary for any of these women; nor was a vocation evident in many of the girls who were simply enrolled by their parents or guardians at very young ages. Nunneries were useful since the only other career for highborn women was marriage. Enclosing wealthy girls within the walls of convents also prevented them from claiming great estates and huge dowries. Thus Katherine Beauchamp was forced to become a nun at Shouldham in 1367 to stop her from claiming inheritance rights to the vast Beauchamp estates.

Katherine's case was typical in England, where *childhood oblation* (donation or offering) for this purpose was quite popular. There were also a variety of other reasons for the practice. Sometimes parents had no one else to care for their children during times of crisis, or when the adults went on a pilgrimage or Crusade. Parents worried about their own shortcomings often believed some of their sins could be expiated by giving up a child, especially an illegitimate one, to a convent. At the very least, these parents thought numerous prayers and Masses would be said for their souls. Still other children were pious offerings—much like donations of land or precious objects. In 1066, Matilda of Flanders and William *the Conqueror* celebrated the dedication of the church of the Holy Trinity at Caen by presenting their establishment with a variety of gifts—including their young daughter Cecilia of Normandy. Churchmen often defended childhood oblation, as John Peckham did in 1282, by explaining that very young girls adapted to life in the convent much more easily than older ones.[4]

For many of these girls, their nunneries were the only homes they every really knew. Gertrude *the Great*, for instance, was enclosed at the age of five, and spent her entire life in a monastery. Thus she called earthly life "this place of exile," and longed to "be set free from the weariness of this life." In an especially poignant passage, Gertrude explained to God: "If mine eyes run down with tears, it is that they have been so long and so wistfully lifted up to thee."[5]

Other women vigorously objected to enclosure. In many poems called *chansons de nonne*, the female characters lamented their fate and revealed bitterness toward those who sent them to the cloister. One says, "May God send a lean year to the one who made me a nun." Another prays, "God give much unhappiness to the one who . . . put me in the cloister." In reality, some victims of childhood oblation were so unhappy they refused to remain in their convents. After growing up in an Augustinian community at Seton, Margaret de Prestewych escaped, married, and became a mother. A few years later (1383), Margaret finally obtained her release from the order by papal approval.[6]

Not all girls were unwillingly enclosed; some demanded the privilege to enter convents in direct opposition to their parents' wishes. Daughters of well-to-do London merchants frequently chose this path because the nunnery provided a higher status and an easier life than they could expect as wives of city merchants. A few *chansons de nonne* speak of the convent as a refuge from the hardships of married life. One character claims, "I want to be a nun because I do not want a bad marriage." Another girl declares, "I do not want to be encumbered with the troubles of a household: I want to go to the convent."[7]

Convents offered women the ability to choose their own lifestyles, and perhaps the power to gain a measure of influence in the world.[8] Religious foundations also presented women with more advanced educational and intellectual opportunities than they could find in the outside world. In addition, the monastery provided women with an outlet for their creative talents—another opportunity usually denied them in secular society. In the fifteenth century, a prospective English anchoress revealed yet another reason that women sometimes demanded the right to follow the religious life; she wished to cast off "secular pomp and illicit worldly life in order to earn the riches of eternal wealth, [by choosing] a spiritual mansion."[9]

Numerous renowned mystics made intimate visionary relationships seem possible and desirable, and thereby inspired other women to embrace the religious life. These visionaries believed that they experienced their reward in this lifetime as well as in the next. Some were especially drawn to Christ in His role as "God the Son," and often reported mystic experiences in which the Baby Jesus appeared to them. In her *Book of Divine Consolation,* Blessed Angela of Foligno (1250–1309) described her many visions of the Holy Infant. Other mystics found most comfort in their visions of "God the Father"—an especially kind and helpful deity. In some of Saint Catherine of Siena's visions, God appeared as "a most piteous and gracious father, who wishes to give us more . . . than we know how to ask for our need."[10]

Many of these women, often termed *bridal mystics*, related sexually gratifying visions of God. The belief that "to be a woman is to be a wife," was so firmly embedded in the medieval mind that religious women tended to express "their mystical experiences in terms of marriage to and sexual union with Jesus."[11] Hence they became spiritual wives. Mechtild of Magdeburg had a visionary relationship with Christ, who was both "an immortal God and a mortal man . . . our Redeemer is become our Bridegroom!"[12] Beatrice of Nazareth (d.1268) stressed the physical satisfaction of the soul given over to the love of Jesus:

> It seems . . . the veins are bursting . . . the bones softening . . . the throat parching . . . the body in its every part feels this inward heat, and this is the fever of love.[13]

The intensity of Beatrice's mystical union with God indicates why other women were inspired to follow a similar path in the hope of reaching the spiritual plateau where this sort of relationship was possible. The convent must have appealed to many of these women as a place where they could shed their worldly cares in the contemplation of Christ's love.

Whether women rushed to embrace the religious life or had it forced on them, convents clearly served many useful purposes for females and/or their families. Still, the female religious was often not appreciated within the church itself. Though the first popular reformed order, the Cluniacs, virtually ignored women, they eventually had to establish a house for females. The primary purpose of this foundation was "to take care of" deserted wives and other female relatives of the many noblemen who had entered Cluny.[14]

During the twelfth century, a "golden age" for monasticism, many new houses were established, and some for women were founded by or with the help of male religious leaders. In this time of expansion, prosperity, and enthusiasm, some churchmen were apparently eager to assist women's efforts to follow the religious life. The Premonstratensians, for example, were so popular with women that, in Flanders alone, some ten thousand women were said to be members of the order by the year 1150.[15] Unfortunately for women, this trend did not last very long; not much later, the men in the order decreed that no nuns should be admitted to any male settlements. This reveals a changing outlook on the part of the ecclesiastical establishment. By the year 1200, the climate of approval for the female religious had begun to deteriorate and many groups were restricting feminine membership.

Early members of another order, the Cistercians, were very ascetic. In the early 1100s, they eschewed all creature comforts like warm clothing, bedspreads, and extra food. They saw themselves primarily as farmers, builders, and writers—work they believed women were incapable of performing. They were equally dismayed by the prospect of spending their time managing women's orders. Hence, by 1228, they had begun refusing to allow the establishment of any new nunneries. This effort failed because convents composed of wealthy and/or titled women simply followed the Cistercian rule by their own choice and placed themselves under diocesan bishops. In thirteenth-century England, the monarch and most of the populace recognized several houses as Cistercian abbeys or priories, even though the abbot of Citeaux categorically denied their membership in the order.[16]

A similar development occurred in many male groups, including the mendicant orders. A new concept in religious life, mendicants were preachers and teachers who served God out in the world, rather than within monastery walls. The first group to win papal approval (c.1207) were the Franciscans (Grey Friars, or Friars Minor) who gathered around kindly, ascetic Saint Francis of Assisi. The Dominicans (Black Friars, or Friars Preachers) were admitted shortly thereafter (c.1215). A more urban group, they were followers of Saint Dominic who focused on stamping out heresy. Because friars tended to be popular, well-supported preachers, they often came into conflict with bishops, monks, and parish priests. Matthew Paris claimed friars shouldered other churchmen aside:

> When great and affluent men lay dying, the friars would be in urgent attendance, greedy for gain, to the loss and detriment of the clergy.[17]

Saint Francis allowed Clare of Assisi to begin the Poor Clares, while Saint Dominic established a house for women at Prouille. These groups were cloistered, unlike the corresponding male orders which primarily lived out in the world, begging and preaching. Both Dominic and Francis established strict rules, attempting to prevent many women from becoming associated with their friars. Despite their isolationist views, the pope eventually had no recourse other than to recognize the swarms of devout women who were following the mendicant life, often without prior approval. In the middle of the 1200s, for example, Amica de Joigny, prioress of Montargis, successfully petitioned Pope Alexander IV to incorporate her convent. Official recognition for such women became widespread in the 1260s, after Pope Clement IV issued a bull formally entrusting the Dominicans with the spiritual care of large numbers of convents.[18]

Problems such as these may have dissuaded some women from joining either monastic or mendicant orders. Other options were available for such a woman, however. For instance, she could become an anchoress and live a permanently enclosed, solitary life of constant devotion. Anchoresses were particularly prominent in England, where women had few religious alternatives; between the years 1100 and 1500, there were always more English anchoresses than male anchorites (this was often true in other countries as well).[19] Anchoresses followed the strictest path of spiritual devotion, giving them a relatively high status as living models of great sanctity and making them popular recipients of charity. In 1480, for example, John Emelyn's pious bequests included *sixpence* for the anchoress at London Wall.[20]

Some anchoresses lived alone in cells attached to religious foundations, walls, or other buildings, but recluses might also form a small group in which each individual resided in a separate cell. Anchoresses could communicate with one another, visitors, and their servants (who made it possible for recluses to live without leaving their cells) through windows hung with heavy black cloths. Fifteenth-century Parisians could often catch a glimpse of Alix la Bourgolle, a well-known and highly respected recluse, attending Mass at the Church of the Innocents by means of the small, latticed window in her cell.

The *Ancren Riwle,* a guidebook written around the year 1220 for three female recluses, expounded on the rules governing English anchoresses. It insisted that they should observe silence during meals, live on charity, and give any leftovers to the poor. The *Ancren Riwle* also advised recluses to refrain from donning haircloths or whipping themselves with leather thongs, and warned them against taking in guests, teaching classes, or allowing their cells to be used as vaults for their neighbors' valuables.

Highborn women who were not drawn to a permanently enclosed, strictly ascetic life might instead join a house of canonesses. This term referred to widows and virgins whose names were inscribed in a church register, and who lived under a rule (or according to the *ordo ecclesiasticum*). They were usually wealthy noblewomen who lived under fewer restrictions than most nuns. Residents in these establishments were often allowed to retain their personal goods, keep maids, and sometimes return to lay society. In many communities the abbess was the only one pledged to live in perpetual celibacy. Since canonesses were usually wealthy and highborn, their religious houses were often quite prestigious. One of the richest abbeys in Germany, for example, was Essen on the Ruhr. A house of canonesses, Essen "owned" more than one thousand estates, and produced elaborate manuscripts—like the famous *Gospel Book of Essen*, which was covered in gold and decorated with precious stones. The power and wealth of Essen were reflected in the figures of its early abbesses (c.950–1200), who were considered sovereign authorities. The canonesses themselves chose their abbess, who was free of all clerical authority other than that of the pope. Abbess Svanhild, who served from 1060 to 1090, represented the peak of this power. Soon after her death, the abbess's powers began to decline until, probably in 1224, the priests of Essen formed their own chapter, which eventually dominated the entire community.[21] This loss of prestige and power was not atypical; many such houses had declined by the thirteenth century, in part because most canonesses were too wealthy, powerful, and independent for male ecclesiastical authorities to condone.

Women might also enter a so-called "double monastery"—a religious foundation that housed both men and women. One of the most prestigious began in 1099 when Robert d'Arbrissel founded the double monastery of Fontevrault. He appointed Hersend of Champagne to be the first superior of this huge community. Perhaps because she performed her duties so well, Fontevrault remained under an abbess' rule. According to Hersend's successor, Petronille, some three thousand men and women were attracted to the order in the first half of the twelfth century.[22]

Around the same time, Gilbert of Sempringham founded the Gilbertines, a double order that vested authority in the male residents. Many wealthy patrons endowed settlements, and thereby helped make the Gilbertines successful and popular. But the number of women in the order gradually decreased. Part of the reason lay in scandalous stories such as that of the "nun of Watton," who was impregnated by a male member at her Gilbertine house. In 1166, Ailred of Rievaulx wrote about this distressing incident, indicating his belief that such scandals could not be avoided in double monasteries. Historian Sharon Elkins reported,

> the story of the nun of Watton has an importance for the history of female monasticism beyond the confines of the tale, for it

> reveals that a monastic leader like Ailred, who admired Gilbert and publicly lauded the spirituality of the Gilbertine nuns, in reality distrusted the monasteries for women and men at the height of their expansion.[23]

The dwindling number of female Gilbertines was not unusual. By 1200, many twin institutions were breaking up. As Ailred of Rievaulx demonstrated, the idea that men and women could cooperate without sexual intimacy was too radical a concept for the church. Saint Bernard of Clairvaux opined that raising someone from the dead was a lightweight miracle when compared with companionship between men and women without the commission of any sin.[24] Since many monastery residents had no religious vocation, perhaps double foundations were an unnecessary risk.

During the 1200s, even many single houses for women deteriorated, in part because the power some abbesses wielded frightened male ecclesiastics. For example, Sanchia Garcia, abbess of the royal Spanish abbey of Las Huelgas de Burgos, acquired most of the powers of a priest. She could punish both clerical and lay officials, hear confessions, and receive vows of obedience from monks.

Friction between male and female orders was another frequent problem. In addition, the clergy claimed that female orders needed male protection, but simultaneously viewed it as an onerous and frightening burden for the monks who had to perform this pastoral chore. The perception of woman as seductress, which became an increasingly popular theme among cloistered male theologians, also caused trouble for the female religious. Historian Jane Tibbetts Schulenburg stated,

> with the reform movements and their emphasis on ascetic piety and clerical celibacy, the initial appreciation of women's active participation in the church was lost and replaced by an atmosphere of heightened fear and suspicion of female sexuality.[25]

Once again, the noticeable absence of a religious vocation in many enclosed women also proved to be a major problem. Agnes de Flixthorpe, for example, was so desperate to obtain her freedom that she fled her religious house at Stamford to live a more worldly life in Nottingham. When the bishop of Lincoln tracked her down around the year 1309, Agnes was disguised as a man—wearing a gilt embroidered robe. She was dragged back to her convent, excommunicated, and condemned to live in chains, in solitary confinement. By 1314, however, Agnes had persuaded the bishop she had reformed, and she was returned to her duties. Apparently she wasted little time before escaping once more into the secular world, with the bishop's men hot on her trail. There is evidently no extant record of what finally happened to Agnes.[26] She was an extreme example of the disruption that could be caused by enclosing women who had no spiritual vocation, and by clerical efforts to keep such discontented nuns in their convents.

Not all frustrated, enclosed women ran away; some who stayed caused a variety of problems by trying to make the convents themselves as worldly as possible. As early as the twelfth century, education was declining in some feminine religious communities, and discipline was becoming quite lax. Boarders and friends became a part of daily conventual life, as did the sight of nuns wandering around outside monastery walls. In the year 1258, a pastoral visit to the sixty-three nuns at St. Savior in Normandy revealed several typical problems. The archbishop of Rouen reported that the nuns did not observe silence or go to confession. Lacking a sufficient number of books, bored sisters had begun to keep pets—dogs, squirrels, and birds. The women also concentrated on fashion, buying new gowns that they kept in their own locked chests,[27] a practice forbidden by the rule of communal property.

As male orders tried to reduce the number and influence of female houses and discipline decayed in many regular monastic foundations, numerous women sought other avenues for embracing the spiritual life. The growth of cities made such options essential since peasant women without dowries migrated to towns, seeking a niche in the new urban environment. In addition, during the twelfth and thirteenth centuries, a heightened religious fervor gripped much of the European laity. This trend was stimulated by wandering preachers who stirred their listeners to imitate Christ and inspired numerous women to minister to the poor and the sick. These women frequently wanted to be less strictly enclosed than most monastic orders allowed; they placed more emphasis on service in the world, rather than on living in self-contained religious communities.

Many women associated with this movement were individualistic religious often called *mulieres sanctae* or *virgines continentes*. A study of several of the most prominent of these women reveals the inter-connection between their spiritual options and the quasi-religious movements. In addition, their hagiographies impart a sense of the religious fervor of the day. For instance, Christina of St. Trond (1150–1224) became known as *Mirabilis* because she fell into a religious trance in 1182. Though she seemed to be dead, Christina levitated to the rafters at her funeral, causing almost the entire congregation to flee in fear. Christina said God had sent her back from purgatory to atone for the world's sins. Many of the *vitae* of the *mulieres sanctae* contained such inspiring, or sensational, miraculous elements.

Forced to marry when she was fourteen, Mary of Oignes (c.1177–1213) persuaded her husband that sex should not be a part of their life together, and then convinced him to work with her at a leper colony. Mary also had accurate prophetic visions. Christine of Stommeln (b.1242), another outstandingly pious woman, began to be tortured by diabolic temptations when she was fifteen. She also endured a variety of "divine" manifestations like stigmata, and blood that gushed forth from many parts of her body. A young woman named Lutgard entered the Benedictine convent of Aywières in 1206, and quickly gained a reputation for holiness based on her visionary abilities and her prodigious fasting. At the Virgin's suggestion, Lutgard fasted for seven years at a time, on three separate occasions, in order to save souls from purgatory.[28]

Despite their highly individualistic lives and affiliations, all these *mulieres sanctae* believed in following the *Vita Apostolica*—the lifestyle of the primitive Christians. The apostolic life was an ambiguous and fluid concept, open to a great many interpretations—which usually included poverty, communal life, loving one's neighbors, and working to support oneself. Many *mulieres sanctae* also emphasized Christ's humanity and wished to imitate His words and deeds, even to the extent of stigmatization. Mysticism and a very emotional involvement, especially a zealous devotion to the Eucharist, were other central elements in their piety.

One of the most widespread and popular quasi-religious options for women was an amorphous group known as "the Beguines," whose primary goals were to preserve their chastity and to live in poverty. Regions with few large cities, like England, rarely had any Beguines. They were most often found in cities in the Low Countries, France, and Germany, supporting themselves as nurses, teachers, and cloth workers. The movement presumably began in Brabant, Flanders, in the diocese of Liège. Mary of Oignes is often called the first *virgine continente* to be connected with a small community of organized Beguines. At that time these women lived individually throughout the city. Some lived in their own homes, and they could even return to secular life. No motherhouse or single rule ever existed, but some Beguines did form self-contained, disciplined associations. Prospective initiates usually went through a period of probation before becoming members. Anyone seen with a man, for example, was summarily expelled. A full member who lost her property, got sick, or was too old to earn a living received financial support from her community. As a result, Beguine houses became retreats for independent widows and the superfluous daughters of moderately well-to-do townsmen. They also came to serve as havens for the homeless.

Numerous lay and ecclesiastical leaders supported the movement's growth. Jeanne of Flanders was an especially influential lay patroness, and her sister Margaret continued this policy after Jeanne's death. Male clerics were often skeptical about non-cloistered females, but the pious fervor of the Beguines struck Jacques de Vitry favorably. After Mary of Oignes died, de Vitry wrote her *Life* as a propaganda effort to gain support for the movement as a whole. He claimed the Beguines were:

> fervent and modest . . . leading an angelic and celibate life, serving the Lord through prayers, vigils, manual labor, tears, [and] supplications.[29]

Despite such support, the Beguines never obtained recognition as an order, partly because they were unmarried women under no man's control. Both the church and secular society were uncomfortable with anyone who could not be neatly categorized. In particular, women who were neither nuns nor wives—the only acceptable roles for medieval females—were considered highly suspicious, if not downright dangerous. The church also called these women distractions to monks. A later thirteenth-century statute restricted the women to residence in certain parishes, and insisted that only priors or village priests could hear their confessions. In the fourteenth century, Pope Clement V promulgated two bulls against Beguines, indicating a belief that heretics often took control of them.[30] There was little proof to substantiate this, although isolated incidents occasionally seemed to confirm it. A former Beguine named Margaret Porete died at the stake in 1310 because she refused to renounce her belief in mystical pantheism. In another case, an entire community of Beguines was put on trial in 1322 at Silesia for repudiating the role of clerical mediation between God and humanity.

The way most ecclesiastical authorities treated Beguines mirrored their general lack of concern for the many women seeking appropriate outlets for spiritual expression and community

Even at an orthodox service women were not safe from being seduced into heresy by demons hovering over them.

life. Jacques de Vitry and others who supported Beguines were probably more far-sighted than those who held the more popular clerical opinion that Beguines were linked with heresies. Possibly the absence of such quasi-religious options caused some women to become disillusioned and frustrated—ripe for the seductive lure of reform movements and heresies.

Chapter Nine

IF IGNORANCE WERE A WOMAN'S PASSPORT TO PARADISE

Women in Heretical Sects

There had always been some differing interpretations of Christian theology, but by the eleventh century, heretics—those who deny or materially alter important aspects of orthodox doctrines or practices—posed a perennial problem for the Catholic church. In that century, the church accused heretics in Aquitaine of defiling the crucifix and participating in orgies, and denounced other heretics for holding secret meetings, worshipping pagan idols, and distributing animal blood as a relic. Though these were typical charges, it is quite possible they had no basis in reality. The church did not merely accuse alleged heretics of doctrinal deviations, but also traditionally added a variety of heinous crimes—especially murder and aberrant sexual behavior—to the charges in order to denigrate heterodox groups and simultaneously rouse popular fervor against them.

In the twelfth and thirteenth centuries, southern France and northern Italy were the major regions where heretical sects flourished. There were small pockets of heterodoxy in Germany and northern France, but virtually none in England. By the end of the Middle Ages, heresy had spread to other countries, and the numbers of sects had greatly increased. During the later Middle Ages, there was a surge of discontent and tension stemming from economic pressures, natural disasters (like bubonic plague pandemics), burgeoning hatred of oppressive masters, and growth of stronger centralized governments. Heresies and reformist movements expressed disillusionment with the established church—a wealthy, powerful, and distant institution that could not protect the populace from plague and other disasters.

People from all walks of life joined heretical sects. Medieval authors attributed feminine membership to gullibility, but there were actually many economic, social, religious, and emotional factors that led both sexes to participate in heresies. Possibly orthodox writers even exaggerated feminine participation in their effort to denigrate heterodox sects. In reality, heresy was not a particularly female phenomenon. Most cults attracted many more male than female adherents, and the majority of women stayed within the true fold—just as most men did. Moreover, among women involved in heresies, motivations varied widely. Not all were passionately devoted to the new movements; some simply followed the lead of their male relatives. Other women were searching for basic necessities rather than spiritual satisfaction. Near Toulouse, for instance, many females from the impoverished lesser nobility went to live with Cathar heretics who fed, clothed, and sheltered them.

Paradoxically, as women's longevity had increased, their position in society had declined. Surplus women, often seen as family burdens, became increasingly alienated from medieval institutions and values. Too few nunneries existed to accommodate them, so other options attracted these unattached women. When the ecclesiastical hierarchy tried to derail non-conformist movements like the Beguines, some of these women instead became interested in reformist or heretical movements. This was particularly true of women who were dissatisfied with the existing power structure and the inferior status of females within that system.

The church created more problems for itself by refusing to discuss doctrinal issues with women. In 1207, a priest succinctly summed up the most common clerical stance during a debate between orthodox theologians and Cathars. This cleric angrily told his noble opponent, an important and wealthy Cathar leader named Esclarmonde de Foix, that spiritual matters were no concern of hers; she ought to go home and tend to her spinning. An early fourteenth-century orthodox council also claimed women were ignorant, and ought to stay that way. In a diatribe against Beguines, this church council particularly condemned these women who "discuss the Holy Trinity and the divine essence, and express opinions on matters of faith and sacraments."[1] Other innocent feminine questioners were burned at the stake, thereby creating an even greater climate of resentment toward the church.

Not surprisingly, reformist and heretical movements sometimes appeared to offer women more support, self-esteem, freedom, and power than did orthodox Catholicism. For instance, the Waldensian reading of the Epistle to Titus (2:1-5) led this cult to allow women to teach and preach. This passage declares that "aged women" should be "teachers of good things," and exhorts them to "teach the young women." Catholic clerics interpreted these same verses to mean only that mothers should be allowed to correct their children when they misbehaved,[2] and thus forbade women to teach or preach. As this disagreement reveals, many individuals termed "heretics" by the church did not think their beliefs conflicted with biblical strictures.

In an era of pious fervor, reformist movements also seemed to adhere more closely to the spirit of early Christianity than did the materialistic orthodox church. Normally an active foe of heretics, Sancia of Majorca, queen of Naples, nevertheless supported the Spiritual Franciscans—a group that had separated from the Friars Minor. They strayed from orthodoxy by denying that Christ and the disciples owned property, and by insisting on living in poverty.[3] Queen Sancia clearly thought their views on apostolic poverty and clerical equality were more correct than the official papal stance. Like other reformers, she never perceived her beliefs as heretical.

Sancia's position illustrates how difficult it can be to distinguish between groups that sought to reform the medieval church and those that were in flagrant violation of its doctrines. Many heterodox cults began with the intent of simply modifying clerical abuses. This was certainly true of the early Waldensians, who intended only reform when they asked the pope for permission to preach on the themes of following the Apostles and living in poverty. Though their request was denied, the group continued to preach, thereby straying into violation of orthodox rules concerning obedience to the pope.[4]

The church was aware of the powerful attraction reformist sentiments and heterodox sects could exert on Christians, so the papacy sometimes reacted violently to any perceived threat—as it did during the twelfth century when a heresy known as *Catharism* gained great popularity in certain regions. Catharism had been well established on the Balkan Peninsula by the early eleventh century, before spreading to northern Italy and southern France. Since most

Cathars were less concerned with dogma than with maintaining high moral standards and attending religious meetings (which we might compare to modern "support groups"), many members knew little about either their own or orthodox Catholic doctrines. There were several versions of their beliefs, though all true Cathars wished to revamp or abolish virtually all Catholic doctrines. Cathars denied that Jesus was God and also repudiated the role of the sacraments. They believed that the godly forces of light fought a constant battle with the earthly, evil forces of darkness. In this continual conflict, souls (light) sought to purify themselves from their bodies, which were part of the kingdom of darkness. Extreme fasting and other mortifications, even committing suicide, were sanctioned to free oneself from worldly desires and earthly institutions—such as the church.

The Cathar sect was divided into two groups, *perfecti* and *credentes*. *Perfecti* were those who had received the *consolamentum* —comparable to the orthodox sacrament of baptism, but performed by words rather than water. Many *credentes* (the ordinary believers) received this only on their deathbeds, so they would not have time to relapse into sin. *Perfecti*, on the other hand, tried to retain their purity by following an extremely ascetic life of poverty, chastity, punishment of the body, prayer, and abstinence from milk, meat, and all other by-products of sexual activity—since they were vehemently opposed to procreation.

Reproduction was the ultimate sin because it condemned additional souls to imprisonment in dark, earthbound bodies. One witness testified before the Inquisition that a dying pregnant woman could not even receive the *consolamentum* since it was impossible for her to be saved. Believers were not encouraged to produce offspring who would share their faith, a stance that probably dissuaded other females from joining the sect so long as they were young, healthy, and energetic. It also encouraged believers to leave the fold. Airmessens, wife of Willelmus Vicarius de Cambiac, defected from the Cathars when a group of *perfecti* publicly scolded her for being impregnated with what they termed a "devil."[5]

Perfectae were theoretically equal to their male counterparts, and could even administer the *consolamentum*. In practice, however, most *perfectae* followed a monastic lifestyle within the walls of hospices—which closely resembled orthodox convents. Other females known as *bonae mulieres* (good women) also lived much like orthodox religious in communities of twenty to thirty women under the charge of mistresses. Many male *perfecti* became itinerant preachers, and even a few women, like Willelma de Campo Longo,[6] took to the roads to spread their faith. Women's access to this role indicates one of the new positions Catharism theoretically allowed females to assume. Other females, especially noblewomen, were financial supporters. Philippa de Moncada, one of the most prominent of the twelfth-century patronesses, contributed money and also opened her castle of Dun to the Cathars. Some women hired Cathar priests, and Eleanor of Toulouse even conducted a secret Cathar service in her chapel while, simultaneously, the pope was saying Mass in the same castle.[7] Esclarmonde de Foix not only helped build Cathar hospices and schools, but even publicly debated doctrinal issues with orthodox theologians at Pamiers in 1207.

The pope eventually became very worried about Catharism's growing popularity in southern France. "Perfect" women who could brilliantly defend their beliefs—as Esclarmonde de Foix did—undoubtedly increased his fear that the Cathar heresy was a very real threat to papal power and the orthodox faithful. Following the murder of his papal legate, Pope Innocent III excommunicated Raymond VI of Toulouse and offered the property of the count's Cathar subjects to any Christians who would help stamp out this heretical sect. Motivated by religion, politics, and greed, a number of warriors responded to the pope's call for a holy war, known as the *Albigensian Crusade*. Though this war was named after the county of Albi in Toulouse where Cathars were particularly numerous, by the late thirteenth century *Albigensian* was used to refer to any Cathar or Waldensian heretic.

One of the largest of the many massacres during this "holy war" occurred at Lavaur in 1211. As part of their strategy to isolate and surround Raymond VI in Toulouse, Simon de Montfort and his "Crusaders" needed to take the castle of Lavaur. After withstanding a two-month siege, the fortress fell. The victorious warriors then executed eighty knights, burned four hundred *perfecti*, and threw Giralda de Laurac, lady of Lavaur, into a well where they stoned her to death.[8] Her execution was a warning to other supporters since she was not a *perfecta*, but had been of great financial assistance to the Cathars.

The "Crusade" officially ended in 1229 with a treaty ceding much of the Albigensian territory to the French crown. This completed the work of the Crusade, which had killed many Cathar leaders and financially ruined other noble supporters. Moreover, in 1231, Pope Gregory IX formally charged the Inquisition—a permanent special court of ecclesiastical judges—with visiting parishes in order to discover and question any heretics living in each region. By the 1240s, the Cathar church was in such disarray that only isolated remnants of the sect continued to exist.

Ironically, another heresy, known as Waldensianism, was started partly as an effort to combat the popularity of Catharism. Peter Waldo, a rich merchant of Lyons, believed his orthodox group could attract Cathars back to the fold by abolishing clerical abuses. Like other reformers, Waldo considered the clergy corrupt and/or indifferent to spiritual concerns. He soon strayed into doctrinal heresy by completely rejecting the role of clerical intermediaries, instead stressing the need for everyone to be able to read and understand the Bible. The common people often confused Waldo's sect with Catharism since, among the poor, the attraction of both groups consisted in their criticism of orthodox priests and bishops and in the holy examples set by their *perfecti*.[9]

Like Catharism, Waldensianism had many high-ranking female supporters, and also allowed women to become *perfectae*. They could act in the same roles as men—preaching, presiding at prayer services, pronouncing the benediction over shared bread, and exercising sacerdotal power. Less elevated female Waldensians were of the *credentes* class, and often lived in communities called *hospicia*. As previously mentioned, Waldensian women could also become preachers and teachers. A thirteenth-century chronicler expressed typical orthodox outrage over the fact that men and women preachers might walk the roads together, lodge under the same roof at night, and even sleep in the same bed. The writer was horrified that the women claimed, "all this . . . they were instructed to do by the Apostles."[10] This was one reason why the church zealously denounced Waldensianism and executed numerous members. Forced to go underground by the fourteenth century, the cult nevertheless continued to exist. It underwent a number of changes and, in some communities, women's priestly powers became greatly restricted.

A variety of "antinomian" or "Free Spirit" cults also surfaced in the thirteenth and fourteenth centuries. Most were loosely founded on similar ideas of asceticism, apostolic poverty, an intellectual form of pantheism (God is all things), and the teachings of Joachim of Fiore (1134–1202). He believed that the *Age of the Father*, which focused on law, and the *Age of the Son*, which focused on faith, would be followed by the *Age of the Holy Spirit*, when mankind would become a part of God. A common thread among many sects was a belief in internal justification; anyone who accepted his or her soul's infusion with God's grace could not sin, so he or she no longer needed external structures like laws, churches, and secular governments.

Though most believers led ascetic lives, clerics often claimed that such sects took the antinomian ideas to their logical but extreme conclusion. For instance, the church asserted that cults it called "Luciferan" and "Adamite" held underground orgies (usually in caves), because they believed it was permissible to do there what was considered sinful above ground. A typical accusation was that a "Luciferan" girl claimed that she continued to be a virgin above ground, while below the ground it was an entirely different story.[11] In reality, the Luciferan sect apparently never even existed, but these fictitious charges helped the church denigrate and exterminate heterodox groups.

Though the Luciferans may have been a product of ecclesiastical fantasies or propaganda, around the year 1200, several antinomian cults did emerge in the Low Countries and Italy. A prophetess named Guglielma, who believed her cult would usher in the *Age of the Holy Spirit*, led a sect in Milan. After she died in 1282, her disciple Mayfreda declared herself the first pope of the new age and even elected a body of female cardinals. Mayfreda was promptly sent to the stake for her heretical (we might term them "feminist") ideas, and even Guglielma was burned posthumously. The ecclesiastical hierarchy had learned not to tolerate ideas like Guglielma's, even when they initially seemed harmless. Among the many victims of this new hardline policy was Margherita di Trento, often called *the Beautiful*, who had helped her lover Dolcino lead an antinomian sect. In 1307, Margherita was arrested, tortured into making a confession, and then burned for her unorthodox beliefs. Jeanne Dabenton suffered the same fate in 1372 for leading the heretical "Society of the Poor."

While antinomian/Free Spirit beliefs flourished on the continent, England developed its own heresy known as Lollardy. It was based on the teachings of John Wycliffe, an Oxford master and priest, who gained acceptance through his royal protectors, Joan of Kent, princess of Wales, and her powerful brother-in-law, John of Gaunt, duke of Lancaster. In the 1370s, Wycliffe spoke out against hypocritical and worldly clerics who lived in luxury, and denounced those who deceived the common people by their dishonest practices in peddling indulgences. Wycliffe eventually went far beyond mere criticism of iniquitous clerics to deny papal leadership, the doctrine of transubstantiation, and the clerical role in the remission of sin. Like Peter Waldo, Wycliffe believed everyone should read, understand, and follow the Word of God, so he attempted to make a vernacular Bible available to all believers.

The popularity of Lollardy rose and fell along with the anticlericalism of the day—a sentiment that was always most noticeable when Rome demanded more money from parishioners. In London, Lollardy was more popular with artisans than with the more prosperous merchants. Apparently the only fifteenth-century members of the merchant class who espoused Wycliffe's teachings were a small number of women. One of these, an eighty-year-old widow named Joan Boughton, was burned at the stake in 1495.

Englishwomen like Joan Boughton may have been attracted to the sect because the laity, including females, could act as priests. Many of Wycliffe's female supporters were arrested, questioned, and/or imprisoned. In 1393, for example, Anna Palmer, an anchoress of Northampton, was arrested for attending Lollard meetings and receiving other members at night. Anna infuriated her captors by refusing to answer questions, and by denouncing the bishop of Lincoln as the Anti-Christ. A less zealous Lollard, Matilda of Leicester, was imprisoned in 1389 and questioned by the archbishop of Canterbury. Though he was dismayed by the subtlety of her answers, he persevered and finally persuaded Matilda to renounce her heretical leanings. She was then allowed her to return to her *reclusorium*.[12] The archbishop's leniency was not uncommon since many women recanted and were released, though some later relapsed back into heresy. Despite the popularity of Lollardy in some regions, Joan Boughton's fate was exceptional since only a very few people were executed for heresy in pre-sixteenth-century England.

Bohemia's religious upheavals were more violent. The leader of the Bohemian sect was John Hus (1370–1415), who espoused many beliefs akin to those of Wycliffe, particularly regarding the great need for reforming the Catholic church. Hus was especially irate about priests who used the tithes and offerings of poor parishioners to buy gifts for their mistresses,[13] and about pardoners who preyed upon the naive faithful with their indulgence selling. As Wycliffe had gained visibility and security through his association with Joan of Kent, Hus also found a pious royal adherent in Sophia, the consort of King Wenceslaus IV. She supported Hus' reforms and admitted him as her principal advisor, and possibly her confessor. Other noblewomen followed her lead. The widowed Catherine of Vraba endowed a living for a Hussite preacher after stipulating that he had to deliver vernacular sermons several times each week. Catherine also founded a community for virgins and widows who wished to serve God by leaving the outside world.[14] Anna of Mochov, a member of Queen Sophia's court, gave Hus protection on some of his travels, and even ejected an orthodox chaplain from a chapel near her home in Usti in order to install a Hussite priest. In 1417, an anonymous orthodox writer termed Anna a "Jezebel" who was undoubtedly on a path leading straight to the fires of hell.

Hus also numbered many poorer females, some of whom were former prostitutes, among his adherents. Reforming "fallen women" was a primary goal of the Hussites, as it had been for many earlier Bohemian reformers. Hence this popular spiritual movement also tried to redress social ills. Like other grass-roots rebellions, the Hussites were vigorously persecuted and many leaders were killed. But even the execution of Hus himself in 1415 did not suffice to bring the cult under control. Following his death, the more radical of his followers gained control of the sect. A combination of spiritual, social, and nationalist motives then caused the Hussites to move "into a full, armed rebellion against the pope."[15]

This development so threatened political and spiritual stability that the Holy Roman Emperor and the pope combined to launch a counterattack against the heretics. Many women joined the Hussite army that fought against German and papal troops. Some women built fortifications and trenches at Prague, while others helped defend makeshift forts during the attack at Vitkov Hill. Women were most commonly employed as nurses or cooks for the male Hussite armies.[16] Whatever their specific jobs, women helped Czech troops defeat five armies sent against them from 1420 through 1431.

By the late fifteenth century, the orthodox clergy was growing desperate in its efforts to maintain control over the populace—especially women—in the face of an increasing number of heresies. For instance, nuns were specifically forbidden to associate with itinerant male preachers who, according to the church, would surely dupe unsuspecting females. Clerics also discouraged nuns

Fifteenth-century witches.
François Garnier, Centre Nationale de la Recherche Scientifique, Paris

from reading about doctrinal questions. Church officials believed books written in the vernacular could lead the educated into heretical thinking, in the same way that songs sung in the vernacular impressed common people.[17] For much of the laity, and all women, ignorance was presumed to be the safest, surest path to paradise. In light of these orthodox attitudes, it is hardly surprising that women sometimes looked to heterodox sects to provide them with the status and compassion they rarely found in the Catholic church.

Chapter Ten

ABRACADABRA

Superstitions and "Witchcraft"

In the year 1275, Angéle de la Barthe was accused of being a witch. On trial at Toulouse, she "confessed" to having fornicated with an *incubus* (defined as a fallen angel who could appear in the shape of a man to satisfy his lust for women). As a result, Angéle supposedly conceived a child who was part wolf and part snake. Her beastly offspring spent two years devouring small children before it disappeared. Quickly convicted on these outrageous charges, Angéle was burned at the stake. Similar accusations, trials, and executions became increasingly common in succeeding centuries, but many beliefs about sorcery, witchcraft, and devil-worship actually existed long before Angéle's time. Following the lines of biblical condemnations of sorcerers and witches, numerous medieval theologians wrote extensively on the subject, trying to define and explain the dangers of witchcraft. For instance, Hildegarde of Bingen warned Christians that Satan was a negative power that could suck everything into a state of evil. Gervaise of Tilbury (c.1214) claimed witches could really fly but, if they spoke the name of Christ, they would fall immediately to earth.

Many of these ideas grew out of popular beliefs about a variety of magical and supernatural phenomena. Medieval scientists assumed that comets portended disaster; common folk thought nocturnal birds were devils who carried away dead souls after dark; and nobles often wore rubies because those stones would protect their rank, fortune, homes, fruit trees, and vineyards.[1] Even clerics endorsed credence in the irrational. They once again relegated women to two opposing roles, as the question of whether females were more like the Virgin Mary or more like Eve generated numerous odd views and practices.

Miracle stories, written by clerics to encourage veneration of Mary, enhanced the premise that pious, chaste femininity was a powerful, almost magical force. One popular example of such literature was the *Tale* (or *Miracle*) *of Beatrijs,* which concerned a young nun who left her convent in order to live with the yeoman she loved. Beatrijs later had to work as a prostitute to support herself and her twin sons. After many years she returned to her nunnery, only to discover that no one knew she had ever been gone. The Virgin had protected Beatrijs by taking her place in the convent until the wayward nun returned. Since few women could aspire to the perfection of Mary, the other side of woman's place in this belief system was even more popular. Churchmen who espoused this view called women "sisters of Eve," and claimed they were especially apt to be lured into evil.

The ambivalence about woman's nature, roles, and particularly her sexual desires also aroused both lay and ecclesiastical men's fears. For instance, a fourteenth-century preacher warned seafarers against allowing a whore aboard ship since her presence would cause the vessel to be rocked by heavy storms. The *Malleus Maleficarum* (the late fifteenth-century witch hunter's manual) declared that olive trees planted by harlots would not produce fruit.[2] The nymphomania associated with the "wild women" who supposedly inhabited certain forests, untamed regions, and mountainous places was probably another product of mixed male fears and fantasies concerning the opposite sex. Many people believed in these creatures, and in "wild men." Like her male counterpart, a wild woman was supposed to be half human and half animal. The male beasts were sometimes portrayed as noble savages who could potentially be tamed. Wild women, on the other hand, were less socially acceptable, partly because they were thought to be obsessed with achieving sexual intimacy with unsuspecting mortal men. It was presumed that a wild woman could even change form to attract unwary knights. These primitive female creatures were often identified with witches since both were believed to have superior knowledge of herbal medications.[3]

The notion that wild women could magically seduce men indicates how greatly men feared falling under feminine sexual spells. They were equally afraid of the female "powers" of menstruation and childbearing. In fact, some men came to believe these "powers" also enabled women to magically control male reproductive functions. In Northumberland in 1435, three men accused Margaret Lindsay and another woman of planting a magic stake that tied up male organs, thereby making the men impotent. In one of the rare late medieval trials where the verdict showed some common sense, the women were acquitted while the men were threatened with excommunication.

Belief in magic and the irrational was a part of life for everyone because God's power seemed far away, while nature was an ever-present force that could be felt, touched, feared, and hopefully propitiated. Perhaps the late medieval fear of women grew partly out of the fact that females were traditionally the intermediaries who attempted to use and appease both natural and supernatural forces. Given little access to accurate scientific or medical knowledge, women often resorted to "magical" remedies and aids as they tried to cope with such responsibilities as family health needs, childbirth, and cultivating crops. In the 1220s, for instance, Caesarius of Heisterbach reported that a woman named Hartdyfa of Cochem had apparently palmed, rather than swallowed, the "bread" used in communion services, since she was fertilizing her garden with the Host (the body of Christ). Caesarius claimed the woman's cabbages were remarkably healthy due to this innovative treatment, but poor Hartdyfa herself was continuously possessed and tortured by demons for her sacrilegious use of Christ's body.[4]

Many beliefs were not restricted to women but were most important to them because they dealt with the everyday facets of feminine existence. For instance, mothers frequently gave coral necklaces or teething rings to their babies because witches were believed to fear this stone. Hence the coral prevented the witch from coming near the child in order to make his teeth hurt. Beatrice de Planisolles of Montaillou even saved her grandsons' umbilical cords to use as lucky charms.[5] Fertility charms were also most frequently designed for women, because producing heirs was one of their most important functions. Tuscan wedding rituals included putting a baby in the bride's arms to stimulate fertility.[6] As men feared, women were also particularly apt to dabble with "love magic"—charms, potions, and other devices that could help them attract and gain sexual power over men. In 1446 Germany, Anna of Wurttemberg, countess of Katzenelnbogen, admitted to having used such a spell to make her husband more affectionate. She took a nutshell containing a spider and held it in her mouth while kissing her husband. This charm was supposed to make him love her forever.[7]

All these superstitions, charms, and other quasi-magical practices were a very pervasive, relatively harmless part of life, but they provided a foundation on which the belief in witchcraft could grow. These credulous beliefs—so much a part of everyday life—were not as threatening as witchcraft, which frightened and enraged people. Women often became victims of this heightened fear. As previously noted, sometimes women were accused of practicing witchcraft merely because they were competing with male physicians. The populace tended to support their favorite empirics, but not "witches." Thus charges of witchcraft made it possible to get rid of successful female lay healers, without rousing public resentment against the authorities who conducted the trials. Maria *la Medica* (named for her healing abilities) was a victim of this ploy. In 1480 Brescia, she was tortured into "confessing" to a variety of prohibited practices, such as invoking Satan's help to effect her cures. As was the case with many other empirics, however, Maria's real crime lay in being a popular and successful female healer.

Since withcraft/heresy accusations were so hard to disprove, defendants in some political cases were also charged with these crimes. Moreover, these cases were usually "show trials; their purpose was heavily propagandistic and the accusations were calculated to shock."[8] Numerous trial records illustrate how useful witchcraft charges were in primarily non-spiritual cases. In fifteenth-century England, for example, a royal family became embroiled in political machinations that culminated in a witchcraft trial. In 1428, Duke Humphrey of Gloucester married a very ambitious lady-in-waiting named Eleanor Cobham. Some thirteen years later, several members of the Gloucester entourage were arrested and accused of using magic to try to kill King Henry VI. Gloucester's enemies claimed his wife Eleanor was implicated in this plot, so they also charged her with conspiracy and twenty-eight counts of sorcery and treason. The facts that Eleanor had a servant known as "the witch of Eye" and that she probably would have liked to become queen made these accusations seem almost reasonable. However, the motive behind Eleanor's arrest and trial was merely to unseat her husband from his position of power, so she received a punishment that was a great political embarrassment to him. After her very public penance, she was imprisoned until her death in 1457, thereby serving as a guarantee for Goucester's good behavior.

A slightly earlier fifteenth-century case, involving other members of the English royal family, was motivated more by greed than by politics. After Henry IV died, his son King Henry V of England arrested his stepmother, Joan of Navarre, and deprived her of her dowry and other possessions. He supposedly did so because a Franciscan friar had accused her of practicing witchcraft. Joan's special treatment during her imprisonment (1419–1421) indicates that these charges merely served as a pretext to borrow her lands—in effect, a forced loan. On his deathbed, Henry himself lent color to this interpretation by specifically naming Joan as one person he hoped would forgive him.

Of all the medieval "show trials," undoubtedly the most famous was that of Joan of Arc, called *the Maid of Orléans*, a case that also illustrates the links among everyday superstitions, "witchcraft," and heresy. Born in 1412 in the village of Domremy, France, Joan grew up in war-torn Lorraine during the ongoing fighting between France and England, which we know as part of the *Hundred Years War*—a conflict that threatened to transfer the French crown to the English king. Around 1425, she supposedly began to hear the voices of Saint Catherine, Saint Michael, and Saint Margaret of Antioch urging her to actively support the dauphin, Charles of France. Miraculously recognizing him disguised among his courtiers, Joan persuaded Charles to let her aid his cause. In the spring of 1429, she led his troops to victory in the Battle of Orléans, and in July, she had him crowned King Charles VII at Reims. Captured in 1430, Joan was condemned by the Inquisition on charges of heresy and witchcraft, and then burned at the stake in May of 1431. Nearly twenty years later, the Inquisition overturned the original verdict and posthumously exonerated Joan. In 1920, the Catholic church canonized her.

Though Joan was a unique woman, there were many typical supernatural elements in her story—beginning with her heavenly voices and her ability to spot Charles, whom she had never seen, among a crowd of equally unfamiliar people. Similarly, many people believed in her powers because her coming had been foretold. A contemporary psychic named Marie d'Avignon had prophesied that a virgin wearing armor would deliver France from the armies of her enemies. Hence, after Joan's virginity was established, her mission was "proved" to be ordained by God. Thereafter many people treated Joan as a magician; the governors of Toulouse asked for help with the city's finances while women wanted Joan to touch their prayer books as a good luck blessing.

The English against whom Joan fought were equally convinced that she possessed supernatural powers—ones from the Devil. The duke of Bedford reported to England that this young girl had laid false enchantments on his troops, causing their defeat at Orléans.[9] The English believed they could never win as long as Joan led the French. Having her tried and condemned by the Inquisition was excellent propaganda since it allowed the English to label Joan a heretic who called up demons and made a pact with the Devil. On the other hand, not everyone believed these charges. Joan spoke the name of Jesus several times as she died, which contradicted the belief that it was impossible for a heretic to speak God's name with her last breath. People also whispered that a dove flew from the stake as she died, and that her heart would not burn—a traditional sign of sanctity. The three prime movers behind her trial were said to have met with mysterious ends; one died while simply having his beard trimmed. Joan herself also made several accurate prophecies—including the recovery of Paris and even her own death.

In addition to illustrating the prevalence of superstitions among the medieval populace, Joan's case reveals that clergy and laity alike had begun to believe that witchcraft—a mixture of heresy, sorcery, and devilish aid—was different and more threatening than its separate components. Her trial establishes a bridge between early views of magic as a relatively harmless individual aberration and the later perception of witchcraft as a diabolic group activity, a heresy led by the Devil—Christ's most formidable opponent.[10]

Trials for such blatantly secular motives became slightly less common by the end of the Middle Ages. By then, witchcraft had become an official "heresy" under the jurisdiction of the Inquisition, and witches were believed to be Satan's personal minions. As German historian Edith Ennen declared in *The Medieval Woman*, "The question of heresy takes on a renewed importance in the fifteenth century. Magic is now regarded as heresy."[11] There are many suppositions regarding exactly why this change occurred. The Crusades may have been a factor since they roused public zeal for stamping out infidels at home and abroad. This incited an atmosphere of intolerance, making Christians feel they should fight all forms of deviance. Heterodox groups that stressed the existence of a cosmic battle between good and evil also played a role by popularizing an image of the Devil as a very real, personal enemy of Christ. Witches were believed to be Satan's weapons in this war, since the Lord of Darkness could use them to destroy the Christian world. Moreover, in the late Middle Ages, economic problems, natural disasters and epidemics, and a growing number of heterodox religious sects produced the need for a scapegoat. In the past, such catastrophes had often been perceived as punishments visited by God upon His wayward flock. But the upheavals seemed of such immense proportions during the late Middle Ages, that people began to believe God would not do these terrible things—obviously magic and satanic interference were at fault. They were traditionally believed to cause a wide variety of calamities, including sterility, birth defects, plague, destructive storms, and famines.

As these and other factors caused perceptions of magic to change, the church's attitude toward sorcery also grew harsher. Clerics soon became obsessed with the supposed links among women, sexual misconduct, and witchcraft. Most churchmen wholeheartedly supported the idea that witches concluded pacts and fornicated with the Devil. In the later Middle Ages, anxiety about feminine sexuality combined with the fear of Satan, presumably because there were so many surplus women who had little access to careers—whether as wives, nuns, or craftspeople. Women's life expectancies had lengthened, so single and/or widowed women were more numerous in the fifteenth and sixteenth centuries than ever before. They thereby provided a highly visible threat to the male-oriented world.[12] A woman who was not under a man's control was an outsider and, by the end of the Middle Ages, all outsiders—such as Jews, heretics, and even unattached women—were regarded as dangerous enemies who, led by the Devil, were bent on destroying Christian society.

Particularly in Inquisition trials, it was most often clerics themselves who defined and spread witchcraft beliefs and fears. The publication of the *Malleus Maleficarum* in 1486, also gave impetus to the witch hysteria. Written by two Dominicans, Sprenger and Kramer, the "Witch Hammer" became the bible of witch hunters. It presented four essential characteristics of the "real" witch. She first had to renounce her Christian faith, a step that turned the ordinary "herb wife" or sorcerer into a heretic. Second, a true witch sacrificed unbaptized infants to Satan (see below). She then had to devote herself to evil. The last requirement was that the witch engaged in intimate relations with the Devil and/or incubi.[13]

The *Malleus Maleficarum* focused the suppression of witchcraft-heresy on women by declaring, "All witchcraft comes from carnal lust, which is in women insatiable." As Jeffrey Richards stated, this book was "a work of pathological misogynism and sex-obsession."[14] Moreover, it directed ecclesiastical judges to use any method necessary to induce confessions, which were obligatory under canon law for conviction and execution. If the accused did not readily confess her crimes, Inquisitors were supposed to lie to her or trick her into admitting her sins. A witch who persisted in her denials was "put to the question"—a euphemism for torture. The judges even had an explanation ready for those occasions when women died from injuries inflicted during such questioning. In a 1493 case, they reported that the Devil had executed the victim while she was in jail.[15] This had the effect of posthumously "proving" the charges against the unfortunate woman.

Obviously, the use of torture to extract confessions makes it difficult for the modern scholar to filter out the truth from these records. Since judges also used torture to force their victims to identify other witches, most names obtained in this fashion are as highly suspect as the rest of their "confessions." In addition, the outcome of trials and confessions was determined in advance, since the Inquisitors developed a formula of specific questions to which they required predetermined answers. One way to obtain the reply they wanted was to change the question, or to translate the Latin query incorrectly. When the victim answered appropriately, the reply was recorded as if she had responded to an entirely different question.[16] Inquisition trial records thus give less evidence of actual witchcraft practices than of the particular responses the judges wanted.

Another "proof" of guilt was the sign of a pact that the witch had made with the Devil. By the sixteenth century, witch hunters had begun diligently searching their female victims' entire bodies for marks that were supposedly symbols of these pacts between Satan and his minions. The Inquisitors believed the marks indicated hidden amulets intended to prevent witches from being punished. Any birthmark, mole, or scar was eventually deemed proof of guilt. The Inquisitors were obviously so determined that they nearly always found what they were looking for, even though it did not exist before they started looking.

None of these techniques seem sensible or morally admirable today, but many Inquisitors were probably deluded rather than evil—they believed they were fighting the Devil himself. Unwittingly or not, however, the Inquisitors fueled the fear of both sorcery and women by defining witchcraft, using procedures like torture to root it out, and focusing on female "magician heretics." As a result of all these tactics, by the end of the fifteenth century the original activity of sorcerers and simple "old wives" had become associated in the public and clerical mind with night rides, black clothing, cannibalism, the evil eye, the renunciation of God, sexual perversions, desecrating the cross and sacraments, and women.

A range of trial records reveal how the beliefs promulgated by clerics changed as they turned heresy and magic into a "cult of witchcraft." For instance, during the thirteenth century, wax image or *volt* magic began being mentioned in trial records with some frequency. In a typical case heard by a Parisian court, Marguerite de Belleville "confessed" that the bishop of Troyes had commissioned her and several others to make a volt, or wax image spell. They gave the figure a godmother and baptized it "Jeanne," because it was intended to cause the death of Jeanne of Burgundy, queen of France. Accusing witches of performing such mockeries of orthodox rituals allowed the church to claim the magicians were heretics.

In the fourteenth century, the church began to believe witches participated in another parody of orthodox rituals—attending organized gatherings of magicians and Devil worshippers. In 1335, four women—Paule Viguier, Armande Robert, Matheline Fauré, and Pierrille Roland—supposedly claimed to have attended such formal witch sect meetings. In the same year at Toulouse, a middle-aged woman named Anne-Marie de Georgel "confessed" to a sexual crime—fornicating with Satan himself—which was another new element in the theology of witchcraft. Moreover, the Devil, described as an awesome black man, had supposedly taught her to make magic potions. Witches were presumed to make these salves with the blood of children, the bones of corpses stolen from graveyards, menstrual blood, and desecrated sacraments. Anne-Marie's case was one of the first times the records specifically mentioned a recipe for such ointments coming directly from Satan.

Also in 1335, another defendant, Catherine Delort, was accused of having had an affair with a shepherd who introduced her to such witchcraft practices as participating in orgies and eating children. By this time, witches were believed to kill children for three main reasons: to sacrifice them to Satan, to provide diabolical food for witch feasts, and to gather essential ingredients for making their magical salves and ointments. Since witches traditionally smothered infants in their cradles, most babies supposedly slain by witches probably died of Sudden Infant Death Syndrome or were victims of deliberate infanticide when their parents "overlay" the newborns in their family beds. In the late Middle Ages, however, these deaths were added to the sins laid at the witch's door so that an old, village "wise woman" was often said to have killed a child who, in reality, had been disposed of by his/her parents.

During a trial in Milan in the year 1390, Pierina de Bugatis "confessed" that her spirit often left her body in order to break into other houses. In common with most witches, however, she passed by the homes of the poor and left them unmolested. This idea—whether actually voiced by Pierina or merely invented by her accusers—reveals the growing fear among both ecclesiastical and temporal authorities of the time that witch/heretics would lead grass-roots rebellions against unfair social and economic conditions.

In the same year, a secular Parisian court heard a "love magic" case against Margot de la Barre, a lower-class prostitute with a reputation for possessing magical powers. A similar case had been heard earlier in this century, when a woman named Isabelle de Ferièves had "confessed" to having created a love charm for Mahaut, countess of Artois. Isabelle described her potion as containing blood, vervain, daisy, and liverwort. Though convicted, Isabelle had not been sentenced to death. But by 1390, when Margot's case was tried, the fear among men that females could magically control male behavior and sexual abilities had increased to such an extent that Margot was sentenced to death for practicing love magic.

In 1450 Lucerne, Else of Meersburg was not merely accused of attending witch meetings, but was also charged with habitually riding to the gatherings on the back of a dog or wolf. Two theories were involved: one was that witches could diabolically control animals and the other was that the beast was actually a demon capable of changing its form.[17] Nine years later, a trial in Andermatt carried this idea a step further; in this case, Catherine Simon was charged with having the ability to change herself into a wolf, a cat, or a fox. She supposedly also used the Devil's help to create avalanches, kill livestock, and cause illnesses. Presumably Catherine was so feared by her neighbors that she was beheaded, her corpse was burned, and then her ashes were thrown into the Reuse River. This ensured that no part of her was left to haunt or terrorize the village from beyond the grave.

A case from 1492 at Langendorf indicates that, by the end of the Middle Ages, widespread popular accusations of sorcery were becoming the order of the day. In this case, the priests and other men of the area reportedly claimed that there were only two women in the whole town who were innocent of witchcraft practices[18]—presumably either another instance of falsified records or of exaggerated popular anxiety.

All these cases indicate a variety of new patterns and directions in the growth and development of witchcraft beliefs. Some historians think these changes resulted from developments in actual practices, while other scholars argue that church thinkers and/or judges invented all of their accusations—charges with no basis whatsoever in reality. Though many beliefs clearly owed more to the ideas of rabid witch hunters than to actual practices, we are unable to conclude that there were no women during this time period who tried to conjure up the Devil and/or who genuinely believed themselves to be powerful sorcerers. There is little or no evidence of women being involved in what we would call "formal witchcraft sects," but it does appear that they were more likely than males to resort to using some types of "magical" aids, especially love magic or charms for healing. Presumably some women—either mentally unbalanced, seeking a greater measure of self-esteem and power in a man's world, or genuinely curious about the workings of the supernatural—did at least dabble in a little, relatively harmless "magic." Unfortunately, deviance of any type was perceived as a threat by God-fearing clerics convinced they had unearthed a horrible pact between Satan and his numerous henchwomen. As the many cases cited in this chapter illustrate, the medieval witchcraft craze had its share of victims, even though the great witch hunts and mass executions were yet to come.

A woman and a clerk are punished in the stocks.

British Library, London

SECULAR LIFE

The Gerade in "Sachenspiegel" Law.

German, ca. 1350

Chapter Eleven

WHIPPED WITH A HANDFUL OF FLAX

Women in Various Legal Systems

Court transcripts from various countries indicate that in many regions, inanimate objects, animals, insects, ghosts, and even the Devil were considered to have legal responsibilities, and could be held accountable for their misdeeds. For instance, Gillon Lenfant and her husband, a cowherd on Clermont manor in England, accused a pig of killing their baby son. The felonious pig was convicted of murder and then executed by hanging.[1]

An equally interesting aspect of medieval jurisprudence was the way some locales settled neighborhood quarrels out of court. In parts of Germany, a housewife could let her hen wander just as far as the woman could throw an egg from her housetop, using her veil as a sling. English villeins traditionally tried to use the least desirable of their animals for tax payments, while their lords always wanted to be given the biggest, healthiest stock. Eventually the rule on some manors came to be that the lord had to accept any gosling strong enough to eat grass without sitting down. A sick hen qualified if it could jump the garden fence when someone startled it.[2] Such customs peacefully settled many village problems without taking them to court. This was important since neighborhood quarrels were considered such a serious threat to peace and prosperity that fomenting disputes in the community was usually a punishable offense. In 1375, for example, an English court sentenced a woman named Alice Shether to an hour in the "thews" (stocks for women) for sowing discord, and for being a malicious scold.

In the early Middle Ages, God was sometimes called upon to preside as judge in trials by ordeal or battle. In one ordeal, the suspect grasped a hot iron and his burned hand was then bandaged for three days. If the hand appeared unscarred when the wrappings were removed, this was assumed to be a miraculous sign of innocence and the suspect was acquitted. The cold water test was reserved for some witchcraft trials long after the 1200s, when most other ordeals were outlawed by canon law. In this test, if the defendant floated when she was thrown into a river or other body of water, she was found guilty. If she sank, she was presumed innocent, although it was not uncommon for the acquitted woman to drown.

It was also thought that God occasionally intervened in the judicial process in order to cancel punishments. Juetta de Balsham was hanged in 1264, but was still alive after twenty hours. Since it appeared God did not want Juetta executed, she was cut down and pardoned.[3] In 1359, a similar sign of divine mercy saved Cecilia Rygeway's life after she was sentenced to die for murdering her husband. Supposedly imprisoned with no food or water, Cecilia survived for some forty days, which King Edward III of England considered nothing short of miraculous. Edward promptly released and pardoned Cecilia.

If God did not come to one's aid, there were other ways to escape punishment. Emma Chaloner beat Alice Attelithe to death in 1261 London and then ran away. Because she had escaped, Emma was *outlawed*—meaning no one was to consort with her, anyone could apprehend her, and all her property was forfeited. Being an outlaw was too dangerous for Agnes Daythef, a vagabond from Oxfordshire, so she took sanctuary at a London church instead of fleeing the area after she stole an expensive surcote.[4] All criminals, even murderers, could find sanctuary for at least forty days inside a church. When her forty days were up, Agnes saved her life by choosing to *abjure the realm*, meaning she boarded a ship, after swearing never to return to England—on pain of death.

Medieval jurisprudence did not even pretend to provide the same justice for all. Equal justice was doled out to people who were equal to each other, a designation that depended upon socio-economic class. Among city women, for example, no mere journeyman's wife could ever be legally considered as "honest" as the wife of a wealthy merchant. In Germany, knights were subject to the law of fiefs—*Lehenrecht*—while burghers lived under the *Stadtrecht* (city law), and peasants lived by *Hofrecht* (manorial law).[5]

Gender played an even greater role in legal inequality. Records from royal English courts indicate that women stood a significantly better chance of being acquitted than did men. Female miscreants sometimes used gullibility as a defense since men thought they were especially apt to be lured into committing misdeeds. Because females were always supposed to obey their responsible male relatives, women might be found innocent if they could prove that their husbands had compelled their criminal participation. An English law code cited the case of a couple who were both convicted of forgery. The husband was executed, while his wife went free because she had merely followed his instructions.[6] If the worst happened and a woman was convicted of a serious crime, pregnancy could at least delay her execution because killing an unborn child was illegal. Convicted by a secular Parisian court in 1390, Jehanne de Brigue received a stay of execution until mid-August of 1391 because she appeared to be pregnant.

On the other hand, women were required to produce more witnesses in court than men needed to obtain acquittals. An Englishman could *wage his law*—prove himself innocent—by getting six witnesses to swear to his probity (witnesses usually swore to the individual's honesty rather than giving evidence about the crime). But a woman had to bring thirty-six men to court to help prove her innocence. Getting these men to swear to her honesty and good character was termed *purging herself thirty-six handed*. Another problem for women was that men were assumed to be their masters. Hence, an Englishwoman who murdered her husband was legally guilty of *petty treason*, just as if she had been a servant who killed his lord or employer. After Elizabeth Walton had her husband killed in 1388, she was burned at the stake for committing this offense.[7] Being a wealthy heiress did her no good, because she had killed her master. Rich men who murdered their wives, however, were sometimes able to buy pardons from the king since no treason was involved.

The widespread view that every female needed a male master resulted in a variety of laws designed to keep women and property under the control of men. Some local French rules were cited in the *Customs of the Beauvaisis*—the observations of customary law in Beauvais, France, that Philippe de Beaumanoir compiled in the late thirteenth century. He reported that women were barred from testifying in court, and that they were not allowed to obtain loans. Females were also unable to participate in legal contracts, a custom

Beaumanoir justified by equating women with "the dumb, the deaf, [and] the insane."[8]

Florentine statutes forbade a woman in that city-state from carrying out any legal transactions without the assistance of a male guardian, called a *mundualdus.* These laws also restricted her from making a will. In thirteenth-century Siena, on the other hand, women could usually make their own testaments. While studying some of these extant documents, historian Eleanor S. Riemer discovered that, "overwhelmingly, women left their property to other women."[9] Though this seems to have been true of women in most countries, the men in Siena considered such economic independence to be prejudicial to male interests so the privilege was later revoked. Though females in Siena and Florence had few legal rights, by the fifteenth century, married women in both cities could petition for restoration of their dowries if their husbands went bankrupt or appeared likely to do so. According to historian Julius Kirshner, some ninety Florentine women retrieved their property or money between the years 1375 and 1431. During the next one hundred years, this figure jumped to four hundred and sixty wives.[10] Moreover, in both Florence and Siena, dowries or their equivalents were most often returned directly to the women without male guardians to administer the funds.

Peasant women in Germany could spend only a small amount of money, a sum determined by law, and all classes of women lacked legal rights. For instance, a woman always had to have a man to defend her in a court of law. The thirteenth-century German legal code called the *Sachenspiegel* (*Saxon Mirror*) stated that a woman's property was always under her husband's guardianship, and she was bound to obey him in everything. German women, however, were allowed to dispose of their own small belongings.[11] As was common in Siena and other locales, they most often left their personal property to female relatives.

Spanish codes allowed childless widows, who lived chastely, to keep any presents their deceased husbands might have given them.[12] In some other regions, all moveable property (*chattels*) was viewed as the husband's permanent possession. Gifts bestowed upon an English wife still legally belonged to her husband, a custom explained by equating men and women with heavenly bodies. This poetic comparison declared that just as the moon has to depend upon the sun for light, women merely glitter in the reflected splendor of their husbands.[13] Thus a present reflected the man's personal wealth, social standing, and generosity; a woman could not own the gift, any more than the moon owns its light.

As the customs of all these countries reveal, men were determined to control property and to keep women out of courts of law. A thirteenth-century justice who wrote a treatise on English law included a typical dictum that women belong at home, not in court.[14] This caused a variety of problems for male as well as female litigants. At a trial in Northumberland in the year 1280, a manor lord brought Christina Rudd as one of his witnesses to the defendant's villeinage. The accused objected at once, claiming women were of too fragile a nature to testify in such a trial. The court agreed, disallowing what it called Christina's "feeble evidence" and allowing the lord's villein to go free.[15]

Similar problems occurred in proof-of-age cases. Noble English girls were normally declared of age at fourteen if they were married, and at sixteen if they were single; boys usually had to be slightly older to be declared adults. A person's legal age was often determined by a proof-of-age trial based on the memories of witnesses, because birth or baptism records were virtually non-existent. Even churches rarely had written records of such details, especially at the village level. The heir could not claim the property until he/she was certified an adult, but in most areas only men were allowed to testify—even though modesty rarely permitted them to be present during childbirth. Thus a man might swear he knew when the child in question had been born because the midwife had told him the date. Records of proof-of-age trials are filled with vague male recollections regarding how they remembered when a particular child was born—such as "I broke a leg immediately afterward," or "I bought a piece of land that same day." Cunning parents who were unwilling to trust to such lucky coincidences tried to "help" potential testifiers remember the child's birth. In England, a new mother named Isabel presented a visitor to her childbed with a silk purse so that he would well remember the date of her daughter Joan's birth. Baptisms and gifts to godfathers served the same purpose.

This all-male procedure clearly left a lot of loopholes, and judges frequently had no accurate information on which to base their decisions. Moreover, the effort to ban females completely from such courts was futile. Even though they could not be witnesses, girls were often the heirs whose ages were in question. In 1283, for example, Olive Bernelee had to appear before a London court to establish her age as seventeen, and thereby become her father's legal heir.[16]

Obviously legal theory and practice rarely coalesced. Though females had no legal standing as adults, women actually appeared at court in a variety of roles. In fourteenth-century Ghent, Callekin van Laerne even went to court to argue her right to protect herself. The jurors decided that she had been justified in wounding a male assailant with a knife. The ruling confirmed that townswomen were entitled to defend themselves, though the court was quick to point out that women were still not allowed to "dishonor" men by grabbing their buttocks.[17] Callekin's case is one indication that the growth of urban centers could help women, since those who held property and did business in towns began to acquire a few more legal rights.

It was often men who wanted the discriminatory customs changed. Though most men believed that, in theory, women should have little access to the judicial system, townsmen simultaneously enjoyed using certain feminine legal rights for their own purposes. In 1280 London, for example, John Gardebois appointed his wife, Avice, as his attorney and charged her with collecting his debts. In fourteenth-century Ghent, Clare van der Ponten served as her husband's legal representative in wool and land transactions. In Florence, Checa Corsini helped her brother Giovanni evade his creditors in 1430, by hiding his assets under her name.[18]

Other women sought judicial protection on their own account. For instance, Idonea le Hukestere brought suit in 1344 against William Simond for butchering her pregnant pig. The London jurors found William guilty and awarded Idonea seven *shillings* for the loss of her sow. Many such cases concerned more valuable property. Isabella de Worstede won her suit in 1373 against a London plasterer, William Grene, who had done a poor job of building her chimney.[19] The court ordered William to repair it at his own expense. Emma Saltere, another London resident, sued Thomas Blankowe and Alice Breton in 1368 for 52*s* they owed her. Since Thomas and Alice never appeared to answer the suit, their property was attached and handed over to Emma. Assessed at a total value of 32*s* 6*d*, the goods included a fur-trimmed blue coat, a chest, and a mattress with coverlet, tester, and linens. If the defendants did not appear within one year and a day, these goods would belong to Emma as partial repayment of the debt.[20]

The death of her husband was often the catalyst that thrust a woman into this sort of financial and legal independence, and a woman's legal rights could also change as new customs or laws were adopted. In 1328, Alianore Wormenhal refused to hand over a number of tenements in Oxford to her husband's heir, because she had been a joint purchaser of the property. The Oxford councillors were in a quandary over this case, so they requested advice from London. The councilmen replied that, according to London customs, Alianore would have a legal right to the portion of the estate that she had helped purchase. The Oxford officials quickly adopted the same rule, and Alianore kept her holdings.[21]

In addition to property claims, women also attempted to initiate other types of suits. For instance, Johanna Wolsy brought a defamation of character suit in 1382 against a London man named Alan who had accused her of complicity in a theft. Alan was supposedly a sorcerer who obtained his information from magic spells, so he was sent to the pillory.[22] Johanna's name was cleared—a somewhat unusual result since women rarely fared well in criminal suits. In 1281, for example, Wenthiliana le Prestre tried to bring a suit against her husband's murderers, but the Herefordshire court offered her little satisfaction—referring her instead to a different jurisdiction. Cecilia le Boteler nearly won her case against her husband's killer in 1323; then the defendant came to court with sixty armed men and "persuaded" the jury to acquit him.[23]

Women had similar problems in rape cases. They could accuse their rapists, but doing so rarely did the victims much good. During the fifteenth century in many southeastern French towns, for instance, there was little official condemnation of gang rapes committed by clubs of young men. According to historian Jacques Rossiaud, this was an almost acceptable way for unmarried youths to acquire experience and pleasure, since they chose to attack the most attractive and desirable females among servants, priests' concubines, and other women on the fringe of society. When the members of these youth groups acquired trades and better community standing as adult men, they quit running with their gangs, got married, and were thereafter considered honest and reputable men. The rape victims, however, were blamed for attracting the attentions of their attackers.[24] With their reputations ruined, many ended up as prostitutes.

An Englishwoman named Rose Savage received no more sympathy and satisfaction than those unfortunate French victims when she accused John de Clifford of raping her in 1282 Oxfordshire. The whole neighborhood knew her allegations were true, but Rose was merely fined for incorrect and incomplete "paperwork" in her suit.

Her case perhaps helps to explain why there were only three rapes reported in the London Eyre from the years 1250 until 1276—and two of those cases were eventually dismissed.[25] A similar trend was noticeable at the manorial level, because women had virtually no influence on the workings of the legal system itself. Englishwomen, for example, had the right to report men's assaults against them but, in many villages, females rarely did so. Historian Judith Bennett believes the low number of reports of male violence against women was related to the fact that males controlled the courts. The result was that men who attacked women often went unpunished, while the female victims were censured for complaining and/or for inciting the assaults.[26]

These local manorial courts were the most active segment of the legal system, especially in the early Middle Ages. Convened by landholders on their own estates, these courts handled various local crimes, neighborhood disputes, and quarrels between lords and villeins. Although village women had no control over the manorial courts, they did have an equal duty to raise the "hue and cry"—letting the community know when a crime was committed or discovered—since everyone had some responsibility for crime prevention and exposure. The English villagers in Warboys raised 124 hues from 1290 through 1353, of which women were responsible for 33.

Naturally, village women also committed some of these crimes, but they did so in much smaller numbers than did men. Out of more than 135 misdeeds listed in the court records from Warboys (1299–1349), only 25 were committed by women. The miscreants included Beatrice Puttock, cited for receiving two stolen geese in 1313, and Margaret Fine, who received an outlawed man named Thomas Galyon in 1316.[27] Being banned from the community was the worst penalty for such village offenders, so it was reserved for "hardened criminals." This was a peculiarly effective punishment in the closed society of medieval villages, where it was almost impossible to exist without the help of one's neighbors. Furthermore, as Margaret Fine's conviction for taking in Thomas Galyon shows, there was nowhere else convenient to go, since receiving prohibited people was also a crime.

Manor courts also dealt with property cases. Even in rural areas, women's legal standing increased somewhat over the years, along with their property rights. When Alice of Rallingbury sued Richard Snouh in 1303 for keeping her off her lands on the manor of Barnet, the manor court returned the land to her for use during her lifetime.[28] Not only did the manorial legal system help women like Alice keep their property, but it even gave a few, more high-born women the opportunity to exercise authority by administering justice through these courts on their own lands. Ermengarde, viscountess of Narbonne (d.1192), ruled and dispensed justice on her estates in the south of France for some fifty years. Similarly, during her husband's absence, Margaret Paston convened her own fifteenth-century manorial courts to hear complaints and arbitrate disputes among local villagers. Occasionally women even held this judicial right in regions where they were otherwise barred from appearing in court.

However, these courts created a variety of problems for both kings and commoners. A landholder who had the power and machinery to dispense justice gained a life and death hold on his/her tenants. In 1279, Angareta de Beauchamp owned the right to convene courts and operate her own gallows on her manor of Spelsbury in England.[29] These privileges were very profitable because courts garnered fines and confiscated property. Hence, unscrupulous manor holders could use this judicial system to fill their own coffers. Yet another drawback was that each manor had its own system. On one, the estate holder might own the right to hear petty cases, but all felony suits would have to be sent to a higher court. Simultaneously, on a neighboring fief, the same manor lord might own the rights to all judicial proceedings. Jeanne de Caumont's (1440s–1470s) legal rights were typical. On one seigneury, she held all judicial rights, while on two others she could hold only "low justice" courts.[30]

To clear up these complications and put judicial profits into their own royal pockets, monarchs in most countries started restructuring their legal systems during the Middle Ages. Royal courts began to handle many types of cases in which various classes and both genders could bring suit. Though this does not imply that everyone was treated equally, people did sometimes use royal justice to redress problems created by local manor courts. The *Jours de Troyes* (royal French court in Champagne) heard such a suit in 1286, when Borgine Baudier petitioned it to overturn her father Huard's conviction and execution for murder by a local court on the lady of Chassins' manor. Three years later, the *Jours* finally handed down an odd decision, ruling that the manor court had acted in a legally correct way, but also deciding that the murder victim was responsible for his murderer's death. The court thereby acquitted the lady of Chassins of any wrongdoing, while simultaneously ordering her to return all confiscated property to Huard's daughters, remove his body from the gallows (after more than three years), and bury him in a churchyard.[31] This case shows two types of secular courts in conflict, and also illustrates that women had access to some royal courts.

Another female plaintiff involved the same court in a dispute with the ecclesiastical legal system. In 1288, Lady Christine de Bar petitioned the *Jours de Troyes* to punish Miles de Jaucourt, who had already been convicted of murdering her son. Since he was a cleric, an ecclesiastical court had tried and convicted Miles, but had imposed no punishment.[32] This was a common problem since the church zealously guarded its right to deal with any and all clerical offenders, even those at the lowest rung of the hierarchy. By removing iniquitous clerics from secular jurisdictions, and then treating most of them quite mildly, this system infuriated much of the lay populace.

Though notoriously lenient with clerical criminals, church courts often severely punished lay offenders. Whippings, ostracism, and excommunication were routinely handed out in the effort to show lay miscreants the error of their ways. Ecclesiastical courts heard a wide variety of cases, and rarely deemed any crime too trivial, particularly if it involved an affront to the church. For instance, a London court of 1476 dealt harshly with the scandalous behavior of Nicholas Haukyns, who never went to church, preferring to sleep late on Sunday mornings. A similar court in 1451 Durham sentenced Isabella Hunter and Catherine Pykring to be whipped twice with a handful of flax for washing their linen on Mary Magdalene Day.[33]

Most commonly, ecclesiastical courts handled "social problems"—such as those concerning marriage or divorce—so they were particularly important to women. Marriage was not officially termed a sacrament until the Council of Florence (1438–1445), but the need for consent between spouses was already being examined during the twelfth century. When a canon lawyer named Gratian compiled the *Concordance of Discordant Canons* (called *Gratian's Decretum*), he included the idea that mutual affection had to exist in order to validate a marriage. He emphasized that such affection could not be present when either partner was forced to marry against his or her will. The church eventually adopted this principle, but its ruling that the force must be strong enough to make a "steady" person capitulate was so vague that force could still be used to make children "consent" to marry. Force was usually a last resort, however, since contemporary wisdom in many regions advised against it. Icelandic women, for example, had been known to maim, or even kill, unwanted husbands[34]—thereby providing violent proof of Gratian's theory.

Catholic dicta also prohibited marriages between blood relatives. This included seven degrees of kinship until Pope Innocent III modified the law to only the fourth degree of consanguinity at the Fourth Lateran Council in the year 1215. Canon law still allowed the pope as Christ's vicar to relax or dispense with these prohibitions, and such dispensations became almost a necessity for highborn suitors. Edmund, earl of March and Ulster, spelled out the problem when he requested a dispensation in the year 1415, complaining that he was related to all the unmarried women he knew of his social rank.[35]

Divorce was theoretically illegal but, as was true of consanguineous marriage, the pope had the option of legitimizing it. The canon legal system recognized a variety of pleas by those seeking annulments. The previously mentioned use of physical force to obtain the required "consent," became a frequent complaint in these trials. Catherine McKesky used this plea when she sued for a divorce from her husband, John Cusake, in 1436 in Armagh, Ireland. Her witnesses swore that Catherine had lamented throughout her forced betrothal, and that her parents had severely beaten her until she agreed to the proposed marriage.[36] The court granted her an annulment. A French court succinctly stated another acceptable cause: a husband who did not engage in proper carnal relations could be divorced "perpetually" by his wife.[37] In 1340, John Henry of Bohemia and Margaret Maultasch, countess of Tyrol, obtained an annulment because Margaret claimed John was impotent. This excuse left Margaret free to marry her presumed lover, Louis of Brandenburg. Few lower-class marriages ended in divorce, but those that did usually involved charges of multiple marriages. Bigamy was also a common plea among the gentry, as was the claim of consanguinity without papal dispensation.

Eventually the church even issued decrees about a variety of topics on the periphery of marriage and divorce laws. Canonists were especially concerned with feminine property rights. For example, they insisted that a woman whose marriage had been properly annulled by the church must be allowed to retain her dowry and other property, unless she had been found guilty of adultery. Similar ecclesiastical codes also required parents to support their children, even when the offspring were illegitimate. These rulings had great significance for women. It was extremely hard for many divorced mothers and those with illegitimate babies to support their children, since there was no law requiring fathers to contribute financial aid.[38] These rules also nudged temporal authorites toward enacting the same types of humane legislation.

Theologians even tried to regulate the role of sex in marriage. Canon lawyers evolved a doctrine of "conjugal debt," which insisted that both partners had a duty to engage in intercourse when either one requested it. One rationale for this rule was that women were by nature sexually promiscuous. As the thirteenth-century canonist, Cardinal Hostiensis, explained, "husbands [have] a moral obligation to keep their wives sexually satisfied, lest they be tempted to stray to other beds."[39] Saint Paul was one of the earliest authorities cited in the debate over conjugal rights since he had declared that marital sex was proper, or at least that "it is better to marry than to burn" (I Corinthians 7:9). But medieval philosophers refined the concept of conjugal debt until only the responding partner was free of sin. Pope Gregory VII (1073–1085) insinuated one distinction into the argument by ruling all coitus was sinful when it was pleasurable—a theory that never achieved great popularity among the laity.

Canonists eventually issued specific laws regarding the conjugal debt, and allowed virtually anyone to petition a church court for restitution of his or her conjugal rights. In 1496, Margaret Elyott charged that her husband, Nicholas, no longer treated her with marital affection. Her witnesses agreed that Nicholas no longer lived with Margaret, so he had to appear before the London court to show cause why he should not be excommunicated.[40] Like most other husbands in his position, Nicholas was merely sent home to fulfill his duties, but he also received a stern warning that another such complaint by his wife might carry stiff penalties.

Although cases involving sexual misconduct, insults to the church, or marital problems were more common, probably to modern readers the most familiar type of medieval ecclesiastical trial was that of the Inquisition. As it spread its wings and attacked more and more heterodox sects, it became especially important to women—who were often victimized by its efforts to suppress heretics and witches. Again, Joan of Arc serves as a good example since her two trials reveal a number of elements common in Inquisition cases, and some of the problems inherent in these courts—such as political and sexual biases. Joan's first trial, and her execution in 1431, were dictated by English political and military necessities, while her second case (1450–1456) was motivated by French political realities. In addition to the machinations of the English, Joan's gender played a large role in her first trial. Joan flew in the face of church teachings on womanly behavior and obedience; rather than staying at home, sewing and having babies, she wore male clothing and led armies. Since it was "known" that God had made womankind subject to male control, it was nearly impossible for clerics to believe He, rather than the Devil, had urged this peasant girl to wear armor and interfere in the male business of warfare. Moreover, the Inquisitors disapproved of any female who preferred the voices of saints that she alone heard, to those of male clerical authorities. In essence, Joan of Arc's real crime was being a very independent, non-traditional woman.

The actual retrial began in Paris on November 7, 1455, with Joan's mother, Isabelle Romée, serving as the official petitioner. The court called a variety of people, both males and females, to testify before it as the rehabilitation trial moved from one town to another. The women may even have been considered the more important witnesses because they could attest to Joan's virginity, modesty, and other "feminine" attributes. After everyone was heard, Jean Brehal (Inquisitor of France) wrote the *Recollectio*, which cleared Joan of the accusations against her. After studying this report, on July 7, 1456, the commissioners of the Inquisition declared the original trial and conviction null and void since the proceedings had been contaminated with fraud and illegalities.

Though the retrial was politically motivated, this verdict seems to have been more reasonable and informed than that handed down by Joan's first judges. The testimony had uncovered a variety of prohibited acts committed by Joan's original judges. For instance, two men had sat behind a courtroom curtain taking notes, but only writing down damning or altered evidence. Much of the original transcript, though not exactly false, was discovered to consist largely of subtle misrepresentations of the truth—a word altered, another left out, and so on. Moreover, Joan had been allowed no counsel, kept in a secular prison with male guards, and threatened and cajoled into signing an abjuration of her "heresies"—but this was later replaced with a different document to "prove" her

Women defending a castle.

The Governing Body of Christ Church, Oxford

guilt.[41] Actually, these were typical irregularities, so most Inquisition condemnations of heretics and witches could apparently have been overturned. Joan's story reveals how easily the Inquisition became an instrument of vengeance or a political tool. The deceit used against Joan also illustrates what the church was willing to condone as it desperately tried to purge heretics, and anyone else it considered undesirable, from the orthodox populace.

Chapter Twelve

DISPLAYED NO WOMANLY COWARDICE

Female Landholders and Politicians

In the early fifteenth century, a young heiress named Jacqueline, countess of Hainault, raised havoc in parts of France, Flanders, and England. Widowed at the tender age of sixteen, Jacqueline was soon forced to wed a second husband, John IV, duke of Brabant. Her dull groom drove Jacqueline to distraction, so she abandoned him. Philip *the Good,* duke of Burgundy, promptly disputed Jacqueline's estate rights since her deserted husband was Philip's cousin—as was Jacqueline herself. Her choice of a third mate, Humphrey, duke of Gloucester, further infuriated Philip, who besieged the countess in Mons. Once he had captured her, Philip sent Jacqueline to live under guard in Ghent. Disguised as a page (a typical medieval ruse according to chroniclers), Jacqueline escaped and attempted to carry on her fight in Holland. She also continued her tumultuous marital career.

After Humphrey, duke of Gloucester, divorced her in order to wed her lady-in-waiting, Jacqueline married the Burgundian governor, Franz van Borselen. This was in direct opposition to the provisions of a treaty she had signed, promising not to remarry without permission from the duke of Burgundy. Philip eventually captured the couple and threatened to behead Franz unless Jacqueline renounced all claims to her estates. Thus, in the middle of the 1430s, after she had struggled for some fifteen years to keep her property, Philip finally succeeded in forcing this tenacious countess to sign away all her lands, rights, and titles.

Though Jacqueline's life was more turbulent than most, the feudal system also gave other women similar opportunities to inherit, manage, and fight for large estates. Moreover, because landholding was the foundation of this system, feudalism sometimes allowed them to wield power based on their estate ownership. Feudalism not only provided land management, it also furnished military induction services, local government, and judicial systems. Political power stemmed from land tenure, while both landholding and political influence were based on personal sworn bonds between members of the noble (landholding) classes. Since political decisions were often based on personal appeals, women could even influence some governmental developments. To understand women's roles in this system, it may be helpful first to discuss the most basic details of feudalism itself, beginning in the years following the fall of the Western Roman Empire.

Feudalism began to develop as the Germanic victors, who deemed loyalty to an oath one of the greatest virtues,[1] were influenced by association with the conquered Romans, who had a number of forms of dependent land tenure. During Charlemagne's reign, his inner circle of men took a sacred, binding oath of *vassalage*, and were then rewarded with royal gifts of land. Out of this practice grew the basic feudal rite, a ceremony known as *paying homage*, at which one man declared himself the subject of another.

In both England and France, the monarch was theoretically the greatest land owner and the overlord of everyone. *Magnates* were high-ranking individuals like dukes who received great expanses of land and paid homage directly to the monarch—making them technically landholders, rather than landowners. These great nobles swore an oath of *fealty* (loyalty and allegiance) to the king at a ceremony of homage—thereby making themselves the monarch's vassals. Since magnates could not maintain single-handed control over their domains, they in turn granted some of their lands to less powerful men (often soldiers of lower descent who had assisted their lords in taking the lands), who then became vassals of these great magnates.

In exchange for their land, all vassals owed their liege-lords fealty, armed service and/or troops, and *aids*. This last item eventually became a fixed amount of money due only at certain times, such as when the lord's oldest daughter married, when his eldest son was knighted, or when the lord himself needed to be ransomed. In most castles, additional vassals (often called *knights*) performed household and military duties, and were thus granted smaller expanses of land called *fiefs*. These were parcels known as *knights' fees* because each estate was supposed to be adequate to provide one armed man for the lord's army.

Villeins (called *serfs* on much of the continent) occupied the bottom of the feudal structure, and lived on manors held by knights or greater nobles. Primarily farmers residing in small villages, this group encompassed over ninety percent of the medieval population through the twelfth century.[2] They were tied to their land, and were thus unfree, at least in relation to their lords. They were allowed to hold the land so long as they provided certain fees to their lords and performed the required personal labor services by working on his manor land, or *demesne*. In the later Middle Ages, it became possible to purchase exemptions from much of this work, which weakened the ties that held feudalism together.

The typical presentation of feudalism depicts secular males in control, but clerics and women were often great feudal lords as well. For instance, Mabille of Bellême (wife of Roger II of Mont Gomeri) inherited great estates in western Normandy and Maine. In addition to being very wealthy, Mabille was also a cruel, avaricious, and unscrupulous lord, belying feudal stereotypes of sweet, gentle womanhood. She led her own troops to take castles and carry on bloody feuds. To settle one squabble, Mabille supposedly poisoned her rival. She apparently hated the monks of St. Évroul even more. Utterly unscrupulous in such fights, Mabille and her troops descended on the unfortunate brothers, who were forced to feed and house the voracious group. In fact, she literally ate the monks out of house and home. Since this was typical behavior for Mabille, she had only herself to blame when an angry, dispossessed vassal murdered her around the year 1079.

Less sensational evidence of women as feudal lords can be found in the late historian David Herlihy's 1971 study of noblewomen as property holders in France (mainly estates near Paris) through the year 1200. Herlihy noted that females were sole landholders in their own right and name in one out of ten cases. Six out of every one hundred references listed women as owners of contiguous lands. In one out of twenty cases, men identified themselves in terms of their mothers' names instead of their fathers',[3] indicating that the mothers were the greater landholders. Though men clearly held much more land than did women, Herlihy's findings reveal that women were feudal landholders.

France provides some of the best examples of women who efficiently ruled family lands as liege-lords. Ermengarde of Anjou governed Brittany while her husband, Alain Fergent, was crusading in the East. Alain fell ill when he returned home, so she again took his place from 1112 until he died in 1119. Among her many accomplishments, Ermengarde abolished the exploitation of shipwrecks by pillaging lords and altered several feudal customs that favored male heirs. Another Ermengarde inherited Narbonne (1130s–1192) from her father. Ruling for more than fifty years, she proved women could be as effective as male landholders. An ally of King Louis VII, Ermengarde of Narbonne led the French royalist party in southern France against the invasions of Henry II and the English/Angevin forces, and fought several wars in defense of her own estates. She was also a protector of the church, and was famous for her judgments in difficult legal proceedings.

Countess Blanche of Champagne increased the numbers of fairs and urban settlements in her region. Blanche also enacted legislation to improve roads in Champagne and to restrict the rights of eldest sons. She was so powerful that she even attended the French *parlement* convened by Philip II in 1213. Just over one hundred years later, another female liege, Mahaut of Artois, was a member of the court of the Peers of France assembled to judge the count of Flanders. Discrimination against female leaders was clearly set aside for these women who governed their own large, important estates. The structure of the feudal system itself allowed women to assume this sort of power. Since land was the basis of wealth, and fiefs were passed through the family, women could hold and/or manage great estates. This gave them the same rights and obligations as their male counterparts.

The belief that estates should be kept "in the blood" helped women inherit and manage their domains. Most women also espoused the idea that property should stay in the family. Mathieu de Bois-Raoul sold his French fief of Boisrault for two hundred gold *florins* in 1361, but his wife, Aelis Catonne, promptly bought it back rather than see it leave the family. In 1380, Aelis passed the estate on to their son Bernard.[4] Because landholders wished to keep estates in their families, when male heirs did not exist, in many regions the property was left to daughters. Frequently, however, estates that fell to women simply added to the possessions of their husbands. The passage of the duchy of Lancaster was a textbook case illustrating the masculine ideal of estate ownership. Blanche of

Lancaster inherited the whole of her father Henry's huge estate after her older sister Matilda died. Her husband, John of Gaunt, became duke of Lancaster in her right, and one of the richest, most powerful men in England. Blanche herself soon died (1369), but John remained duke of Lancaster for more than thirty years. At his death, Blanche's estates passed to their son, the future King Henry IV.

Because women like Blanche were not recruited to fight, they presumably could not fulfill all the conditions of vassalage that were the basis of landholding. Though a woman could inherit a fief, theoretically she could rule it only through her male relatives. A common way of controlling women and their estates was to use them as pawns on the matrimonial field. This practice allowed noblemen to maintain their hold on their own lands, while simultaneously augmenting their property. The bride's role in such a case was negligible. She was important as the bearer of future heirs, but her main identity was as an appendage to the desired estate; she was simply passed, along with her lands, from her father to her groom.

When these heiresses became widows and/or regents for minor sons, however, they often achieved superior status and freedom of action. Even men assumed widows had both the duty and the right to protect their estates and assure succession for rightful heirs. In the 1070s, the widowed Countess Richilde ruled Flanders and Hainault for her son. Similarly, Garsenda de Forcalquier ruled Provence from 1209 until 1225 for hers. These female lords had to be very assertive since their neighbors often seized the opportunity offered by "womanly frailty" to annex more land. The favorites of King Edward II of England—Hugh le Despenser and particularly his son Hugh *the younger*—were quite successful at taking estates away from women. In the 1320s, the younger Despenser even imprisoned and threatened teen-aged Elizabeth Comyn, a co-heir of the Pembroke lands, until she signed over most of her inheritance to him.[5]

Guidinild of Catalonia, on the other hand, proved women could fight for and manage their own property. In 1026, she mobilized her forces and led them to recapture her family holding of Cervera. Guidinild then proceeded to build a fortress to defend her estate from other avaricious male lords.[6] The feudal system allowed such feminine militancy because troops were recruited from the lord's or lady's own household, vassals, and relatives—old friends and acquaintances who were used to following their liege-lord—rather than professional soldiers from the general populace.[7] Therefore, despite the pervasive view that women could not be warriors, females often participated to some extent in military ventures. In 1129, while besieging Frederick of Bogen's castle of Falkenstein, Henry *the Proud* of Bavaria received an urgent summons from his father-in-law, Holy Roman Emperor Lothar III. Henry left the siege of his rebellious subject's castle in the capable hands of a woman—his sister Sophia. Lothar had requested Henry's assistance because the emperor had encountered serious difficulties while besieging the city of Spires (Speyer, Germany). This important city was defended by another woman—Agnes of Saarbrücken. Frederick II, duke of Swabia, had left his wife Agnes in charge of Spires, and she managed to retain possession of the city for nearly a year.[8]

A number of discrepancies clearly existed between the ideal of simple, docile females (which many women were) and the reality, which included women who were competent estate managers and military leaders—either with or without their husbands. Men tacitly recognized this fact since, although not recruited to fight personally, female estate owners were required to fulfill the other feudal duties of any vassal. Women raised armies for wars and often personally defended their own castles. In 1338, "Black Agnes" kept King Edward III's troops out of Dunbar Castle in Scotland. Agnes and her ladies humiliated the English soldiers by pretending the intense five-month siege was just a petty nuisance. Female liege-lords also owed the same loyalty to their overlords that male vassals were required to pledge. Nichola de la Hay fulfilled that obligation admirably by refusing to allow the enemy to annex the castle of Lincoln. She started her defensive measures as a vassal of King John, and then continued to hold Lincoln for his son, the boy king Henry III, during the decisive siege of 1216.

Leading the defense of a castle was the most common military role for a woman. The feminine position in other types of warfare was more complicated, and thus harder to assess. Most women who led or accompanied their troops did not actually take to the field armed and on horseback. Instead they often stayed with the wagon/supply encampment well behind the front lines.[9] On the other hand, even these women who did not personally wield weapons fulfilled their feudal obligations. Moreover, as Megan McLaughlin stated:

> when a woman is said to have been present on the battlefield, to have worn armor or to have carried herself bravely, it seems reasonable to consider her an active participant in war.[10]

These women played roles much like those of male army leaders or "generals."

Vassals holding estates from women liege-lords were obliged to swear fealty to them, just as they would to male lords. Pons of Mont Saint-Jean swore a typical oath to Blanche of Champagne in 1219. He first vowed to be Blanche's loyal man. Pons then promised to aid her in any military ventures, particularly those against Erard and Philippa of Brienne or Adelaide of Cyprus. (Adelaide and Philippa claimed Champagne as their inheritance, so both were attempting to oust Blanche.) These were no idle vows. Blanche could, and did, lead her armies of knights and vassals to battle. In 1218, she and her troops burned Nancy and then won a fiercely fought pitched battle.[11]

Women could also inherit and manage land at the lowest level of the feudal structure, as revealed by the many extant records listing peasant women who paid *fees* (called *entry fines*) to acquire the right to hold plots of manorial land. Many of these fees were very low, indicating the property was quite small. An Englishwoman named Alice paid a typical entry fine of a mere two *shillings* in 1286/7 to retain the inheritance of her mother, Molecous.[12] Women rarely controlled large plots because, in the absence of a male heir, land was usually split among all daughters and/or other heirs.

English court rolls often cited women, rather than their husbands or sons, for non-payment of fines and other infractions. For example, a Broughton villager named Agnes Kateline was fined in 1309 for not keeping her ditches repaired. This widow had a grown son, but she held at least one tenement in the village independently of him.[13] Another English peasant, Juliana Strapnel, held lands on the Essex manor of Ingatestone as a tenant in her own right. She apparently owed the same fees and work services as any villein. In 1275, Juliana had to pay a moderate annual rent and provide her lord with two days of plowing, and one and a half days each of weeding and harrowing on his demesne. She also had to participate in the haymaking on her lord's lands, reap one acre at grain harvest time, supply a man to work on three other occasions, and help in the nut gathering.[14]

In addition to this plethora of services, manor lords often benefited from the many fines exacted by their own manor courts. In

1324, for instance, Alice Barley of Foxton, Cambridgeshire, paid her liege 3*s* 4*d* for *pondbreche*—illegally refusing to let her lady's bailiff repossess a lamb that Alice had rescued. In 1350, Agnes Chilyonge of Manningham was obliged to pay a *leyrwite* of *twelvepence* for committing adultery. Agnes de Broughton appeared frequently in the manor court records of Broughton village from 1297 until 1332. Among the fines charged to Agnes were numerous brewing fees, a citation for making a concord without license to do so, and a charge for receiving a prohibited woman.[15] Although fined often, Agnes was no habitual criminal. Most of her "fines," those for brewing, could more properly be called "licensing charges" (in effect, a small business tax), since villeins had to pay their lords to obtain the right to run a brewery.

Because the manor lord held all the land, forests, streams, and animals, villeins also had to pay a small fee for using any portion of the lord's land. Fishing his stream (*piscary*), collecting firewood or housewood (*estover*), baking bread in his oven, and grinding flour at his mill were other privileges obtained by paying small fees. Even taking pigs to the lord's woods required a payment, called *pannage*. Such fees were often paid in kind, that is, with goods rather than money. The Abbey of Marmoutier, for example, gave Fulk, count of Vendôme (d.1066), a family of pigs to compensate him for confirming the abbey's right of *pannage*. The abbey residents gave the boar to the count of Vendôme, but they apparently thought it more fitting to give his wife, Petronilla, the sow and piglets.[16]

In addition to allowing females of all classes to hold property, the feudal system gave some women wider scope for political intervention. Governmental decision making was such an intimate affair that noblewomen could sometimes use their closeness to the seat of power to influence political developments, and make a variety of personal appeals. In the year 1220, Isabelle of Angoulême requested assistance from her son, King Henry III of England. Isabelle first tried to justify her own actions by explaining why she herself had married Hugh de Lusignan, instead of carrying out the planned match between him and her daughter Joan. Isabelle wrote,

> His friends would not permit that our daughter be united to him in marriage, because her age is so tender . . . it was proposed that he should take a wife in France, which if he had done, all your lands in [Poitou] and Gascony would be lost. We, therefore . . . ourselves married the said Hugh . . . and God knows that we did this rather for your benefit than our own.[17]

After this inventive rationalization, she proceeded to address the real issue, her plan to recoup property and money she believed were due her.

Not all women's appeals were so self-serving. In 1406, Joan Beaufort, countess of Westmoreland, wrote to her brother, King Henry IV of England concerning one of his vassals who had accrued many debts while fighting for the king in Wales. Joan urged Henry to provide the loyal servant and his family with better lodgings and financial aid. Since this support was one of a lord's feudal responsibilities, Joan was only urging Henry to do his duty. Frequently females did serve as the consciences of powerful men, reminding them of their obligations. Nor was it necessary to be a king's close relative in order to appeal to him. In the 1320s, an anchoress named Alyne of Wigan petitioned King Edward II of England to restore her pension. She had lost her means of support when her patron forfeited his lands because he had taken part in a rebellion against the throne. King Edward immediately had Alyne's pension restored to her.[18] Elizabeth Woodville fared even better. She lay in wait for King Edward IV and then begged him to pardon her father and brother. Elizabeth's intervention was so successful that not only did the two men receive pardons and recoup their lands, but Elizabeth also married Edward and became queen of England in 1465.

Because men believed state treaties were most effective when sealed by marriages between the pact-making countries, they also allowed women what might be termed an "inadvertent importance." Men intended women to be docile pawns in their schemes, but the emphasis on political treaty/marriages instead opened the door to more active feminine participation. Women frequently took over the whole process, beginning with the betrothal negotiations. The marriage arranger was a very significant person, and as the mother of the girl (or even the boy) involved, a woman often negotiated the betrothal contract. Eleanor of Aquitaine had served as regent of England, as well as managing her own duchy of Aquitaine, so she was an experienced negotiator when she changed the history of France by choosing a wife for the future King Louis VIII. The redoubtable queen journeyed to Spain to visit her daughter Eleanor, queen of Castile, and to look over her three marriageable granddaughters. Since Berenguela was already betrothed, Eleanor of Aquitaine's only viable options were Urraca and Blanche. Though Urraca had been intended as Louis' bride, Eleanor decided on Blanche instead. The old queen based her choice on both intuition and political savvy; she was convinced the name Urraca was too foreign for the French to accept, and perhaps she saw in this granddaughter the abilities that later made Blanche one of the most capable regents ever to rule France.

Once the negotiations and ceremonies were over, women—from brides to widows—might refuse to be manipulated in the desired manner. A typical conflict came to a head in Scotland during the middle of the fifteenth century when the king of France asked Mary of Guelders, queen regent of Scotland, to assist the embattled queen of England, Margaret of Anjou, with financial and/or military support. Though Mary was a vassal of the French king, she refused at first on the grounds that her relative, Philip *the Good*, duke of Burgundy—who had negotiated her marriage—did not want anyone to help Margaret. However, Mary eventually did agree to aid Margaret's cause, in exchange for the surrender of the important castle and town of Berwick to Scotland. Mary's divided loyalty allowed her to achieve a level of autonomy since she could not possibly satisfy everyone.

An equally unexpected development occurred in another area of personal-political machinations—the use of war as a method of acquiring estates and influence. Women were supposed to function as pawns for this estate-building technique, in which men used their armies to annex property from helpless female landholders. But some women instead used war as a tool to increase their own holdings. Around the year 941, for example, Ava, lady of Auvergne, acquired several estates through her own military prowess. After she had captured this property, she gave it to her husband, Abbo, for use during his lifetime. Ava specified that, after Abbo died, the confiscated estates were to be given to the Abbey of Cluny.[19]

Militant women who attempted to build and secure large estates sometimes became involved in disputes with other family members. When family feuds escalated into international conflicts, females might even achieve fairly widespread influence. One such dispute revolved around the question of which branch of the family—that led by Duke John IV de Montfort or that of Joan de Penthièvre—should rightfully inherit a vast expanse of ducal lands in Brittany. This squabble not only lasted some sixty years, but its effects spilled over into the *Hundred Years War* and had repercussions in France, England, and Brittany.

A woman attacking a knight with her distaff.
Beinecke Library, New Haven

Women were actively involved on both sides of this conflict. Late in 1341, the French king threw Duke John IV into prison, so his wife, Joan of Flanders, took over her husband's military role. She led the burning of the enemy's camp and supervised the defense of the castle of Hennebont against besieging war machines. Her rival, Joan de Penthièvre, also maintained her own troops, and even arranged the murder of a key supporter of the English/de Montfort faction in 1350. Despite her best efforts, however, in 1365 she was finally forced to sign the *Peace of Guérande*, conceding most of the duchy to John IV de Montfort.

In spite of the treaty, the conflict between the two branches of this contentious family continued off and on for years. The feud entered its final phase with merely a few changes in the cast of characters. In 1404, the current leader of the de Penthièvre faction, John of Brittany, died, but his widow, Marguerite de Clisson, carried on the fight, captured John VI (the new de Montfort leader), and even enlisted the aid of the dauphin of France. While Marguerite and her party kept John VI in prison, his wife, Joan of France, made a dramatic appearance before the Estates General of Brittany. Displaying their two young children, Joan pleaded for help to save her husband's life. She led the allies she had garnered by her emotional appeal in besieging the de Penthièvre castle until John VI was released, and Marguerite fled the country. The feud was finally over—a conflict that demonstrated the political impact of women who refused to accept their supposed inferiority and inability to govern or fight for their estates.

Mathilda of Tuscany persuading Pope George VIII to receive King Henry of Germany.

Biblioteca Apostolica Vaticana, Vatican City

Chapter Thirteen

NEVER BETTER RULED BY ANY MAN

Women as Consorts, Regents, and Rulers

In 1180, a woman named Mary of Antioch became regent of what was left of the Byzantine Empire for her twelve-year-old son. Unfortunately, she quickly alienated much of her court and country by taking a lover, and then allowing him to become her most powerful advisor. Her stepdaughter led the faction that attempted to oust Mary and her son Alexius II. Mary of Antioch's popularity plummeted after she outraged the Greek populace of Constantinople by staging a disastrously unsuccessful assault on the rebels taking sanctuary in the most important Byzantine cathedral. The empress' position further deteriorated when her late husband's relative, Andronicus Comnenus, entered the fray, claiming he wanted to free the boy emperor. In the ensuing struggles, the Greek populace massacred the unpopular Latins—Mary's supporters—living in the city. Mary of Antioch was soon captured, and her son was forced to sign her death warrant. For a short while, Andronicus reigned jointly with young Alexius II, but in 1183, the 'protector' had the child-emperor murdered. With only a very tenuous claim to the throne, Andronicus then tried to solidify his position by marrying Alexius' twelve-year-old widow, Agnes of France. This ploy was unsuccessful; in 1185, their subjects ousted the couple, and killed Andronicus.

This very involved palace coup vividly illustrates two extremes of women's roles in royal politics and government. Though not always a wise decision maker, Mary of Antioch was a spirited, ambitious woman who determined her fate by her own actions.

The unfortunate Agnes of France exemplifies the opposite feminine position. Forced at a very young age to move far from home in order to marry a boy, Agnes was then compelled to wed an old man, her first husband's murderer. Few women found themselves in such excessively infelicitous circumstances, but the role Agnes played was not atypical. Women were supposed to be pawns for male-run governments, queens in name but not in power. Like Agnes of France, most women conformed to male expectations; but some did not.

In an examination of the broad spectrum of feminine roles in medieval state governments, it is helpful to begin with some of the requirements for queenship. Like men in other classes, kings and their advisors had a variety of expectations for the royal consort. Theoretically, the "ideal" mate should bring the monarch and his country some advantage, such as great riches. As a widower, the German king, Maximilian of Austria, chose to wed wealthy Galeazzo Maria Sforza's daughter, Bianca Maria, in 1493. Though he had no personal affection for Bianca, and in fact did not know her, Maximilian desperately needed her huge dowry to help him attain the crown of the Holy Roman Empire. Similarly, other royal brides were accessories accompanying the transfer of their lands. Anne of Brittany (1477–1514), the daughter and heiress of Francis, duke of Brittany, became queen of France twice because her duchy was so important. After seven years of marriage, her first groom, Charles VIII of France, died before the couple produced a son, leaving Louis, duke of Orléans, as his successor. In order to retain Anne's duchy of Brittany, King Louis XII then divorced his wife—who has gone down in history as Saint Jeanne of France—and promptly married Anne, making her queen of France for a second time.

Occasionally a woman's primary advantage was not her property but her lineage. A usurper, or any ruler who felt his hold on the throne was tenuous, might need such a bride. Henry I of England, for example, was the son of William *the Conqueror*—who had acquired the throne more by his military prowess than through his exalted bloodlines. Moreover, Henry took the throne after a rather mysterious hunting accident killed his brother, William Rufus. Strictly speaking, the rule of primogeniture dictated that the crown should have then gone to an older brother, Robert *Curthose* of Normandy. With so many counts against Henry's "divine right" to rule, choosing the best wife was an important step in securing his crown. He selected Edith, princess of Scotland (1080–1118), because she had an impeccable lineage for a prospective English queen. Her mother, Saint Margaret, queen of Scotland, was a direct descendant of the Anglo-Saxon king, Alfred *the Great*. Edith made herself more popular with her Norman subjects by taking the name of Matilda—which was easier for them to pronounce. In fact, she was so well-liked by everyone that she became known as "Good Queen Maud" (or "Queen Mold").

Still other monarchs were most concerned with securing beneficial allies, or favorable peace terms. Their wives were merely useful pawns in military or political alliances, or in peace treaties. Anne, princess of Byzantium, played this part in the year 989. Her brothers, Basil II and Constantine VIII, the co-rulers of the Byzantine Empire, sent her to faraway Kiev to complete a treaty with the prince of that region, Vladimir I. Anne was evidently none too happy with her role as sacrificial peace offering, and the unfamiliar foods, climate, customs, and people in her new home made her desperately ill. Since her marriage contract/treaty included the provision that Vladimir convert to the Greek Orthodox church, God supposedly repaid Anne by producing a miracle to save her life. For whatever reason, Anne did survive her illness and lived on for another twenty-one years.

One of a royal couple's primary duties was to produce an heir to the throne, a necessity that sometimes forced kings into several marriages. It took King Louis VII of France three tries before he met with success. Around the year 1136, Louis married Eleanor of Aquitaine (see below), but their marriage was annulled in 1152. Since he had no sons, Louis took a second wife, Constance of Castile. She died in 1160, while giving birth to their second daughter. Louis may have been getting desperate by that time; before the year was out, he had taken a third wife, Adele of Champagne. She finally presented Louis with the son he needed, the future Philip II *Augustus*.

In addition to the numerous advantages—money, land, royal blood, treaties, and heirs—that kings might require of their brides, monarchs traditionally expected their wives to conform to certain behavioral standards. The "ideal" conduct for a royal wife was much like that expected of any highborn woman. She was supposed to be obedient, chaste, sweet-tempered, pious, and kind. Some queens conformed so well to this stereotype that they also produced a variety of more tangible benefits for their royal husbands. When Conrad II became king of Germany in 1024, his wife, Gisela of Swabia, proved to be a definite asset to the new monarch. A negotiator of great wisdom, she served as an influential advisor to Conrad. Gisela advanced church reforms, furthered learning, and patronized chroniclers and teachers. After Conrad died in 1039, she smoothed the path for the transition between her late husband's government and that of their son Henry III. Gisela was a particularly skillful diplomat, and contemporary writers often extolled her ability as a peacemaker. This was a common queenly role because women were presumed to be especially peace-loving.

Monarchs also expected courage and wisdom from their wives, virtues exemplified by Constance of Sicily. The posthumous daughter and heiress of Roger II, king of Sicily, she was over the age of thirty when she married the German king, Henry VI. She brought the kingdom of Sicily into the Holy Roman Empire and produced an heir, the future Frederick II. Constance was wise enough to realize that provable legitimacy was exceptionally important to the baby she carried. She also knew that at her age of forty, and after some eight years of a previously barren marriage, extraordinary measures were called for to establish beyond any doubt that she was the infant's mother. She therefore stopped her entourage as they were traveling to Italy to join Henry in 1194, and gave birth to her son very publicly. The fanfare with which Constance advertised Frederick's legitimacy was a most intelligent move.

Despite the traditional belief in women's inferior intellect, kings often proved they had high opinions of their wives' talents. Occasionally a monarch even allowed his consort to assume a position approaching that of a co-ruler with an official status in the government. The energetic and intelligent Queen Adelaide of Maurienne (r.1115–1137) was such a partner to her less able husband, King Louis VI of France. Adelaide not only encouraged Louis to govern well, but she also personally made benefactions to churches, confirmed donations, appointed clerical officials, and settled judicial cases. The queen participated in signing a variety of charters, including those granting royal protection to religious foundations and others giving communal privileges to towns. Adelaide helped Louis VI in executive and policy-making decisions, and even wrote safe-conducts in her own name.[1]

It was more common for a king to think his wife wise enough to be entrusted with the regency if he died while his son was still a minor. This important duty required firmness and wisdom because the accession of a child-monarch often led to rebellions and lawlessness among the nobility. In 1295, a child named Ferdinand IV inherited the throne of Castile. His youth plunged the country into chaos, but his mother and regent, Maria de Molina, quickly curbed this lawlessness. She was such an admirable ruler that when her grandson, Alfonso XI, inherited the crown in 1312 at age one, Maria was again called upon to take up the reins of government.

When monarchs did not need regents, they usually insisted that women stay completely out of the male business of government. The consort was traditionally expected to provide herself with other interests—ones deemed more suited to feminine nature and abilities. Her proper concerns included maintaining a serene and happy relationship with her husband, caring for her children, seeing to the efficiency of her household staff, and displaying compassion for the needy. Philippa of Hainault's contemporaries often extolled her as a model queen since she was an excellent wife and mother who occupied herself with all the appropriate feminine interests. But her influence also touched on many other facets of life in mid-fourteenth-century England where she carved out a niche for herself as more than merely an appendage to her husband, King Edward III. Her pet economic project involved promoting the cloth industry on her dower lands in Norwich. Once the artisans of that area learned to make cloth themselves, they no longer had to export the vast amount of wool they grew. Finished cloth was a much more profitable item than was the raw material, so this greatly ameliorated the financial position of the wool-producing residents of Norwich. Philippa's cultural activities included an interest in literature; she was reputedly a patron of both Chaucer and Froissart. She contributed to English education by endowing Queen's College. Her pious and charitable work also led her to commission construction of several hospitals.

Queens like Philippa of Hainault needed such outside interests because most men were quite determined to keep them out of official government business. Men cited a variety of reasons for their prejudices against women rulers. A fourteenth-century Scandinavian man might have used the story of Ingebjorg of Norway as "proof" that women should not govern because they were too emotional and apt to let their hearts rule for them. By the year 1319, the widowed Ingebjorg had garnered a great amount of power in her son Magnus' regency governments in both Norway and Sweden. Then she married a Danish nobleman named Knut Porse, and began to use her position solely to elevate and enrich her new love. Eventually, the regency councils of Sweden and Norway curtailed her influence on her son and stripped away all her governmental authority.

Men also claimed that women lacked firmness, and were simply too incompetent to govern well. Agnes of Poitou exemplified these shortcomings. The daughter of Agnes of Anjou and her first husband, William V of Aquitaine, Agnes of Poitou became queen of Germany as Henry III's second wife. She was crowned Holy Roman Empress in 1046. Agnes had a variety of interests and was actually quite intelligent. A well-educated patroness of artistic and literary endeavors, Agnes was also an influential supporter of the Cluniacs. When her husband died in 1056, however, she was sidetracked from these personally fulfilling interests to assume command of the regency government on behalf of her six-year-old son, Henry IV. Unfortunately, her hold on both her son and the government was so tenuous that many great nobles were able to acquire additional power and property for themselves. Henry IV was finally removed from Agnes in order to suppress this realm-wide anarchy, and she abdicated the regency. She spent the remainder of her life in Italy as a pilgrim, a papal supporter, and a penitent. Agnes' regency was pointed to as a justification for the dictum that allowing women political influence produced great disturbances.

Fifteenth-century England suffered a similar loss of peace and prosperity due to Queen Margaret of Anjou. Though her marriage to Henry VI in 1445 was intended to secure peace between France and England, many of her new subjects viewed her as a symbol of England's defeat. Too young and naive to understand the need for tact and compromise, Margaret's forceful personality made a potentially difficult situation much worse. In fact, she proved to be one of the most disruptive forces ever to hit the medieval English political scene, since she was extremely strong-willed but not very wise.

When Henry VI became incapable of ruling due to his mental illness, Margaret felt obliged to govern in his stead lest his throne be usurped. She did not realize, however, that she was far too aggressive to suit the male courtiers and advisors around her. Margaret directed several bloody battles, traveled to Scotland and France to negotiate for military aid, and, in general, tried to wield too much absolute power. Not only did most official correspondence have to be dispatched along with her own letters, but she also demanded to be kept informed of every detail about negotiations, finances, and military reports. The way she played favorites, sowing dissension among the individuals at Henry's court and among his possible supporters, was further evidence that she was not politically astute. A firm believer in absolute monarchy based on the sovereign's divine right to rule, she resented any attempt at governmental intervention on the part of Henry's subjects. Thus Margaret also alienated many advisors and the English Parliament. Margaret's aggressiveness, military leadership—both successes and failures—and inept political machinations all helped cause the *Wars of the Roses* (a series of skirmishes among the nobility) and allowed Edward IV to usurp the throne.

When applied to Margaret of Anjou, the typical male stereotype of naive womankind seemed quite accurate, but the idea that women were sweet, kind, and gentle creatures fell far short of the mark. Although men traditionally claimed women were too weak to rule, females like Margaret of Anjou caused men to fear women would take total control if given any opportunity to do so. There was even some historical basis for the belief that females craved power and would use any means to retain authority. A notorious example was that of Empress Irene of Byzantium who became regent for her son Constantine VI in the year 780. Wanting to stay on the throne, in 797, Irene deposed her son and had his eyes put out, since a blind son was unable to threaten her rule.

In an effort to prevent such occurences, men tried a variety of tactics to enable them to maintain control over female heads of state. One popular ploy was to force an heiress to wed a man who could reign in the woman's stead—a maneuver which frequently did not produce the desired result. Constantine VIII of Byzantium kept his daughter Zoe (b.978) tucked away in the women's palace in Constantinople for some fifty years. In 1028, however, he finally admitted she would have to be his heir, so he married her to sixty-year-old Romanus Argyrus. Romanus was an able ruler, but he was none too exciting a husband for the new empress—who was discovering the exhilarations of freedom and sexual intimacy for the first time. Zoe whiled away her time with a succession of lovers until 1034, when she and her latest paramour murdered Romanus. She promptly married her lover, who thereby took charge as Emperor Michael IV. When he died in 1041, he named his nephew Michael V as successor. Michael V then made a fatal mistake by arresting Zoe to prevent her from interfering in the government. A popular uprising reinstated the empress and even dragged her sister Theodora out of her convent, so the two women could rule together. The sisters had never been close, so Zoe could not tolerate this partnership for long. Theodora returned to the convent when Zoe married Constantine Monomachus, a man who capably ruled Byzantium, even after Zoe died (c.1049), until his own death in 1055.

Zoe and her country were actually quite lucky in the men she married, since many a man chosen to rule in a queen's place was not so competent—as illustrated by Queen Tamara of Georgia's story. After inheriting the throne in 1184, Tamara was forced to marry in order to outwit the many nobles who believed any woman was too feeble to rule. But her husband turned out to be incompetent, weak, and greedy. Tamara finally banished him. By 1191, she had suppressed the rebels and proved herself an able ruler. Georgia became prosperous, peaceful, and a center of artistic and literary development under this queen's administration.[2]

In twelfth-century England, rather than forcing an heiress to wed, some nobles tried to simply replace her on the throne with a male. This scheme backfired so badly that two women actually ran the country at various times. When King Henry I died in 1135, his heiress was his daughter Matilda, known as *the Empress* because she was the widow of the late Holy Roman Emperor. Despite the oaths they had sworn to support Matilda, some magnates opposed her because she was a woman. Others feared she would be supplanted on the throne by her new husband, Geoffrey of Anjou, with his alien interests and French relatives. Hence, many nobles instead backed Henry's favorite nephew, Stephen of Blois, who promptly seized the throne. The Empress retaliated and eventually captured King Stephen at the battle of Lincoln. For a few months in 1141, Empress Matilda virtually took his place as monarch. She might have ended the war had she not alienated a number of clerics, many nobles, and almost all the citizens of London. The Londoners resented her arrogance, her fierce pride, and her heavy tax levies so much that they refused to allow her to stay in the city.

Stephen's wife, Queen Matilda of Boulogne, was an equally valiant military leader, but she was wise enough to gain the support of the London populace. This was not hard to accomplish since she arrived in the city shortly after the Empress departed; the Londoners would have probably welcomed any foe of Empress Matilda. While her husband languished in the Empress' prison, Queen Matilda established herself in London and rallied Stephen's army. The queen finally obtained Stephen's release and they regained the throne, though they were never able to defeat Empress Matilda. The civil war finally ended with a treaty naming the Empress' son, Henry of Anjou (King Henry II), to succeed Stephen.

Many Englishmen who supported Stephen were disconcerted to discover that their affable king was weaker than either his wife or his female rival. Nor was this the only occasion on which women leaders shocked men. A mid-tenth-century regent named Toda of Navarre is an example of a woman who astonished everyone by her unpredictable actions. Toda was driven to these desperate measures because her grandson had acquired a well-deserved but unfortunate sobriquet—Sancho *the Fat*. A seasoned ruler with some forty years of experience to her credit, Toda realized Sancho's obesity was a major obstacle in his path to regaining the throne of Leon. Since the Islamic and Jewish doctors of Cordoba had an excellent reputation, Toda took her grandson to them for a weight reduction course around the year 960. Sancho did indeed lose weight, though he never actually became slender. But Toda's Christian neighbors were horrified by her actions. They were even more appalled when she allied herself with the Muslim Cordobans and used their military aid to retrieve Sancho's crown.

A fourteenth-century English queen, Isabella of France, was equally unconventional and ruthless. She assumed power by taking a lover and then disposing of her husband, King Edward II. In all fairness, however, Isabella did have valid reasons for hating Edward and for thinking England would be better off without him. After Edward began lavishing his affections on Sir Hugh le Despenser and his son, Hugh *the younger*, they persuaded the king that Isabella was plotting against him with her French relatives. In 1324, Edward II took away Isabella's estates, put her on a meager daily allowance, and removed her friends and servants from court. Though Edward had ousted Isabella from favor and confiscated her estates, he still dispatched her to France to negotiate on his behalf. Then the foolhardy king sent young Edward, the twelve-year-old heir, to join his mother. One of Edward II's enemies, Roger Mortimer, was already in France, after having escaped from the Tower of London.

Isabella soon proved herself more astute and aggressive than her husband. Realizing that all the elements for a successful palace coup had come together, she used this fact to her advantage. She and Roger became lovers, and then swept young Prince Edward up in a plot to overthrow his father. In 1326, the three conspirators landed with an army in Suffolk, captured the king, and presumably had him murdered. Isabella's lover served on the regency council for Edward III and she herself became equally powerful. Their misuse of this newly acquired power did not endear Isabella and Roger to their subjects. Mortimer was more tyrannical than Isabella, but she too was denounced as greedy, extravagant, and immoral. The young king solved this crisis by personally assuming the reins of his government. In 1330, Edward III had Mortimer condemned by Parliament and then executed. Having lost her authority as well as her lover, Isabella retired to her dower lands, though she later appeared occasionally at court. Perhaps her role in her husband's murder disturbed her conscience, because she took the veil shortly before her death in 1351.

Unlike Queen Isabella, Catherine Sforza never murdered any of her husbands, but she killed plenty of other people. In fact, though she was generally a very good ruler in the cities of Forli and Imola, she nevertheless became infamous for her cruelty. Belying men's stereotypes, Catherine was an excellent military leader who was respected and even feared by her troops. Far from being weak and sentimental, Catherine once refused to relinquish the castle she held, even though her opponents were holding her children hostage and threatening to kill them. Catherine always revenged herself on rebels by brutally executing them. After her second husband was murdered in 1495, she went on a rampage and had a large number of people—including some twenty children—put to death. Under attack by Cesare Borgia in 1499, Catherine reputedly sent his father, Pope Alexander VI, a container of poison- or plague-contaminated messages. The failure of this dastardly scheme was quickly followed by her defeat at the hands of Borgia and his allies. Though later released from the papal prison, she never regained her position since the populace greatly feared her return. Most men who tried to take away her cities failed, but Catherine's own cruelty finally defeated her.

Other women were equally spirited, but did not confuse justice with revenge or firmness with cruelty. Blanche of Castile, the intelligent, capable, and well-educated daughter of King Alfonso VIII of

Castile, was twelve years old when she married the future King Louis VIII of France in the year 1200. Twenty-six years later, when Blanche was thrust into a position of authority by the death of her husband, she proved to be an exceptionally competent ruler. To several northern French nobles, however, the accession of an underage king, Louis IX, with his Spanish mother as regent seemed to offer excellent conditions for a rebellion against the crown. The rebels' hatred of their foreign queen was fueled by malicious, and almost certainly unfounded, rumors that she had a lover. In January of 1229, Blanche personally led a daring winter attack against the castle of Peter Mauclerc, count of Brittany, and gained a temporary success. She eventually negotiated treaties that secured royal power in the northern half of France, and guaranteed peace with England until the year 1240.

At the same time, Blanche also had to deal with problems in southern France during the *Albigensian Crusade*. In 1229, she helped conclude a treaty with Raymond VII of Toulouse, thereby attaining a bride for her son Alphonse and placing extensive portions of southern France under royal dominion. The queen then arranged a profitable marriage for her oldest son with another heiress, Margaret of Provence. Blanche continued to influence Louis, and even served as regent while he was crusading in the 1240s. She negotiated with foreign dignitaries, presided over the royal council, received their oaths of loyalty from merchants and nobles, and supervised royal officials. In fact, part of Louis IX's success must be attributed to his mother's skillful regencies. As Christine de Pisan later declared, no man ever ruled France any better than Blanche.

Like Queen Blanche, when Isabella of Castile tried to take over her kingdom (which she inherited from her brother Henry IV of Castile in 1474), she first had to fight for it. Her opponent was Henry's daughter Juana, who believed the crown was rightfully hers, even though it was popularly assumed she was illegitimate. Isabella was only able to vanquish Juana after some five years of civil warfare. At the same time, Isabella's husband Ferdinand II became king of Aragon. He also wanted to govern Castile, but Isabella and her people would not permit him to do so. Ruling together, Isabella and Ferdinand defeated rebellious nobles, firmly administered justice, took control of the religious military orders, and restructured and revived the Inquisition. Before this reign, Castile was isolated both by the Pyrenees and by the problem of dealing with the Moors. Ferdinand and Isabella conquered the

Islamic kingdom of Granada and became involved in European politics. In addition, Spain became one of the first European countries to colonize the New World, thanks to Isabella's support of Columbus' voyage in 1492.

Margaret of Denmark was another of the ablest medieval monarchs—either male or female. Unlike Castile, where a native woman was preferred to an alien man, much of Scandinavia firmly resisted female rulers. Margaret therefore took care always to govern in the name of a male relative. She inherited the Danish throne in 1375 from her father, King Waldemar IV. Her husband, Haakon VI of Norway, died in 1380, leaving Margaret as regent of Denmark and Norway for her five-year-old son, Olaf V. After he died in 1387, she acted as regent for her great-nephew, Erik of Pomerania. Wiser and stronger than he, Margaret continued to rule in all but name, even after Erik came of age. She achieved internal peace by forbidding private warfare, strengthening the financial position of the Danish throne, and protecting peasant freeholders from avaricious nobles. To break the Hanseatic League's stranglehold on Scandinavia, Margaret created the Union of Kalmar, which temporarily brought the countries of Sweden, Denmark, and Norway together under one crown. This released the entire region from economic and political domination, and increased the area's own financial resources. Margaret of Denmark thereby prevented Denmark, Norway, and Sweden from becoming helplessly embroiled in Germany's disintegration.

As the accomplishments of the preceding three women prove, female rulers did not always conform to male stereotypes concerning women's lack of leadership qualities. Like their masculine counterparts, women displayed a wide variety of governing styles and skills. A final example, that of Eleanor of Aquitaine, shows a whole range of feminine political activities. Though she began her political career as a pawn, she ended her life as one of the most powerful individuals in medieval Europe.

The daughter and heiress of William X of Aquitaine, Eleanor was forced to marry the future Louis VII of France (c.1136). Young, vivacious, forceful, and flirtatious, she was incompatible with her pious, serious, and not exceptionally strong husband. While on Crusade together at Antioch in 1147, it was even rumored that Eleanor committed adultery with her uncle, Raymond of Poitiers. She was apparently as eager for a divorce as was her jealous husband, and their marriage was finally dissolved in 1152. Shortly thereafter, Eleanor chose a younger husband for herself, Henry of

Anjou—soon to be King Henry II of England. Though she had produced no male heir for Louis, she presented Henry with several sons, as well as daughters.

Now mature, Eleanor was still spirited and ambitious, but had begun to prefer power and political activities to flirting and having fun. For nearly fifty years, she not only administered her own region of Aquitaine, but also occasionally helped rule England. At first, she acted as regent for Henry, who was frequently in France. In later years, the couple became estranged. While Henry was dallying with his mistress, Rosamund Clifford, romantic legend hints that Eleanor was busy hiring a sorceress to magically enchant toads to suck out "Fair Rosamund's" blood. Though this idea is implausible, it is true that Eleanor caused strife both in England and on the continent by plotting with her sons for a rebellion against Henry. Even after quashing his sons, Henry continued to be so fearful of his wife's immense political power that he virtually imprisoned her, beginning in the year 1174.

Released from captivity when Henry II died in 1189, Eleanor once more vigorously entered the political fray. Her son Richard I *the Lionheart* spent most of his reign crusading in the Holy Land, so Eleanor again helped rule England. And when Richard was captured while returning from the Crusade, it was his mother who collected the huge ransom—thirty-five tons of silver—required to free him. After Richard's death in 1199, Eleanor's youngest child, John, became king. He had continuous difficulties with rebels and rival claimants to his throne, but his mother's support helped him retain his crown. Though she retired to Fontevrault, she remained a powerful advisor to King John until her death in 1204.

Twice queen, Eleanor of Aquitaine was a consort in France, a regent in England, and a ruler in her own great duchy of Aquitaine. She was an exceptionally competent administrator, an advisor, a traveler, a patron of literature, a founder of hospitals, an instigator of rebellions, and a skillful negotiator. Eleanor was equally adept at taking direct action and at manipulating events from behind the scenes. During her long lifetime—three times the length of the "average" medieval woman's lifespan—she personally covered nearly the gamut of possibilities for feminine political influence and governmental roles. Though Eleanor was a most unique individual, she ably represents the other medieval women who expanded their formal, ritualistic roles as consorts and heiresses into more politically active ones as rulers, advisors, schemers, partners, and regents.

A lady and a nobleman playing chess.

Bayerische Staatsbibliothek, Munich

CULTURAL LIFE

Carnival games in Germany, 1482–1520.

Bayerische Staatsbibliothek, Munich

Chapter Fourteen

EAT, DRINK, AND BE MERRY

Medieval Amusements, Entertainments, and Ceremonies

From birth to death, January to December, people of all classes and both genders marked the passage of their years and lives with a panorama of colorful pageants, rituals, and ceremonies. These festive events, along with a variety of popular games and sports, offered an important release from the harsh reality of everyday medieval life. Naturally, like children of any era, medieval youngsters enjoyed hiding, chasing, running, and playing with toy soldiers, dolls, and pets. Peasant children generally had only a few toys, such as simple stick horses, but wealthier youngsters might have more elaborate playthings like rocking horses and musical instruments. Noble boys conducted mock battles with wooden weapons, while their sisters played with dolls—which often featured wigs made from real hair.

Medieval adults also participated in many games and sports. Queen Elizabeth Woodville especially enjoyed bowling with her own set of ivory pins.[1] A lower-ranking sports enthusiast named Margot of Hainault appeared in Paris in the middle of the 1400s. Margot was a twenty-eight-year-old amateur tennis champion when she defeated many of the best male players in Paris. Similarly, some manuscript illuminations show pictures of women beating their male opponents at chess games. On the other hand, such skill might be dangerous; a mid-thirteenth-century London woman named Juliana Cordwaner was stabbed to death by her male opponent during an unusually acrimonious chess game. Like tennis and bowling, the popularity of chess cut across class lines, attracting commoners such as the unfortunate Juliana and nobles like

Mahaut, countess of Artois. When Mahaut died in 1327, her list of possessions included a number of chess sets in costly materials—such as one made of silver and ivory and another fashioned of jasper and crystal. Chess became so popular that William Caxton even printed *Game and Playe of the Chesse* in the 1470s, one of the earliest books he produced.[2]

Everyone also enjoyed watching and participating in a variety of rougher sports. Among the lower classes, throwing and wrestling contests were particularly popular, as were cock fights and bear baiting (which might actually involve several different types of animals). For peasants and townspeople, leisure activities frequently centered around taverns. Many had extremely bad reputations because prostitutes often gathered in them, and excessive drunkenness and gambling were equally common. Not only did men occasionally lose their shirts at the gaming tables, but some were even obliged to leave the rest of their clothing with the inn or tavern keepers in order to pay their bar bills.[3]

The nobility's favorite pastime, hunting, was popular with a broad spectrum of people until highborn landholders began enacting laws to restrict it to their own class. The nobility maintained its prerogatives through a system of preserves that set aside almost all forest land to be used only by titled landholders. Despite these laws, London citizens demanded and received the right to continue hunting in certain parks.[4] Nobles even imposed chivalrous ideals—a sporting code—on this pastime. *Beasts of venery* like red deer and boars thus ranked higher than *beasts of the chase* like roe deer and marten. A similar social scale regulated hawking—a favorite sport among noblewomen. Only the most high-ranking individuals could have falcons. Depending upon their status, others had to be content with goshawks or the even lower-ranked sparrow-hawks.[5] Many medieval works of art depicted highborn ladies enjoying both hunting and hawking. In the fifteenth century, Beatrice d'Este, duchess of Milan, was noted as a particularly skillful enthusiast of both sports. The traditional courtly explanation for such feminine ability was the poetic assertion that women were excellent falconers because they resembled such birds: they were beautiful and difficult to care for. But the cleric John of Salisbury alleged that females were good hunters because bad people were always more predatory than good ones.[6]

Jousting was originally another popular sport reserved for the nobility, but tournaments eventually became more of an entertainment than a sport. Early ones were serious sporting events that helped noblemen attain honor and experience in preparation for wars, and kept them in fighting trim. By the fifteenth century, however, tournaments had become orderly, chivalrous, and romantic spectacles.* The fanciful invitations issued for the *Pas de la Dame Sauvage* held at Ghent in 1470 show that the martial spirit, so prevalent at earlier tourneys, had greatly deteriorated. The tale concocted for this tournament concerned an imaginary land and a beautiful lady for whom the host, Claude de Vaudrey, had pledged to joust. Vaudrey carried out this theme by arriving at the arena with a group of men and women who were dressed in hairy costumes, simulating savages. Another fifteenth-century tournament, *L'Arbre d'Or*, was equally romantic in spirit. Anthony *the Great Bastard of Burgundy* hosted this event in 1468 to celebrate the marriage of Margaret of York and Charles *the Bold*, duke of Burgundy. The story Anthony fabricated for the occasion told of a lady for whom he had promised to break one hundred and one lances.[7] Throughout this particular tournament the golden tree motif was much in evidence.

Feminine participation also helped make such events more entertaining than martial. A monastic chronicler of 1348 wrote about a band of some forty "wanton" women who provided part of a tournament spectacle. Attired as men in parti-colored garments bedizened with silver and gold, the ladies paraded through the lists on chargers and palfreys. They later "forgot" their marriage vows and participated in a number of lewd activities, according to the outraged chronicler.[8] In 1438, a tournament at Ferrara included a unique competition for the female spectators. The ladies competed in a foot race for their own prizes—three large pieces of very fine cloth.[9] More frequently, women "defended" mock towers, bestowed tokens on their favorites, or handed out rich jewels and other prizes.

Already popular spectacles, as tournaments became less warlike and more entertaining, they turned into festivals of music, dancing, trysts, fights, and betting. Tournaments therefore drew a very wide segment of society; horse dealers, haberdashers, moneylenders, fortune tellers, acrobats, mimes, troubadours, wandering

* The first event of such a tournament was usually a joust or tilt, a fight between single knights. After several tilts came the tourney, a battle pitting two groups of knights against each other. The entire tournament usually included several days of jousts, tourneys, feasts, and a variety of other entertainments.

scholars, and prostitutes joined other onlookers—ordinary townsfolk, peasants, and nobles.

Like tournaments, plays were popular entertainments available to spectators of all classes. The first medieval plays were directed by church officials and performed with clerical casts inside monasteries or churches. By the eleventh century, liturgical drama had become a popular way to explain biblical history to illiterate parishioners. In fact, plays soon had to move outside into the churchyard as the productions grew longer and the staging became more complex—involving much scenery and numerous props. Costumes were elaborate, as were the special effects, which often utilized intricate machinery. Laymen participated in the enlarged casts and the language began to change to the vernacular. Instrumental and vocal music were also important dramatic features, so a troop of costumed singers and musicians performed just offstage.[10]

The subject matter reflected the link between drama and the church. Writers composed miracle plays borrowed from the legends of saints and martyrs, and they virtually exhausted the Bible as a source. Late medieval dramatists even wrote "morality plays," like the well-known fifteenth-century English drama *Everyman*. These plays used personifications of vices and virtues rather than actual biblical or saintly characters, but were acceptable because they taught orthodox moral values. Another side-effect of the church's involvement in drama was the absence of actresses. Clerics insisted that men or boys must dress in women's clothes and assume the female roles. One of the few documented exceptions concerned the nuns of Barking who produced and acted in *Visitatio Sepulchri*. This was the third, and last, in a series of liturgical dramas that the abbess of Barking, Katherine Sutton (c.1363–1376), penned as an attempt to liven up the Easter services. Katherine even made costumes so that her nuns could act out these plays.

By the fifteenth century, the dramatic arts had largely moved out of the cloister and the church. Even though the later plays were often managed by the laity, usually under the auspices of town guilds, women continued to be banned from the stage. One exception occurred in the late 1400s when Englishwomen produced, and reputedly acted in, their portion of the Chester play-cycle, *The Assumption of the Virgin*. In the same century, an eighteen-year-old girl was chosen for the role of Saint Catherine in a drama produced at Metz. Her performance was so moving that a nobleman named

Henri de Latour fell in love with her. Even though she was only the daughter of a glazier, Henri was infatuated enough to marry the actress.

Henri's unsanctioned and "unequal" marriage must have confirmed the often-stated fear of orthodox thinkers that actresses were so seductive they could lure men to their downfall. Churchmen inveighed against female dancers for a similar reason—their sensuous movements might excite lusty thoughts in their male audiences. Clerics denounced even male dancers since the activity itself was deemed lewd and frivolous. Unlike dramatic productions, however, dances could be held in informal, private settings, so people tended to ignore these ecclesiastical denunciations. In later years, highborn females were sometimes even called upon to perform at state functions or celebrations. Margaret Stuart of Scotland and Isabella of Lorraine participated in exhibition dances in 1445 at a ball in Chalons. Dance eventually became a staple of court entertainment, particularly for special events. At Lucrezia Borgia's wedding festivities in the 1490s, for instance, a group of dancing women provided part of the spectacle. Though it violated ecclesiastical strictures, Lucrezia's father—Pope Alexander VI himself—claimed he enjoyed watching women dance more than any other entertainment.[11] Just as moralizing clerics feared, men often did particularly enjoy watching the sensuous movements of female dancers.

Churchmen had similar reservations about females who might use music* to enchant or bewitch males. Once again, clerical strictures often fell on deaf ears—partly because it was easy to sing and play instruments alone or in small groups. Music was so popular that most castles contained violins, harps, lutes, organ, flutes, and horns. Isabeau of Bavaria, queen of France, and her contemporary, Valentine Visconti, duchess of Orléans, were both noted harp players. Less high-ranking musicians sometimes used their talents to become professional or semi-professional entertainers. By the fourteenth century, women playing lutes, pipes, fiddles, and bells were a common sight in the taverns of Frankfurt. The luckiest, or

---

* Early music was composed of several established types of monophonic songs—structured forms with single melody lines (like the more formal liturgical Gregorian chants). Polyphony probably began to evolve shortly after the year 1000, but was not common until c.1200s.

perhaps most talented, entertainers acquired jobs in private homes. Mahaut, countess of Artois, hired a woman singer named Noël in 1319, and then added a female organist to her group of household musicians the next year.[12] Magnates' households traditionally included resident musicians, as well as other entertainers—like jugglers, fools, and dwarves—some of whom might also be women. From 1421 until 1434, for instance, the Burgundian court employed a female fool, a blond dwarf called *Madame d'Or*. When Isabella of Portugal married Philip *the Good*, Madame entertained her by fighting with a giant as part of the *entremets* (entertaining banquet intermissions).

In contrast to women like Madame d'Or who were very nearly members of the families they served, most female entertainers led a wandering, hand-to-mouth existence. Some were known as *jongleuresses*—lower-class female vagabonds whose acts often included acrobatics, juggling, and feats with animals, as well as a variety of dances. One of their most popular routines was based on an act originated by Saracen women. With blackened faces and Eastern costumes, jongleuresses enthralled their audiences by dancing upside down on their hands. Unfortunately for these women, many secular authorities equated all such performers with prostitutes.

Theologians also condemned these female entertainers, but many churchmen reserved their harshest criticism for minstrels—of either sex. They were primarily singers rather than poets, and some also accompanied themselves on the harp or lute. Clerics hated minstrels because they sang secular verses about love, carried scandalous items of current gossip from place to place, and were presumed to use seductive music and poetry to lure people from the paths of virtue. The visionary Mechtild of Magdeburg believed that God relegated all such itinerant singers and musicians to the eternal fires of Hades. Her mystical dreams revealed,

> The miserable minstrel who with pride can arouse sinful vanity
> weeps more tears in hell than there is water in the sea.[13]

Minstrels, dancers, and other performers sometimes settled in one locale and formed entertainment guilds. Early fourteenth-century Parisian records listed eight women as members of the guild of minstrels. Jealousy and disputed territorial rights occasionally led to fighting between wandering performers and entertainment guilds.[14] The competition was understandably keen for the lucrative work of performing before wealthy patrons. When Queen Isabeau of Bavaria entered Paris at the end of the fourteenth century, a group of anonymous young women sang sweetly beside the fountain in the rue St. Denis, which bubbled with spiced wine. King Louis XI enjoyed a more risqué entertainment when he entered Paris in 1461. A number of nude women, portraying sirens of the ancient world, paraded before the king and his entourage. Though anonymity was the norm, a few female performers left brief glimpses of themselves for posterity. The records of Westminster in 1306 noted that several female minstrels enlivened the knighthood ceremony for Prince Edward (later King Edward II), including a woman with the colorful stage name of *Pearl in the Egg*. Around the same time, the treasury paid Maud *Makejoy* for entertaining Prince Edward with her dancing and acrobatics.

Many of these entertainers would gather in cities and castles during certain festive times of the year since they were particularly apt to find work on such occasions. Rather than abolishing early customs, clerics had achieved an amalgamation of festive pagan and Christian elements to help them control parishioners. Hence, they superimposed an ecclesiastical year over other medieval calendars, organizing the year around alternating seasons of penance and joy that followed the life of Christ. Various holy days (holidays) commemorating the Virgin Mary and numerous saints were interspersed throughout the year. Seasonal games and amateur or professional entertainments were an important feature of most of these holy days.

Christmas (December 25th–January 6th), the most festive event of the winter, corresponded to the ancient feast of Saturnalia. Celebrants symbolically put the old year to death, while ushering in the new one with minstrels, divinations, wassails, jongleurs, gifts, feasts, music, and skin-clad mummers (dancers). Many ancient customs became part of English Christmas celebrations; mistletoe was the Druids' holy plant, and the Yule log was a carry-over from winter solstice celebrations. Some superstitions probably also originated in ancient traditions—like the belief that the first person to cross the Christmas threshold let good luck enter with him. Bad luck, on the other hand, befell those who allowed their home fires to die out during Yuletide. Several medieval Christmas carols are still popular today, such as "Deck the Halls," "Good Christian Men Rejoice," and the "Twelve Days of Christmas" (a medieval counting song).

Certain foods, like *humble pie*, a concoction of animal entrails, also became associated with Christmas celebrations. Huge amounts of food were common; in the mid-1200s, King Henry III of England hosted a Yuletide banquet that included six hundred roasted oxen, and a seasonal pie that weighed one hundred sixty-five pounds and measured nine feet in diameter. On some manors, a lower-class man was named *lord of misrule*, and he could demand feasts and entertainment for the peasants. Another form of this custom, the *Feast of Fools* or *Feast of the Ass* elevated the status of the lower clergy called sub-deacons for one day.[15] On this occasion, clerics often wore masks or costumes, danced lewd jigs, and paraded about entertaining the townspeople with indecent gestures and songs. Nuns also sometimes held their own Yuletide feasts at which they elected an *abbess* to preside over similar revelries.

Much of the period between Christmas and Easter—the most important medieval religious holy day—was a time of penance known as Lent. But even these somber days were interspersed with a number of more light-hearted occasions. Twelfth Night and several other festivals from Christmas to Midsummer had themes based on the New Year's advent, and on promoting fertility. Naturally clerics found little to recommend such ceremonies. They often condemned Valentine's Day, for instance, because it involved a variety of entertainments based entirely on the pleasures of very earthly love and romance. One of the most popular English activities on this day was a guessing game known as "Lady Anne," which ended with couples pairing off and leaving the circle, presumably to play other more private games. Peacock eggs, pomegranates, and cakes colored with red and purple were traditional foods on Valentine's Day.[16]

Even Easter itself occasionally included festivities related to fertility. One of the more outrageous ceremonies occurred in 1282, when an English parish priest forced the maidens of his village to dance and sing in honor of Bacchus. As he accompanied the girls, the priest himself danced, sang, and carried figures representing human reproductive organs waving from a pole. The church instituted sepulchre rites and resurrection plays in an effort to stamp out such pagan rituals. There were also sexual overtones to the celebration of Hocktide—the second Tuesday after Easter. In England, a contest between village men and women was common on this holiday. It usually involved capturing members of the opposite sex and forcing them to take off their shoes or pay some other kind of "tax." In the later 1200s, the ladies of the royal court even forced King Edward I into bed during Hocktide, and made him pay a forfeit.[17]

An offspring of ancient summer solstice rituals, Midsummer was celebrated on the Eve of St. John (June 23rd), and was the greatest summer festival in both England and Germany. Customary observances included drinking, feasting, dancing, playing lewd games, building bonfires, carrying torches through the farms or streets, and rolling burning wheels down the hillsides. London officials marched with dancers, music, arms, and torches around the city which was ablaze with great bonfires, while all the houses were lit up and garlanded. Many midsummer games concerned divining the future. For instance, a girl might remove the petals of a rose one by one to discover if "he loves me" or "he loves me not."

During the second half of the year, celebrations tended to focus more on harvests and food than on sexual symbols. In July, St. Swithin's Day celebrated the summer's abundance. Apple bobbing contests, foot races, and seasonal foods like plums and currant bread were typical features of this holiday. Similarly, at the end of the August 1st celebration of Lammas Day, villagers participated in candlelight processions and acted out a ritual in which bread was ceremoniously saved for the following year. In the fall, English farmers labored to complete their winter planting, but peasants still set aside some time for festivities. The English lyric, *Mirie it is while sumer ilast*, reflected the spirit of this harvest season—a time to celebrate the fruits of summer's labor and to prepare for the coming winter. Halloween usually featured jack-o-lanterns, apple bobbing contests, and bonfires. Children wore masks and pretended to be wandering spirits as they went "souling." If neighbors did not give them soul cakes, the "spirits" played pranks. In November, St. Catherine's Day and a number of other women's feast days were celebrated with bonfires and Catherine cakes. Harvest suppers, dances, and dramatic games were also common at this time.[18]

Just as those rituals marked the year's passage, so there were numerous festivities denoting life's journey. From birth to marriage to death, medieval people acknowledged the progress of their lives with a variety of ceremonies. The birth of an extremely high-ranking individual, for example, was usually an occasion for many festivities. Dances, songs, a procession with torches, and minstrel performances were part of the celebrations in 1312 to honor the birth of a son (the future Edward III) to the English royal couple,

Isabella of France and King Edward II. For noble babies (and usually for infants of any class), the christening ceremony occurred soon after birth, lest the Devil take an unbaptized child's soul. At the baptismal font, one godparent held the child's body as the other two sponsors each held a foot. The priest totally submerged the child to prevent a devil from getting a hand on the infant. The godparents solemnly vowed to keep the baby away from water, fire, trampling horses, and dogs for seven years.[19] They usually gave expensive christening presents to the highborn baby.

Royal betrothals and weddings were also festive events at which ostentatious trappings were considered necessary, rather than optional. In the middle of the thirteenth century, a variety of festivities surrounded Sanchia of Provence's marriage to Richard of Cornwall (brother of Henry III of England). Sanchia's ship had docked at Dover, so the wedding party processed in great style from that port to London. Along the route, the populace showered the bride with gifts, held burning candles to light her way, rang bells, and blew horns to honor her. After the wedding at Westminster Abbey, a splendid banquet provided feasting for thousands of poor people, and similar festivities continued throughout the month of December.[20]

Other classes naturally had less elaborate marriage celebrations. Most unions started with an informal or formal betrothal contract. By the 1200s, marriages in some regions also had to be preceded by reading the *banns*, the public proclamation of the upcoming nuptials. English priests made these announcements on three separate days before allowing the wedding to take place. The basic ceremony—regardless of social status—usually began at the church door with a symbolic transfer of endowments, the families' consent, and the individual vows. The neighbors endeavored to remember the details of this public ceremony so they could later testify that the wife had been properly married and endowed. The couple would exchange rings and vows, and then the wedding party was supposed to move into the sanctuary for a Mass and nuptial blessing. In practice, weddings did not always adhere to this pattern. A few began and ended inside the church, while many others did not include a Mass.

Among peasants, the wedding ceremony often began and ended at the church door where the couple exchanged rings, and the bride's father gave her away. Even though the two families would have already reached an agreement regarding dowry and dower, they usually announced the terms at the church door for public remembrance. The peasant bride's family might also pay the *merchet*, a "license fee," before the couple spoke their vows and the groom gave his bride a ring, in much the same manner as in today's ceremonies. This ritual was often followed by a feast with the entire village in attendance.

There were a number of other medieval rites of passage, such as the solemn rituals that surrounded a man's induction into knighthood. This ceremony normally included prayers, and the candidate's receipt of a special attire befitting his new status. Victims of leprosy also frequently had separation ceremonies since they were not allowed to remain in contact with the uninfected populace. The afflicted person usually wore a black burial pall during this ritual to symbolize his/her death to the outside world. A new queen's coronation was another rite of passage, as well as an integral part of the brilliant spectacle of royalty. This ceremony invested the queen with qualities suited to her new position of leadership and publicly separated her from her subjects by emphasizing her superior status. After Elizabeth Woodville married King Edward IV in 1464, she was crowned at Westminster. Clothed in a regal purple mantle, Elizabeth walked under a canopy leading a stately procession of nobles and prelates. The archbishop of Canterbury anointed her head, and she was crowned with great solemnity before hearing Mass.[21]

When a woman dedicated herself to a religious vocation, a solemn ritual denoted her passage into this new way of life. A twelfth-century English enclosure ceremony for an anchoress reveals some typical elements, such as the blessing of the postulant with holy water and incense. She also heard numerous scriptural readings and recitations. Just before entering her sanctified *reclusorium*, the postulant heard Mass and the Office of Extreme Unction, emphasizing her departure from worldly concerns.[22] Once inside her cell, the newly-made anchoress' door was symbolically sealed and she was free to begin her life of contemplative service to God.

The final rite of passage was equally important. In most classes, this began with preparing the body for burial by washing it and then wrapping it in a white shroud, or winding-sheet. But for wealthy men and women, an ostentatious funeral could serve more than one purpose. When Margaret Paston prepared for her husband John's burial in 1466, she not only wished to honor him, but she also wanted to remind everyone of their position as wealthy and locally important landholders. Hundreds of burning torches and candles surrounded John's coffin, which was covered in opulent gold cloth. The funeral "baked-meats" were similarly lavish. Margaret served a thousand eggs, twenty gallons of milk, and great quantities of poultry, beef, pork, and beer to the ravenous mourners. Though peasants and townspeople were usually buried with less expense, the common people sometimes sang, danced, and played games during vigils for the dead. Numerous church and civil records illustrate that such festive elements were frequently included in folk rituals honoring the deceased. In 1284, a Ludlow guild forbade games and the presence of women other than family members at vigils. A London council of 1342 also railed against such assemblies, citing practices like fornication and theft at night watches.[23]

Another ceremony was sometimes performed for years after the deceased was buried. This was originally a simple commemorative service performed by monks on behalf of the nobility. It soon became common practice among the wealthy to endow anniversary Masses, votive lamps, and chantries. Margaret of Denmark gave a huge sum of money to establish a chantry in the early 1400s, which would benefit the souls of all the men who died fighting for her country.[24] Anniversary services often included processions, alms-giving, and hospitality for the mourners. Despite two subsequent marriages, John of Gaunt, duke of Lancaster, held such annual services for his first wife, Blanche of Lancaster, from 1370 until 1399, the year of his own death. In 1374, the ceremony was highlighted by a solemn high Mass at St. Paul's Cathedral. John also draped Blanche's tomb with black cloths, and surrounded it with forty wax candles and twenty-four torches held by poor men wearing Lancastrian livery.[25]

This extravagance reveals the great value medieval people placed on these earthly ceremonies, and also indicates the importance they traditionally attached to the afterlife. The story of Blessed Ellen of Udine illustrates the lengths to which people might go to assure themselves of a place in heaven. After Ellen's husband died, she took a vow of silence, followed a strict penitential lifestyle, and gave generously to chantries and other charities. She explained her asceticism to her confessor:

> I wear a hair shirt because of the silken undergarments . . . with which I used to clothe myself. Thirty-three stones I put in . . . my

> shoes because I have so often offended God with my leaping and dancing. I flagellate my body for the impious and carnal pleasures with which I indulged it during my marriage.[26]

The hardships of medieval life perhaps helped make festive ceremonies, games, and entertainments very popular, but the joys and tribulations of earthly life remained secondary to the next world's demands. Nor is it surprising that medieval people usually took care to store up credit with God. Like Ellen of Udine, many a woman danced away her youth, only to become extremely charitable, ascetic, and pious as she grew old.

A woman teaching.

Bibliothèque Nationale, Paris

Chapter Fifteen

"THE WORKING OF A WOMAN'S WIT"

Women's Roles in Learning and Literacy

Kamar of Baghdad, a concubine of ninth-century Prince Ibrahim of Seville, was unusually well-educated for her time. When jealous courtiers accused her of being too scholarly and clever for a woman, she reeled off the angry reply:

> By Allah, what men are these who despise the only true nobility—that which talent confers. The most shameful thing in the world is ignorance, and if ignorance were a woman's passport to Paradise, I would far rather that the creator sent me to hell![1]

Like Ibrahim's courtiers, most medieval men preferred their women ignorant. In fact, they often claimed God gave women less capable minds so they would have to obey men. In the 1350s, a French noble named Bertrand du Guesclin voiced the common sentiment that "in woman there is no more sense than there is in a sheep." Similarly, an Italian visitor reported that in fifteenth-century England "the working of a woman's wit was considered of small account."[2]

The belief that the female mind was inadequately equipped for learning provided a useful excuse for opposing women's education. In addition, clerics frequently opposed feminine learning on the grounds that literate females would spend their time composing love letters or reading heretical literature. Secular males often stated that their wives should not be more educated than they, and also stressed that reading was "suitable" only for nuns. Historian Edith Ennen noted yet another problem: "the enormous cost of study restricted the number of burghers' sons who could afford to go to [a] university." Ennen thus concluded that fathers rarely even considered spending such a large amount of money on their daughters' schooling since the girls would later need dowries and, furthermore, could not put their education to any practical use.[3]

In the early Middle Ages, denying women access to education was not especially discriminatory. Even among men, usually only the clergy was literate, and many clerics themselves had virtually no academic skills. Moreover, manuscripts had to be laboriously copied by hand onto expensive parchment. Hence, even if people could have read them, books were too costly and rare for most individuals to acquire. In the 1040s, for example, Countess Agnes of Anjou had to pay an enormous price—two hundred sheep, a large amount of wheat, numerous pelts, and a variety of other goods—to get her hands on a copy of a collection of Latin sermons.

The main forms of early medieval written literature were letters and sermons. Since monasteries were the repository of scholarship, theologians did most of this writing—which was almost always in Latin. By the thirteenth century, however, a large body of vernacular writings began to take the place of Latin works. This development encouraged people to read since it was no longer necessary to know a second language. Vernacular literature thereby helped increase literacy among the laity, while opening up a wide variety of new genres.

In the early Middle Ages, most works were composed and transmitted orally. But in the middle of the 1300s, the French composer Guillaume Machaut described the benefits of a new practice—reading silently to oneself. When he received letters from his young love, Péronnelle d'Armentières, Machaut gloated, "The secret that lay within was not revealed to all, because I read them between my teeth."[4] This new privacy also enabled authors to branch out into different themes and genres because they could now work without an audience—which sometimes changed or condemned a writer's material. Moreover, since this was quieter and faster than reading aloud, monastic libraries could lend books out for shorter periods of time and accommodate larger numbers of scholars at big tables in one room. In the new manuscripts themselves, spacing was provided between words, confusing abbreviations and letters were changed, and many books began to include alphabetical indices and chapter divisions.[5]

Paper was another important innovation since it was durable and fairly cheap. After paper made its way from the East into

Europe during the twelfth century, guilds of professional lay copyists soon began to spring up near universities. They prospered by mass-producing a variety of relatively inexpensive manuscripts on paper. At the end of the Middle Ages, a new invention—the workable printing press—made still cheaper books accessible to more of the populace. Increased availability and variety of subject matter had a salutary effect on literacy by giving the average man and woman new incentives to learn to read.

All these innovations were helpful, but probably the most important change was the increase in educational opportunities. In the early Middle Ages, there were several types of schools connected with religious foundations that trained boys to become monks, priests, or clerks. During the twelfth century, a greater variety of institutions began to be established, and many of these were secular schools. Guibert de Nogent (1053–1124) reported that the number of professional teachers, mainly wandering scholars, had multiplied greatly during the course of his lifetime, contributing to the spread of literacy among the laity.[6] Later scholars often settled down, establishing schools that offered reading, writing, accounting, and language courses. Because learning was no longer only for those destined for clerical careers, wealthy merchants and craft guilds also founded secular schools.

Not everyone appreciated all these educational institutions; universities were often especially unpopular. These were ecclesiastical schools, run and attended by clerics and those training for clerical careers in such fields as medicine, law, theology, and accounting. Much of the laity called universities unnecessary and too exclusive, and condemned the students for their wild and disreputable behavior. In 1381, the Cambridge University manuscripts were burned by the townspeople, who had an ongoing quarrel with the transient students—a typical college-town problem even then. A poor townswoman, Margery Starre, was thrilled by the destruction. She threw the ashes into the air shouting, "Away with the learning of the clerks!"[7] This was a common attitude among the lower classes toward the privileged few who went to these schools.

Women like Margery may have been especially inclined to hate universities because females were not allowed to study or teach at these institutions—regardless of rank, wealth, or intelligence. There were a few isolated exceptions to this rule in Spain and Italy. A Latin scholar named Lucia de Medrano, for instance, lectured on the classics at the University of Salamanca, while

Francisca, another Spanish woman, filled the Chair of Rhetoric at Alcala, dubbed "the Athens of Spain."[8] In Italy, Dorotea Bocchi (or Bucca) spent some forty years (c.1395–c.1435) teaching philosophy at the University of Bologna, where her classes were among the most popular with the students.

Stories about female university scholars and teachers more often emphasized the difficulties they faced; in fact, women usually had to conceal their gender in order to circumvent prohibitions against their participation. According to Christine de Pisan, Novella d'Andrea covered herself with a veil when she substituted for her father, Giovanni d'Andrea, a fourteenth-century professor of law. Christine claimed this was a protective measure—the veil prevented Novella's male audience from becoming distracted by her beauty. A somewhat different story was related by a Viennese abbot named Martin of Leibnitz (d.1464). He wrote about an anonymous young woman in Cracow who dressed herself as a male scholar in order to attend the university there. She was so intelligent that her deception worked perfectly for some two years. Eventually, however, her real identity was discovered and she was expelled from school. She then entered a nearby convent, where her superior education equipped her to teach novices and boarders.[9] Such tales—of somewhat dubious historical accuracy since versions of them were told in more than one university town—underlined the fact that feminine participation at the university level was nearly non-existent.

Despite its attitude toward women in universities, the ecclesiastical hierarchy did not condemn all women's education. At least in the early Middle Ages, the female religious was often encouraged to undertake various studies. Though scholarship for nuns was rarely seen as a priority, many did receive a relatively high-quality education. The most scholarly orders even studied the natural sciences, astronomy, medicine, the classics, theology, and the writings of the church fathers. At the convent of Hohenburg, for instance, the sisters knew how to calculate the time of night by the position of the stars.[10] Cecilia of Normandy, an eleventh-century religious at the Trinity at Caen, was so learned that she received advanced grammar lessons from Arnoul Mauclerc, a famous orator and dialectician.[11] An English nun called Clemence of Barking translated the *Life of St. Catherine*—thereby proving that both Latin and French literacy flourished in some English convents, at least through the twelfth century.

After Clemence's time, however, the advanced education offered by early convents was rarely available. Instead of mastering Latin and the classics, most nuns read romantic poems and ballads written in the vernacular. Between the years 1080 and 1162, at least three letters and one treatise for English anchoresses were written in Latin by Goscelin, St. Anselm, and St. Ailred. Around the year 1220, however, the *Ancren Riwle,* an advice manual for three anchoresses, was composed in Middle English. Only later was it translated into French, and then into Latin. Similarly, in the middle of the fourteenth century, Richard Rolle wrote the *Form of Living* for an anchoress (probably one named Margaret de Kirkeby) in Middle English. It is significant that Rolle composed many of his other writings—ones for male anchorites—in Latin.[12] This suggests that after the twelfth century Latin literacy was no longer prevalent among English religious women.

Scholarship had declined to an equal extent in most European convents. Though Marguerite d'Oingt, prioress of Poletins near Lyons, was quite adept at writing Latin, she was aware that her nuns could better understand her work if it was composed in their native tongue, the French-Provençal dialect. In the late thirteenth century, Marguerite wrote a book about her mystical visions, as well as the *Life of Saint Beatrice,* in the vernacular.[13] By this time, what frequently passed for Latin education among French and Belgian nuns was simply memorization and familiarity with content.

For laywomen, opportunities either to teach or to study varied according to wealth, social class, geographical area, and trends in pedagogic philosophy. In England, anchoresses sometimes taught girls, but educational opportunities remained minimal for those who were poor. In the year 1500, eight-year-old Elizabeth Gairard, a tradesman's daughter, was among Sir William Barbour's thirty London students. He taught her to say the *Lord's Prayer*, the *Hail Mary*, and the *Creed*,[14] indicating that the curriculum at such lower schools (at least for girls) still consisted largely of rote memorization, not necessarily reading instruction. By that time lay teachers were replacing clerics and tutors, but there was little increase in the number of schoolmistresses. Guild records contained the name of one female member, Matilda Maresflete, who taught religion in Boston, Lincolnshire, in 1404. Fifteenth-century London records mentioned few female teachers. A grateful, wealthy grocer left a *scolemaysteresse* a legacy of twenty *shillings* in 1408, and one teacher called Elizabeth Scolemaystres was noted residing in Cripplegate during the 1440s.[15]

In some other countries, the rise of secular education allowed females a slightly larger measure of participation. By the eleventh century, France had "elementary" schools that allowed a few female students to attend. Only two female tutors were recorded in the 1292 Paris tax rolls, along with one schoolmistress named Dame Tyfainne of the rue aux Ours. A schoolmaster named Guillaume paid a 5*s* tax that year, while Tyfainne owed only 2*s*—possibly indicating that female instructors were in less demand than male ones. However, slightly less than a century after these tax rolls listed only three female teachers, there were twenty-one schoolmistresses—such as Jacqueline de Transvere and Denisette de Nérel[16]—registered along with the schoolmasters.

In Italy as well, educational authorities focused on boys, but girls were often able to obtain the rudiments of basic literacy. Florence had four major Latin schools, and some ten thousand children attended the grammar schools in the 1330s. Few girls received any formal schooling beyond this lower level, which perhaps explains why Italian women were seldom recorded as teachers. In 1304 Florence, however, a well-educated, married woman named Clementia was termed a *doctrix puerorum* because she taught basic Latin to boys.[17]

In late thirteenth-century Germany and Flanders, educational opportunities began to increase with the emergence of parish or municipal schools, which were less expensive than tutors and convents. The parish schools of Cologne were open to burghers' daughters, and a 1320 decree in Brussels allowed girls to attend secondary schools there. In fact, throughout this region it became relatively common for burghers' daughters to acquire a little "elementary" education. Germany also had some female teachers, although many fourteenth- and fifteenth-century ones were so poor that their debts had to be forgiven. They may have had trouble earning sufficient wages because a wide variety of rules strictly regulated their behavior and the subject matter they taught—reading, writing, and arithmetic. Despite these restrictions, one woman in mid-fifteenth-century Ueberlingen became so popular that parents began sending even boys to her classes. When a schoolmaster complained about his female competitor, however, the city forced her to pay a fine for each boy she taught.[18]

Wealthy families could bypass all the prejudices against women in public institutions by hiring tutors and governesses, thereby designing excellent schools within the walls of their own courts. In this home academic setting, noble girls usually received practical and religious training in preparation for acquiring and pleasing socially prominent husbands. Their reading material included legends and stories of saints, as well as biblical tales and prayerbooks. Women also occasionally learned writing, foreign languages, and Latin. The private tutors who served these wealthy families were often themselves well-educated members of the lesser nobility. In the 1390s, for instance, Mary Hervey instructed Blanche and Philippa, the daughters of Henry IV of England. Mary taught the girls to read with the help of two "ABC books."

Because so many highborn children were educated at home, women achieved an inadvertent educational role as tutors to both boys and girls. Mothers frequently provided the first lessons for their offspring. Blanche of Castile, for example, reportedly took time out from her duties as regent to teach her son, King Louis IX of France, to read. Books of instruction were so scarce that women who wished to teach their children sometimes had to produce their own texts. Lady Dionysia de Mountchesny commissioned Walter of Bibbesworth to compile a French textbook for her daughter. This book included scenes from childhood, drills in naming body parts, aspects of a child's daily routine, riddles, proverbs, and the names of plants and animals. There was even a section on occupations in which a woman named "Muriel" was pictured threshing and hackling flax, and "Dame Hude" was shown spinning yarn.

Whether from their mothers, home tutors, or convent schools, a surprising number of wealthy medieval women did manage to acquire reading and writing skills, at the very least. Hence, noblewomen were often particularly interested in educational and literary progress. It was partly due to their efforts that literacy increased, private libraries swelled with volumes, and new genres of literature developed during the Middle Ages. Even some men tacitly acknowledged women's importance in the transmission of learning. The *Sachenspiegel*, a thirteenth-century German code of law, stated that books should be passed down through the female line because women read them more frequently than did men.[19] King Henry V of England apparently saw nothing wrong with literate women. He even borrowed two books—*The Chronicle of Jerusalem* and *The Journey of Godfrey of Bouillon*—from his aunt, Joan Beaufort, countess of Westmoreland (c.1410s), and then forgot to return them.

A number of wills demonstrate that many women like Joan Beaufort accumulated private libraries. Alice Chaucer, duchess of Suffolk (d.1475), owned numerous books, including a copy of Christine de Pisan's *Le Livre de la Cité des Dames* (*The Book of the City of Ladies*). Perhaps Alice had some interest in progressive feminist ideas. Although her books were almost all on religious subjects, Cecily Neville, duchess of York (d.1495), also seemed to have an interest in women writers, such as Catherine of Siena, Bridget of Sweden, and Mechtild of Hackeborn.[20] Mahaut of Artois (d.1327) made her castle at Hesdin into a center for literary endeavors, and even carried some of her favorite books along on her travels. Mahaut's manuscript collection included a copy of the Bible, a Psalter, a Gradual, several *Books of Hours*, the *Lives of the Saints*, the *Miracles of Our Lady*, the works of Boethius, the recently written travels of Marco Polo, and several romances. Her library indicates that she was able to understand both Latin and vernacular works.

Mahaut's library also reveals some of the new directions medieval literature was taking. While early literary efforts were almost always Latin treatises about religious subjects written by clerics, the rise of courtly literature in the early twelfth century led to the emergence of a group of professional poets who composed secular works in the vernacular. In southern France where the trend began they were known as *troubadours*, while in the north of France they were called *trouvères*. An early form of courtly poetry, the *chanson de geste* (song of action), glorified fighting and militant heroes, and was therefore more popular with men than with women.

Ladies were more enthralled by the courtly love embodied in chivalric romances, so they often supported this genre. Eleanor of Aquitaine, for instance, was a patroness of numerous renowned troubadours—such as Bernard de Ventadour, Bertran de Born, and presumably Marie de France. Eleanor may have passed her admiration for troubadour poetry on to her daughter, Marie of Champagne (d.1198), who also became a literary patroness. Marie and her husband, Henry *the Liberal*, made their court a renowned center for troubadours, including: Gace Brulé, one of the first lyric poets of northern France; Andreas Capellanus, who presumably composed his famous work *De Amore Libri Tres* (*Three Books about Love*) at this court; and Chrétien de Troyes, an innovator of the Arthurian romance. In Chrétien's introduction to *Lancelot*, he even thanked Marie for encouraging his work and making suggestions for improvements to the *Lancelot* story.

The introduction of courtly literature seemed to open the door to many new styles and topics, thus allowing a variety of themes and genres to flourish—again thanks to women patrons. German noblewomen, for instance, frequently aided writers who were experimenting with the novel—a new form that is often said to have originated in England with Geoffrey Chaucer. Several fifteenth-century German authors dedicated such books or translations to Princess Matilda of Rottenburg in recognition of her support. Similarly, in fifteenth-century France, Margaret of York, the third wife of the last Valois duke of Burgundy, Charles *the Bold*, supported a variety of literary innovations. She was a patron of the translator and printer William Caxton, and she pioneered many of the literary efforts at the sophisticated Burgundian court.

Despite numerous literate women and influential patronesses, however, men still espoused the theory that females were innately less intelligent than men. Both laymen and clerics also continued to deny women access to educational institutions. Men frequently claimed to be protecting feminine virginity by forbidding young girls to study with male teachers—a provision they also hoped would protect men from being tempted by attractive female students. At the same time, men used biblical strictures to prevent females from teaching. This often meant that girls could not obtain an education from women teachers, because there were none available. The male attempt to "protect" women thus resulted in protecting their minds from exposure to higher levels of knowledge.

Equally unfortunate for women was the direction male scholarship was taking as it moved away from the liberal arts into more specialized subjects, such as law, medicine, and theology. These degrees prepared men for government, university, and other clerical careers. Women scholars, on the other hand, were isolated from the rest of society. Barred from universities, and thus from entrance into the professional arena, female students received an education that could not be used as a stepping stone into any career. By the sixteenth century, society as a whole was becoming far more literate. In common with men, more women gained basic literacy skills in this period, but simultaneously the gap between educated males and females widened alarmingly since women rarely had access to more than what we would term a "grade school" education. As their schooling lagged farther and farther behind men's, women found themselves less and less able to compete in the marketplace, and in a wide variety of careers.

Christine de Pisan at work.

British Library, London

Chapter Sixteen

THAT WHICH TALENT CONFERS

Women in Literature and Art

In the late twelfth century, Marie de Ventadorn supported several male troubadours and, in addition, even wrote her own romantic poems. Nor was Marie the only female troubadour; some twenty women from southern France are known to have written poetry, thereby introducing a feminine note to the primarily masculine tone of courtly literature. Most if not all of these women did not depend upon their writing skills to make a living, so they were not restricted to composing for a certain audience. They generally used the same poetic conventions as their male counterparts, but many of their extant works are more personal and less stilted than similiar poems written by medieval men.

This emotional realism is quite noticeable in works that extol the pleasures of physical love. The early twelfth-century poet Castelloza wrote to her lover: "no joy ever sustains me except for yours." Castelloza longed for:

> a place where I would kiss you and embrace you, for, with that new life could come into my body, which you make yearn for you greatly and covetously. [1]

In contrast to this verse, so evocative of joyous intimacy, many other poems resounded with the sorrow of lost love. Abandoned women and unfaithful men were common themes in courtly poetry, but once again, female troubadours treated these subjects with greater accuracy and sympathy for feminine emotions. One anonymous woman eloquently bemoaned the fact that, although she and her lover had shared fully in the pleasures of love, she alone had to bear the sorrow when he ended their relationship. Azalais de Porcairques (born c.1140) expressed similar grief, lamenting: "I've lost the joy of my solace." The loss of her philandering lover was like winter in her heart: "Now we are come to the cold time . . . the ice, and the snow, and the mud."[2] More than three centuries later, a Spanish poet named Florencia Pinar bitterly lashed out at callous men for intentionally deceiving and ensnaring women in passionate traps. Comparing women who love faithless men to caged partridges, Florencia lamented,

> Now weep, who once had thought
> not once of ever being caught;
> instead they live deceived, decoyed
> by them they sought most to avoid.[3]

Though the faithless lover motif remained popular, women also contributed to a variety of other literary themes and genres. As early as the 840s, a noblewoman named Dhuoda had composed an educational and moral treatise, known as *The Manual of Dhuoda,* for her son William's instruction. Her manuscript, like that of many later women writers, was not only innovative but was also highly colored by her own intimate emotions. Dhuoda's husband, Bernard of Septimania, had separated her from their oldest son for political reasons, so she sent her book to him with this anguished preface:

> Knowing that most women in the world have the joy of living with their children, and seeing that I, Dhuoda, am withheld from you . . . and am far away . . . I am sending you this little work of mine. I would be happy if . . . the presence of this little book calls to your mind . . . what you should do for my sake.[4]

A century later, another articulate and creative woman, Hroswitha of Gandersheim (c.935–c.999), became the first known medieval dramatist. A cloistered noblewoman, she wrote her plays to entertain and inspire her nuns, who presumably read them aloud rather than actually staging these works. Basing her dramas on biblical stories and saints' legends, Hroswitha frequently focused on women. In a play entitled *Dulcetius,* she depicted womanly Christian virtue of such strength that it could defeat the Roman Empire. This drama pits three virtuous maidens against Emperor Diocletian and his top military leader, Dulcetius. When Dulcetius tries to rape the three virgins, God answers their prayers for salvation. Instead of kissing beautiful young girls, Dulcetius ends up passionately embracing the kitchen pots and pans. After his delusion ends, the infuriated governor is understandably impressed by the piety and power of his three captives. He gives them a chance to renounce their faith and be allowed to live, but all three maidens refuse to recant their devotion to God. Two of the girls are burned and the third is pierced by numerous arrows. No wounds appear on their bodies, however, because God takes them directly to heaven before the Romans can harm the virtuous maidens. According to Hroswitha, martyrdom was their ultimate victory, proving feminine steadfastness could defeat male might.

Hildegarde of Bingen also helped develop both literature and drama by composing the earliest known morality play—a drama that taught the Christian philosophy of virtue triumphing over vice, but did not use biblical figures or saints as the characters. As is true of Hroswitha's plays, there is no conclusive evidence that Hildegarde's drama was ever actually produced. Her *Ordo Virtutum* had female characters for its spiritual heroes, but she utilized personifications of virtues rather than real people. This play's protagonist is *Anima*—a soul searching for the path to heaven. *Humility* and her sister virtues are all female soldiers, fighting for *Anima* against a male persona, *Diabolus*—a very worldly devil.

Like Hroswitha and Hildegarde, many female writers were religious women, since they were usually the most literate women, particularly in the early Middle Ages. The first known female poet of Germany was Ava of Melk (d.1127), who presumably became a religious after her husband died. She used older literature as a guide and her sons as scribes when she created her poems, five of which are extant. Abbess Herrad of Landsburg composed and designed an innovative book called the *Hortus Deliciarum* (*Garden of Delights*). Beautifully illuminated, this manuscript's illustrations were an integral part of its message and were nearly as important as its text. Herrad chose this format because it allowed even the illiterate to benefit from her book.

Other religious women contributed to the body of hagiography (lives or legends of saintly individuals), treatises that often served as entertaining vehicles for the transmission of moral doctrines. Sister Illuminato Bembo, for example, extolled the virtues of her holy friend and companion, Saint Catherine of Bologna (Caterina dei Vigri). Completed in 1469, *The Mirror* of Sister Illuminato praised Saint Catherine for her hard work, prudishness, virginity, charity, and sympathy. Illuminato was most impressed by Catherine's humility and obedience to her superiors—attributes that apparently transcended the grave. The nuns believed their dead leader would soon be canonized so they wished to enshrine her corpse, seated in a tabernacle/chair in the choir. Sister Illuminato ordered Catherine to let her stiff body "unbend," and this appeal to "holy obedience" caused the future saint to loosen her dead limbs so the nuns could seat her.[5]

Unlike female hagiographers, visionary women wrote or dictated their own mystical experiences, conveying revealed truth in a more introspective way. Their writings often contained personal explanations of their ecstatic visionary relationships with God. In her *Booke of Gostely Grace,* Mechtild of Hackeborn (c.1241–1298), vividly described God's heart as a beautiful garden and vineyard complete with lovely streams of clear running water. She entered His heart and worked the land alongside Christ. Jesus helped her when a task was too heavy, and Mechtild said, "then was it to bear but a light burden."[6]

God's physical beauty was a recurring theme in visionary writings. In her early fourteenth-century manuscript *Speculum* (*Mirror*), Marguerite d'Oingt described Christ: "[His] body was so beautiful that one could see in it the angels and saints as if they were painted there."[7] In her *Exercises,* Gertrude *the Great* concentrated on Christ's "ravishing face," and often expressed her desire to "gaze upon the beauty of thy divine countenance." She wrote that the "divine splendor" of His face "satisfieth the longing desires of all saints." Gertrude also enjoyed a mystical, "ravishing union" with Jesus, and was as happy "as a bride amidst the raptures of the king her spouse." She prayed to Christ, "O thou who art my chosen delight; let me faint and die in thy embrace." In her visionary dialogue, Jesus promised to satisfy Gertrude with "delights of which my Godhead is the source." Christ also told her:

> If thou wilt be mine, my beloved . . . thou must love me with tenderness, with wisdom, with strength; so shalt thou taste the sweetest delights I promise thee.[8]

Dictated in the early 1400s, *The Book of Margery Kempe* combined elements of both the hagiographical and mystical genres. From a literary perspective, this laywoman's manuscript is important because it was the first known autobiography in the English language. Margery revealed her mystic experiences, testified to the intensity of her spirituality, and demonstrated her devotion to God. She not only looked inside herself; she also related intimate details of her life, her travels, and her search for understanding and salvation. One intimate detail of this search concerned her ambivalence about marital relations. She reported that she tried to persuade her husband to live with her under vows of chastity, but he refused. Margery lamented, "He would have his will and [I] obeyed with great weeping and sorrowing"—giving us an intriguing picture of the Kempes' love life. Margery was actually torn between her own physical and spiritual desires; these mixed emotions allowed her to enjoy herself, while simultaneously fearing that she and her husband:

> displeased God by their inordinate love and the great delectation that they had . . . from their pleasure of their bodies.[9]

Women's secular biographies and memoirs also frequently included very intimate glimpses into their lives. Anna Comnena's (1083–1148) *Alexiad,* a far-ranging "biography" of her father, Emperor Alexius Comnenus, and the history of his reign, contained many such details. Anna related information about contemporary medical knowledge, Byzantine protocol, and important current events—such as the First Crusade. In addition, she included word portraits of a wide variety of women. For instance, Sichelgaita, the wife of Robert Guiscard, emerges from the *Alexiad* as a fearsome, armed Amazon of a woman. Anna evidently admired strong females. She praised her mother, Empress Irene Ducas, because she "displayed no womanly cowardice,"[10] even during times of extreme danger. Her brother received no such encomiums. Anna included an intimate account of her deep disappointment when he was born, because he would eventually rule Byzantium. This was a role she had hitherto considered her own (because she was the first-born child), and one for which she had been trained. Anna deplored the system that gave the crown to her brother, not because he was better qualified, but merely because he was a male.

Women also wrote a variety of other types of "non-fiction"—such as the educational manuals that had become so popular by the fifteenth century. Female writers who penned these manuscripts frequently chose traditionally "male" subjects to discuss. In a popular treatise known as *The Book of Saint Albans,* Juliana Berners compiled information on hunting, hawking, fishing, and heraldry. This work demonstrated that Juliana had closely and accurately observed wildlife, heraldry, and veterinary practice. Because warfare was an important activity for the nobility, military manuals like Christine de Pisan's *Le Livre des fais d'armes et de chévalerie* (*Book of Feats of Arms and of Chivalry*) were also among the most sought after books. In addition to presenting concrete, detailed, and accurate information about fighting, Christine argued for Christian-chivalric values and for a purely defensive army. This added a personal touch to what might otherwise have been merely a routine technical treatise. Although her views were highly idiosyncratic, her manual was so popular that it was translated into English. William Caxton, the first printer in England, even produced a printed copy in the 1480s.

Christine was unusually prolific; among other works, she wrote poetry, a biography of King Charles V of France, educational treatises for her son, *The Book of Three Virtues,* and *The Book of The City of Ladies*—a volume we might term "feminist" in theme and tone. A Parisian illuminator named Anastaise was one of the real women Christine mentioned in *The City of Ladies.* She enthusiastically praised this artist, who had done some work for Christine herself. She claimed all of Paris was talking about the beautiful borders of flowers and sophisticated background details that Anastaise painted in manuscripts. Unfortunately, this is the only known record of a woman who may have been one of the best miniaturists of her day.

This dearth of information is typical, though it is perhaps not surprising for an era when most artists—both men and women—did not sign their works. Anonymity was preferred because the church condemned artistic pride as sinful, and because artists were not perceived as uniquely creative individuals. Art was expected to be useful above all else. The artist used his hands to create functional works, and was thus considered a craftsman or manual laborer. Since there was no division between arts and crafts, manuscript illuminations and elaborately embroidered cloths were no less important art works than large paintings or statues. The sculptor, illuminator, or embroiderer was perceived as a conduit through which God worked, rather than as an individual endowed with exceptional talent.

It is especially difficult to discern the feminine role, since biases in favor of artistic anonymity and the societal strictures against feminine involvement have left the modern scholar with only tantalizing glimpses of a very few women participants in most fields of artistic endeavor. Moreover, the slight documentary evidence that is available sometimes merely leads to confusion. In the eleventh and twelfth centuries, for instance, there were apparently four nuns named Diemudis who worked as artists in one region. There is so little known about any of them that some scholars believe two or more were actually the same woman. Only one, an eleventh-century nun of Wessobrun, stands out from the crowd. This particular Diemudis is credited with having used a very sophisticated style to copy and illuminate at least forty-five manuscripts—including the works of Saint Gregory the Great, Saint Augustine, and Saint Jerome. Her reward for this prolific work illustrates why artists can be so difficult to track down. Rather than receiving money or widespread name recognition, which might have resulted in more documentary evidence of her work, Diemudis was honored by being depicted holding a plume on her grave.[11]

The evidence is somewhat less ambiguous about women patrons, who were an important link in the chain of artistic progress. Despite some drawbacks, the patronage system did give artists enough security and recognition to allow them to experiment with new techniques and styles. Because artists could not create without backers, the numerous women who hired them to produce artworks were an important part of creative evolution. In the fourteenth century, Jeanne d'Évreaux, queen of France, hired an artist to create a sophisticated gilt statue of the Virgin and Child for the abbey of St. Denis. Late in that century, another French queen, Isabeau of Bavaria, commissioned an artist to produce a gold statue studded with jewels. This beautiful piece portrayed her, along with King Charles VI and their children, worshipping at the feet of the Virgin and Child.[12] Isabeau gave the statue to her husband for a New Year's present.

In contrast to the relatively well-documented role of these patronesses, little information exists about women artists creating such statues and other works. Not surprisingly, the presence of women in heavy architectural and monumental art was especially rare. Euphemia, abbess of Wherwell in Hampshire (1226–1257), was one of the few women who made a documented contribution to architectural design and construction. Her innovative designs for a chapel and a new hall made these structures safer from fire and more permanent than previous buildings at the abbey. Similarly, her waterway/sewage system improved sanitation for the abbey infirmary. Euphemia also designed and landscaped a large garden and meditation area.

Feminine assistance to male family members—architects, builders, and sculptors—was probably slightly more common. In fifteenth-century France, Marguerite de Feschal directed the construction of her Loire Valley château, *le Plessis-Bourré.* Her husband was a master builder/designer, but he was required at King Louis XI's court so frequently that Marguerite had to complete most of the work on her new château.[13] This was a difficult job, because the absence of blueprints left most architectural details and designs up to the builders and overseers themselves. A thirteenth-century German laywoman named Sabina von Steinbach also assisted a male master, possibly a relative named Erwin who was a builder and sculptor. It is believed that Sabina finished the statues at Strasbourg Cathedral that he had begun. A scroll on the statue of St. John reads: "Thanks be to the holy piety of this woman, Sabina, who from this hard stone gave me form."[14]

Even painting was a craft that was seen as an unacceptable occupation for women—especially wealthy noblewomen. Probably less high-ranking girls sometimes learned artistic skills from family members who were already artists. Miniatures occasionally depicted women working as artists. An extant fifteenth-century French illumination, for example, shows a female artist at work while her apprentice mixes pigments in the background. But, in general, the great artistic progress of the Middle Ages did little to elevate the status of female artists. They were rarely perceived as equal to male painters, and even those who were comparable to men received little recognition. In some poor nunneries, women who created exquisite illuminated manuscripts had to sell those volumes to wealthier men's institutions. If the monks put on new bindings, the books appeared to have been entirely produced by the brothers.[15] Male historians also neglected or obscured the exact nature of women's artistic activities. Margaretha van Eyck, the sister of famed painter Jan, is known to have been an artist but, unlike the well-documented role of her brother, the extent of her own participation is lost to posterity.

Women artists usually concentrated on painting miniatures—book illustrations or illuminations—rather than large-scale projects. Manuscript painting was an established, highly respected art form in the Middle Ages, and one which was strongly associated with the monastic tradition of bookmaking. Around the year 970, for example, a Spanish artist named Ende illuminated and then signed an exceptionally beautiful copy of the *Beatus Apocalypse*—a popular, often-copied manuscript in medieval Spain. Though her vivid pictures of fantastic dragons, demons, and angels made her work justly famous,[16] little is known about Ende herself. She may have been a nun, or have simply been boarding or working at the convent. Even some 500 years later, women were still finding that convents provided them with the best artistic opportunities. Tommasina del Fiesco of Genoa retired to a nunnery after her husband died and began a "second career" writing, copying, and illuminating a variety of manuscripts.[17] Possibly Tommasina was fulfilling a lifelong creative desire which had been denied her in the secular world.

There was even one female artist-saint, the previously mentioned Catherine of Bologna, though most art historians now think her creative efforts were restricted to a few small religious paintings and manuscript illuminations. Sister Illuminato apparently believed St. Catherine was a role model for other women, and preferred not to encourage females to follow artistic careers. She therefore made short work of Catherine's creative activities, by simply stating in one sentence that the future saint delighted in producing religious art for her convent.

Sister Illuminato's reticence is surprising since artistic work was a relatively acceptable occupation in female religious houses. It was probably common for nuns to teach each other these skills, as a number of artist-bookmakers did at the Dominican convent of St. Catherine at Nuremberg. At this house in the mid-1400s, calligraphist Margaretha Karthauserin worked with an illustrator named Barbara Gwichtmacherin to produce a number of volumes that bear her signature. Another nun named Margareta Imhoff also assisted Margaretha. She had apparently learned the craft by helping Kunigunda, yet another sister at Nuremberg. Kunigunda had finished a *New Testament* only a few years before Margaretha began her work.[18] These four nuns demonstrate the convent tradition of transmitting artistic skills from experienced workers to novices.

Though it seems to have been somewhat less acceptable for laywomen to work as artists, during the late Middle Ages, there were some female illuminators and other painters in most countries. In late fifteenth-century Flanders, the number of women in the Bruges guild of painters increased until females accounted for some twenty-five percent of the members. In Frankfurt, at the end of the fifteenth century, a woman named Juttchen was frequently mentioned as a painter of puppets.[19] Paris evidently had a longstanding tradition of women artists, since a variety of fourteenth-century records briefly noted several female illuminators. A few of these women may have also worked as sculptors or, more likely, as painters of statues. A medieval statue was almost always painted in bright colors after the sculptor finished.

Bourgot de Noir is more famous than most of those women, perhaps because she was associated with a male artist. Since her father, Jehan, was a painter, he presumably trained Bourgot at home. From the 1350s through the 1380s, Bourgot and Jehan worked together on numerous projects. Their level of financial success indicates they were excellent illuminators, and they usually worked for people who could afford to hire the best. They numbered a king, a duke, and Yolande, countess of Bar, among their patrons. While Bourgot and Jehan were completing a commission from King Charles V of France, he even gave them a house in Paris.

Like manuscript illuminations, artistic clothwork was associated to a large extent with cloistered artists before it became a medieval industry, as well as a recognized artistic endeavor. Though modern readers may be tempted to deny embroidery as "art," historians Rozsika Parker and Griselda Pollack insist that in the Middle Ages there were no:

> rigid . . . divisions between art made with paint or stone and art made with thread and fabric, . . . a variety of forms and media were linked by their ritual functions.[20]

Especially in the early Middle Ages, noblewomen both in and out of the convent produced beautiful woven or embroidered works of art. Empress Judith of Bavaria (802–843), for example, was renowned for her ability to make a variety of creative and appealing embroidered items. Berthe, a ninth-century countess of Roussillon, is believed to have created her own designs when she embroidered a tablecloth. She later sent the finished article, complete with intricately stitched biblical verses, to a church in Lyons.[21] Around the year 1200, Joanna, prioress of Lothen, and her nuns Alheidis and Reglindis, wove a series of brilliant tapestries depicting the history of their convent.[22] Agnes of Meissen, abbess of Quedlinburg (1184–1203), and her nuns made at least two wall tapestries. One of these, which portrayed the marriage of Philology and Mercury, was of superior workmanship and detail. The embroidered altar frontal sewn by Joanna of Beverly, a fourteenth-century English nun, demonstrates the continuing tradition of convent participation in this art form.

Even before Joanna's time, however, many embroiderers were lay professionals. Several such women had been listed in the 1292 Parisian tax survey—like Jehannette *la broderesse* of the rue Perrin

Gascelin.[23] Among the nobility, ornamented clothes and other items were particularly popular when expensive materials, such as gold, silver, and jewels, were employed in the decoration. The costliness of these materials was matched by the fantastic designs of the needlework and the skill of the seamstress. Since seams had to be virtually invisible, the artist might camouflage them with embroidery or rows of pearls. The ideal stitches were so tiny and delicate that the garment appeared to be made of one continuous piece of cloth.[24] The English style known as *Opus Anglicanum* (c.1300) was the culmination of medieval artistic embroidery. This entailed laying gold and silver threads onto the fabric in such a way that the garment would sparkle and flow in procession.[25] A beautifully sewn and expensively bejeweled garment was indeed a work of art—and a costly one. A lay artist-craftswoman, Roesia Burford of London, made a *cope* decorated with coral in the early 1300s that Isabella of France, queen of England, considered a great artistic achievement. She bought it from Roesia for an extremely large sum of money, and then donated the vestment to the pope.

In 1239, King Henry III of England commissioned another professional laywoman, Mabel of Bury St. Edmunds, to make a *chasuble* and altar veil ornamented with gold and studded with pearls. The best masters of London appraised her work and pronounced it of excellent quality and free of defects. King Henry himself was obviously pleased because he later employed Mabel to embroider a standard for a wall in Westminster Abbey. This banner was of ruby samite, and was decorated with gold. The king chose the materials and subject, but the composition and design were Mabel's own.

Despite commissions by influential patrons like King Henry, women's participation in artistic clothwork became increasingly restricted. As the demand for works embroidered in the *Opus Anglicanum* style increased dramatically, it was imported all over Europe. Thus production shifted from women in home workshops to guild workrooms controlled by men. As in other crafts, laws were eventually enacted to prohibit females from participating in this field of artistic endeavor. By the fourteenth century, most recorded payments were being made to men.[26] While wives and daughters probably continued to assist their menfolk in creating textile works of art, they rarely became independent mistresses after this time.

Marie of Burgundy reading.
Österreichische Nationalbibliothek, Vienna

EPILOGUE

All the preceding facts and stories show that the Middle Ages was truly a "man's world," but they also reveal that women engaged in a wide variety of activities and made contributions in numerous fields. In some ways, medieval women actually enjoyed more opportunities for achievement and status than did females in later centuries. The personal nature of medieval feudalism allowed women to wield a level of power rarely achieved by women in the absolute monarchies (served by huge male bureaucracies) of later centuries. Nor was the highly touted Renaissance woman any luckier in the field of education. A man's schooling could further his career, but most often the learning acquired by sixteenth-century noblewomen restricted them to narrow areas of scholarship and select audiences of admirers. While female lay healers had thrived in some areas during the Middle Ages, increasingly repressive legislation enacted from the fifteenth century on virtually annihilated feminine participation in later health care professions.

The business activities of female merchants also decreased. Few sixteenth-century women were as economically productive as their medieval counterparts. Women on the fringe of society faced even more problems in the post-medieval world. Prostitutes who enjoyed a measure of acceptance during much of the Middle Ages became victims of active repression and harsh punishments in later centuries. Non-titled single women of the sixteenth and seventeenth centuries were accused of witchcraft and summarily burned at the stake in far greater numbers than were their medieval counterparts. In fact, the wide variety of roles open to women in the Middle Ages, with its female doctors, judges, and feudal rulers, foreshadowed the possibility of women's increased status, which is only now beginning to be realized in many developed nations.

Moreover, lest we are tempted to believe that our own age is much more enlightened, we should note that women are still subject to discrimination. In our own time, many females do not report violence against them because both courts and society are frequently unsympathetic. Similarly, only recently has the medical community begun to even think about researching such health problems as heart ailments specifically among women, rather than merely adopting the conclusions gathered by studying men. Though modern American women have many legal, business, and educational rights and opportunities denied their medieval counterparts, polls and studies continue to reveal discrimination, harassment, lack of access to top management positions, and unequal pay for women. These indicators must continue to remind us that men's attitudes and women's problems have not always changed a great deal since the Middle Ages.

APPENDIX I

Class Structure

Feminine status was partly dependent upon marital status; a married woman generally had less freedom than a widow, but her standing was usually higher than that of an unmarried girl. A woman's rank also depended upon the position of her family and husband. Classes certainly existed, but they were not simple homogeneous groups. Each division consisted of numerous subclasses.

The most elevated class included royalty, great landholders (the magnates), lesser nobles, and knights. According to John Boswell, by the thirteenth century, nobility was viewed as an:

> inherited, personal characteristic, conferring . . . privilege, possessed in varying degrees by all . . . from knight up, and wholly wanting in everyone else,

no matter how wealthy.[1] The titled nobility itself encompassed several degrees; in fifteenth-century England, "dukes" ranked highest, followed by "marquis," "earl," "viscount," and finally "baron." Even the most minute differences in rank could matter a great deal, especially during marriage negotiations.

City residents were also divided into a wide range of social and economic positions. As cities grew, they began to include merchants, master crafters, artisans, hucksters, and journeymen. They were freemen (as opposed to the lower class bondsmen), but all these urban dwellers ranked lower on the social scale than the noble classes, even though some actually became wealthier than much of the lesser nobility. The richest of these families often bought country estates and huge houses, and imitated the menus, clothing styles, and furnishings of their "betters." Moreover, in the later Middle Ages, many wealthy merchants' daughters married impoverished nobles' sons. Even before that time there was enough overlapping to blur the dividing line between great merchants and the landed gentry. Families like the Pastons almost defy classification. Both city merchants and rural landholders, one of the family even became Sir John (II) Paston. Slightly lower in rank and wealth were the well-off merchants and city burgesses who helped govern their cities by assuming positions of responsibility, like that of mayor or alderman. A range of less prosperous tradespeople and artisans separated these burghers from the poorest urban residents, who were often less well-off than were their rural, peasant counterparts.

Even the peasantry had its own range of subclasses, based on economic position, legal status, and social standing. In much of Europe, the peasantry could be roughly divided into two groups: "plowmen" were relatively self-sufficient farmers tilling their own lands, while "laborers" earned wages, usually by farming someone else's land. Plowmen sometimes became quite wealthy, and held many plots of manor land. At the other end of the spectrum were the poorest day laborers (called *cottars* because a hut or cottage was usually all they had) who tried desperately to grow enough food on the village commons to feed themselves and their families.

Another factor separating individuals in this class was whether the plowman or laborer was free or unfree. In the later Middle Ages the ability to buy one's freedom altered some former class divisions. In England, tenants who held land under a lord and who were forbidden to leave that land except under certain conditions were known as *villeins*. They were unfree with relation to their lords, but they held certain legal rights. On the continent, bondsmen and women were often called *serfs*, and most had fewer rights and less freedom than did their English counterparts. In all regions, bondsmen and women usually owed their lords more rents and services than did their free neighbors. Moreover, the status of villeins and serfs remained lowest because, in most regions, they were not allowed to join the clergy or to appeal their legal suits in royal courts.

APPENDIX II

Money

Most often the specific amounts of money we cite were English and French units—loosely based on the weight of a pound of silver. But actual coins corresponding to these amounts did not exist for all monetary units. The main English coin, the silver *penny*, was based on the Roman *denarius*. England kept the Roman spelling—*denarii* (plural)—or sometimes *denares*. In France the comparable coins were called *deniers*, but both countries abbreviated them as "*d*." Twelve *denarii* or *deniers* equaled an English *shilling* or a French *sou*, both based on the Byzantine *solidus* and written "*s*." Twenty *shillings* made a "£"—the *pound sterling* in England, and twenty *sous* made a *livre tournois*—*lv.*—in France. Around the year 1300, one English *pound sterling* was worth approximately five French *livres tournois*. Some records, however, indicate similarities in value between the two currencies. In 1292 Paris, 12*d* was the lowest tax assessment and 8 *lv.* was close to the highest tax. In London, some twenty years later, few people paid less than 16*d* or more than £6 in taxes.

Recently, H. A. Miskimin attempted to establish what these units were worth in modern terms. He stated, for example, that American wheat sold for about $32 per quarter (eight bushels) while early fourteenth-century English wheat averaged 6*s* per quarter. London wills allowed him to equate approximately £60 with $50,000, but he found that most houses sold for twenty-five to fifty *pounds*.[1] Either housing costs were low by our standards, or £60 was worth much more than $50,000 at current monetary values. Moreover, other extant London wills indicate that an annual income of £7 was deemed quite sufficient for a fifteenth-century merchant.[2] Using Miskimin's equations, the average "middle-class" London family could apparently live well on a yearly sum of between $5,800 and $6,300 in current terms.

Obviously inflation and other variables make it difficult for us to know exactly what medieval money was worth in today's values. Hence it is probably more useful to compare medieval wages with contemporary prices. On a typical thirteenth-century English estate, a carpenter earned 3*d* per day, while a mason received 2½*d*. At the same time, these workers paid 1*d* for a pound of soap, 1½*d* for a pound of candles, and 4½*d* for a gallon of butter. They could have afforded nine *pence* for a pound of pepper, but cloves—at ten *shillings* per pound,[3] or about three months' wages—were probably out of their reach.

Monetary values or what could be purchased with a given amount naturally fluctuated, depending upon region and time period, as the cost of living rose and fell. During the 1370s in the city of London, beer went for five *shillings* a barrel. Nearly a century later, the price had apparently dropped because Sir John Howard recorded buying beer in 1463 London for a mere two *shillings* per barrel. Sir John also noted that in another town he could buy beer for 20*d*[4]—4*d* less than the 2*s* he had to pay in London.

For our purposes, financial records help us compare women, since they are often the only indicators of cost of living, social class, economic position, job importance, and personal competence and status. We can assume, for instance, that a countess whose lands garnered an annual income of several thousand *pounds* must have had larger, more profitable estates than did a noblewoman with an income of a few hundred *pounds* a year. Another example is that a fifteenth-century laundress who made under £2 a year was either in a less prestigious and lucrative job or was less adept at her work than was a skilled silkwoman whose income was reported in the same records at nearly £8 per year. A thorough search of the records gives us the answer that doing laundry, no matter how well, was a less profitable job than silkwork. No laundress was recorded as making much money, but several silkwomen made a great deal. These comparisons are a great help because there is frequently little personal information available, especially about urban and peasant women.

APPENDIX III

Life Expectancy for Women

In the fifth through seventh centuries, the mortality rate for females was very high; few reached what we would call "middle age." During those centuries, grooms in many Germanic tribes gave dowries to their brides and/or their fathers-in-law. The fact that brides were valuable enough to be "bought" suggests there were fewer women than men during this era. By the seventh century, the Frankish *wergild* (price paid to the family for a relative's death) for childbearing women had risen to three times the amount paid for a freeman. This is another indication that life in this period was particularly difficult for women, who had to withstand primitive medical practices, poor nutrition, and a variety of other hardships.

In the eighth through the tenth centuries, highborn women probably had a slightly better chance for survival. Peasant women may not have fared so well. A survey of records from estates near Paris in the early ninth century shows that for every one hundred and thirty-two male serfs there were only about one hundred women.[1] The evidence suggests that women at this time were still finding it difficult to survive the harsh conditions of life, particularly childbearing and heavy manual labor. The statistics may also indicate that among the poor, girl infants were deliberately culled out to provide a better chance for the survival of sons, who were the more valuable workers. Whatever the cause, a peasant female's life expectancy at birth was not much more than twenty-five years—shorter than the life span of the average male peasant.

By the tenth century, several agricultural improvements began to raise the possibility of increased longevity for everyone. The improvements included: a more efficient heavy plow, triennial crop rotation, replacing oxen with horses, water mills, and a more modern harness. These innovations gave a tremendous boost to agricultural productivity, and enabled peasants to grow greater quantities of protein-rich food, such as peas and beans. This gave everyone a more nutritious diet, which aided health and increased life spans. The availability of more iron- and protein-rich foods also made most classes of women better able to survive childbirth.

During the eleventh through thirteenth centuries, the Crusades and numerous other wars decreased the male population to such an extent that statistics begin to reveal a relatively greater life span for women. An indirect bit of evidence supporting the case for increased female longevity was that the Germanic institution of the male dowry gradually disappeared. This reinforces the idea that, at some time during the twelfth or thirteenth century, the number of women began to equal the number of men in many regions.[2]

In the middle of the fourteenth century, however, the plague made life more precarious for everyone. Originating in the East, this pestilence swept across Western Europe—with recurring outbreaks for three more centuries. For women who did not succumb to the plague, the growth of urban areas apparently resulted in increasing the average female's life expectancy in the fourteenth and fifteenth centuries. As opposed to the situation in rural areas, in the cities of the late Middle Ages, women sometimes outnumbered men. In 1395 Bologna, there were approximately one hundred women for every ninety-six men. Records from Nuremberg at this time reveal a 100:84 ratio of women to men.[3] Possibly these figures point more toward women's tendency to migrate to towns than to their longevity. Nevertheless, such statistics do indicate that urban areas probably offered greater security for women, while city work was usually less physically demanding.

Though women's life spans seem to have increased by the late Middle Ages, their status apparently fell as their numbers rose. Female infants were "worth less," so their numbers may have been reduced by parents and other guardians. The evidence definitely suggests that girl infants were much more likely to be killed than boy ones. Thus only those females who survived infancy had a longer life expectancy than had their predecessors from earlier eras.

GLOSSARY

aids – financial subsidy or tribute paid by a vassal to his/her lord.

anchoress – female religious; a recluse.

Assize – statute regulating market weights and/or measures; in England the weights and measures of ale and bread were fixed by an Assize that tied the price of those items to the price of grain.

Assize of Nuisance – London body that "viewed" and then ruled on suits concerning a variety of property and housing matters.

bondswoman – *See* **villein**.

bull – an official papal letter; pope's edict, decree, or mandate.

chivalry – code of upper-class manners. In theory, it regulated a man's education, actions in war, and behavior toward the church, his lord, his equals, and women.

commune/city-state – a municipal corporation; especially in Italy, an autonomous administrative district consisting of a city and its surrounding territory.

convent – *See* **monastery**.

courtly love/literature – poetic theme emphasizing the beauty, wisdom, and virtue of highborn ladies; usually incorporated poet's love and admiration for a specific noblewoman, often his patroness.

demesne – manor land set aside for the lord's use and worked for his benefit; that portion of a lord's lands not held by any tenants.

dowry/dower – In Roman areas the *dos* was the bride's dowry, but in early Germanic regions it was the gift from the groom to his bride—or her family. In either case, throughout much of Europe, the presence of a *dos* or dowry remained the most important factor in sealing a legitimate marriage. The dower (often known as *dos* in England) was the part of the husband's property with which the bride was "endowed"; it was to provide her maintenance if she outlived her husband. After her death it reverted to his heirs; it also reverted in many regions if the widow remarried. Dowry (*Maritagium*) was property or money given by the bride's family for her marriage. It was used by the husband until his death, when it served as another part of the widow's maintenance. At her death it reverted either to her family heirs or to her children.

Divine Office – songs corresponding to Masses celebrated on feast days.

entry fine – fee paid by deceased tenant's heir to enter, or take over, work, and hold a plot of land.

Eucharist – sacrament commemorating and renewing Christ's sacrifice—the Host is Christ's body and the Eucharistic cup or chalice becomes filled with His blood; this service is called *Holy Communion*. (*Also see* **transubstantiation**.)

excommunication – papal/ecclesiastical punishment—the withholding of church membership, privileges, and sacraments from a person.

fealty – solemn oath proclaiming allegiance and fidelity to one's lord; the obligation to defend, remain loyal to, and provide armed service for one's lord.

First, Second, and **Third Orders** – put briefly, the First Order is that of priests; the Second Order consists of nuns and religious brothers; and the Third Order is for lay people who continue to live in secular society but who are directed by (and affiliated with) a religious establishment, usually a monastic order.

friars – mendicants; non-cloistered men who have taken religious vows.

guild – association of people engaged in the same craft or pursuit; in the Middle Ages there were separate guilds for various merchants, craftsmen, town governors, doctors, etc.

hagiography – stories or biographies (often semi-legendary) of saints.

Hanseatic League – coalition of northern German towns, including Cologne, Lubeck, and Breslau, which essentially controlled trading in northern seas.

high justice – *See* **low justice**.

Holy Roman Empire – theoretically the Christian version of the fallen Roman Empire. An attempt by many of Charlemagne's successors to recreate his great empire; it began in 961 with Otto I *the Great*. The medieval Holy Roman Empire most often consisted of a loose amalgamation of German and Italian territories under an emperor, usually a German king, who was crowned "emperor" by the pope. Called "Roman Empire" by Conrad II in 1034, Frederick I named it the "Holy Empire" in 1157 to stress the quasi-divine nature of imperial power. The term "Holy Roman Emperor" was first applied in 1254, and the conception of such an empire lasted until the nineteenth century.

homage – act by which one acknowledged the suzerainty of one's lord, and became his *vassal*. This formal, ritual act was usually accomplished during a ceremony that, after the ninth century, included the oath of *fealty* (a reinforcement of homage). The ritual act of homage was carried out by kneeling before one's lord, placing one's hands between his, and swearing a solemn oath to be his loyal man henceforth.

hue and cry – method of alerting neighbors to crimes that had been committed or those in progress; a legal responsibility of all to raise a loud cry upon discovering a crime.

Hundred Years War – series of wars, battles, skirmishes, and sieges between England and France that actually lasted from 1337 until 1453; started when Edward III of England challenged the right of Philip IV to the French throne (Philip inherited from his uncle Charles II, who was also Edward's uncle) and Philip retaliated by declaring all English lands in France forfeited. Though several wars and treaties came close to securing the French throne for an English monarch, Charles VII finally pushed the English out and retained the throne—partly thanks to Joan of Arc's help.

interdict – papal/ecclesiastical punishment of withholding sacraments and Christian burial within the district under an interdict.

knight – mounted, armed soldier in feudal lord's army; noble boy served first as page, then squire, then ceremonially inducted into this military rank/honor at around age 18.

Liber de diversis medicinis – fourteenth-century English medical manual.

London Eyre – records of London sittings of this periodic court of itinerant justices.

low justice – the ability of manor courts to hear only small cases—misdemeanors, etc.—in contrast to manors that had the rights of *high justice*, allowing those courts to hear even felony cases and to have, and use, gallows.

magnates – greatest ranking nobles; wealthiest holders of most land.

manor – lord's estate including rights of holding and granting land, holding court, and certain rights over the landed tenants.

marginalia – illustrations or illuminations in the borders of books.

Ménagier de Paris – title, as well as the name of the main character/narrator, of a book of practical instruction written by a wealthy Parisian merchant for his much younger bride.

misteries (mysteries) – guilds of those people who had attained mastery level skills at a craft. Although any trade or craft was a mistery, the greatest were occupations like goldsmith or butcher.

monastery – convent; dwelling of monks or nuns living a common life; in the West it usually refers to those communities living under the

Benedictine rule. Sometimes the term "convent" is used to denote a community of nuns or monks while "monastery" refers to the physical structures or buildings in which the community lives.

mulieres sanctae – pious women who lived non-conformist religious lives, particularly during the twelfth century.

reclusorium – cell for an anchorite, anchoress, or recluse.

regrating – buying a finished product and reselling it.

rule (living under a rule) – guidelines for a religious life set up by the order's founder; generally specifies certain offices at various times of day, vows to be taken, work to be done, rule of silence, rule of communal property, etc.

scriptorium – monastery building or section where copying was done, and where manuscripts were produced in many houses.

Second Order – *See* **First**, **Second**, and **Third Orders**.

serfs – *See* **villein**.

stigmata – wounds received by Christ dying on cross.

tertiary – member of a monastic Third Order. (*Also see* **First**, **Second**, and **Third Orders**).

transubstantiation – idea/doctrine that the bread and wine are substantially changed into the body and blood of Christ during the Holy Eucharist was first used in an offical church document in 1079 and appeared frequently thereafter. Aquinas used the word *transubstantiation* to mean the whole substance of one changed to the whole substance of the other.

usury – charging interest on money loaned out.

villein – unfree English villager; had legal rights in relation to peers; bondsman/woman—he/she was bound to the lord and the land. On the European continent, unfree peasants had slightly fewer rights, and were known as *serfs*. (*See* Appendix I.)

virgines continentes – *See* ***mulieres sanctae***.

vita – a "life"; biography of saintly person.

Wars of the Roses – series of skirmishes in England (c.1455–1485), largely between nobles and their retinues; fighting between Yorkist party (for King Edward IV) and Lancastrian party (for King Henry VI).

wills – documents bequeathing real property and estates, as opposed to *chattels*, small personal items, which were disposed of in *testaments*. Women could sometimes make testaments but not wills.

NOTES AND CITATIONS

To conserve space, we have put some citations together and given only abbreviated titles here—full source information is listed alphabetically in the bibliography. For more sources, especially on the women mentioned throughout the text, see Echols and Williams, *An Annotated Index of Medieval Women.*

For example: see #2 below where both Peire Vidal and Bertran de Born are cited under the same number, though each has separate page numbers listed. To find complete source information for these two poets, look under Bonner in the bibliography and find: Bonner, Anthony (ed.). *Songs of the Troubadours* (1972).

Chapter One — Literary Theories

1 Ferrante, *Women as Image...*, p. 92.

2 Bonner (ed.), *Songs...*: Peire, p. 169; Bertran, p. 142.

3 Lind (ed.), *Lyric...*: Dante, p. 127; Petrarch, p. 191.

4 DuVal (trans.), *Cuckolds...*, pp. 1, 8, 9.

5 *Fifteen Joys of Marriage* quoted from *Oxford...Prose,* pp. 373 & 378.

6 Ariosto quoted from Lind (ed.), *Lyric...*, p. 263.

7 De Meung quoted from Luria, *A Reader's...*, p. 53.

8 Dunbar cited from Gies, *Women...*, p. 38. Chaucer cited from Baugh (ed.), *Chaucer's...*, p. 391, line 590.

9 Marbode: Gies, *Women...*, p. 38. Albertus Magnus: Ranke-Heinemann, *Eunuchs...*, p. 157.

10 Ferrante, *Women as Image…*, pp. 21 & 30.
11 Tertullian: O'Faolain, *Not in…*, p. 132.
12 Lucas, *Women…*: Gratian, p. 6; Alan, p. 8; Adam, p. 10. Aquinas quoted from Aquinas, *Summa Theologica*, p. 466.
13 For Thomas of Chobham see Braswell, "Sin…," pp. 81–100, and Farmer, "Persuasive…," pp. 517 & 522.
14 St. Bernardino cited from Origo, *World…*, p. 58.
15 Quoted from Anderson and Zinsser, *A History…*, p. 307. For more about Beatrice de Dia, also see Morrall, *Medieval Imprint…*, p. 109; Thompson, *Literacy…*, pp. 138–139; and Thièbaux, *Writings…*, p. xi.
16 Willard, "A Fifteenth…," p. 116.
17 Fox, *A Literary…*, p. 273.
18 Pisan, *The Book…*, pp. 206 & 86–87.
19 Willard, "The Franco-Italian…," p. 343.
20 Pisan, *The Book…*, pp. 4–5 & 256.
21 Ibid., pp. 34 & 212.
22 Hadewijch quoted from Bynum, *Holy Feast…*, p. 241.
23 Gertrude: *Exercises…*, p. 24. Mechtild: Howard, "The German Mystic…," pp. 181–182.
24 *Julian of Norwich: Showings*, Long Text, pp. 293 & 325.
25 Blumenfeld-Kosinski, "Christine…," p. 289.
26 Willard, "Franco-Italian…," p. 355.

Chapter Two — Homes, Food, Clothes

1 St. Bernardino cited from Ennen, *Medieval…*, pp. 233–234.
2 Aquinas cited from Bishop, *Middle…*, p. 236.
3 Elizabeth: McFarlane, *Nobility…*, p. 110.
4 Eleanor: Labarge, *Baronial…*, p. 51, and Labarge, *Simon…*, p. 100.
5 *Household...Dame Alice*, pp. 119–121 & 124.
6 Eleanor's servants: Anderson and Zinsser, *A History…*, pp. 131 & 132.
7 Elizabeth's ladies: Scofield, *The Life…*, I, p. 377.
8 Maud: Hardy, *Philippa…*, pp. 66, 87, 128. Jane: Griffiths and Thomas, *Making…*, pp. 175 & 195.
9 Sweet woodruff: Freeman, *Herbs…*, p. 43.
10 Richard II's bed: Leach, *Soup Stone…*, p. 40.
11 Lord Neville's will: Rosenthal, *Nobles…*, pp. 184–185.

12 *Cawdelle de almaunde* recipe from *Two Fifteenth...*, p. 16.

13 For recipes, see *Horizon Cookbook...*, pp. 585, 660, 548, & 532, respectively. For other examples and more information on foods, see Sass, *To the King's...*; Wason, *Cooks...*; and Hieatt and Butler, *Pleyn Delit....*

14 Pies: *Horizon Cookbook...*, p. 90. A recipe for cooked blackbird pie can be found in Cosman, *Fabulous Feasts...*, p. 204. But "pies" as entertainments were obviously not cooked with the animals inside. Sass, *To the King's...*, p. 54, advises using a false crust baked on top of an empty pie shell. The live birds or other animals are then inserted just before the pie is brought to the table.

15 Pope Clement VI: Burnham, "Patronage...," p. 375.

16 *Household...Dame Alice*, Aug. 17, 1413.

17 Opals: Kunz, *Curious...*, p. 148. freckles: *Liber de diversis...*, p. 22. herbs: Duby, *Private Life...*, II, p. 361.

18 Contini, *Fashion...*, p. 71.

19 Hartley, *Costume...*, p. 96.

20 Castle of Vincennes: Harksen, *Women...*, p. 21.

21 For many details on clothing, see Brooke, *Early...* and *Later....*

22 Labarge, *Baronial...*, p. 132–137.

23 Lester and Oerke, *Accessories...*, pp. 354–355. Also see: for royal and clerical gloves, Sherman, "The Queen...," p. 262; for symbolism of gloves, Leach, *Soup Stone...*, p. 93.

24 Sacchetti, "Fashions...," pp. 167–169.

25 Braswell, "Sin...," pp. 86–87, and Chaucer, *Tales...*, pp. 512–513, lines 415–430.

26 Nicolosa: Hughes, "Invisible...," p. 26.

27 O'Faolain, *Not in...*, p. 169.

28 Erembourc: Géraud, *Paris sous...*, p. 72. fees: Power, "Position...," p. 425.

29 Servant's duties: Anderson and Zinsser, *A History...*, p. 358.

30 Clemence: *Fifty Earliest...*, p. 97. Agnes: *Calendar of Wills...*, I, p. 252.

31 Paris, *Chronicles...*, p. 54.

32 Lubeck: Ennen, *Medieval...*, p. 170.

33 Isabel Gregory: *Fifty Earliest...*, p. 91.

34 Joan: Kendall, *Yorkist...*, pp. 337 & 342. Perrette: Contamine, "*Peasant...*," p. 494. Home improvements: Roncière, "Tuscan...," p. 192.

35 For city food, see Harksen, *Women...*, p. 17; Wason, *Cooks...*, p. 111; and *Horizon Cookbook...*; the recipe for *brawn* is on page 84.

36 Margherita: Anderson and Zinsser, *A History…*, p. 374. Regensburg will: Ennen, *Medieval…*, pp. 217 & 220.

37 Germany: Ennen, *Medieval…*, pp. 217 & 220. aprons: Hartley, *Medieval…*, pp. 59 & 69. symbolism: Thrupp, *Merchant…*, p. 147.

38 English sumptuary laws: Brooke, *Later…*, and Holmes, *Later…*, especially p. 19.

39 Labarge, *Baronial…*, p. 146.

40 Quoted from Ennen, *Medieval…*, pp. 220–221.

41 Nannina's trousseau: Anderson and Zinsser, *A History…*, p. 399.

42 English odd jobs: Boulding, *Underside…*, pp. 468 & 484. Katherine Rolf: Anderson and Zinsser, *A History…*, p. 130.

43 Britton, *Community…*: Emma, pp. 26, 31, 217; Joan, pp. 26, 203, 251.

44 Fossier, *Peasant…*, pp. 48–9 & 70. Also see Clarke, *Archaeology….*

45 Peasant homes: Davis, *Life…*, pp. 262–263.

46 Technological advances: Dresbeck, "*Techne…*," p. 111.

47 Tuscan homes: Roncière, "Tuscan Notables…," p. 170.

48 Ladurie, *Montaillou…*, pp. 4, 8, & 9.

49 For more about peasant foods, see Bishop, *Middle…*, pp. 242–243, and Tannahill, *Food…*, pp. 218–226.

Chapter Three — Medicine

1 Women's deaths culled from *London...1276*: Lettice, p. 10; Juliana, p. 42; Amice, p. 14; Beatrice, p. 19; Agnes, p. 7; Isabel Paternoster, p. 58; Isabel Scrul, p. 59; Edith, p. 35.

2 Boccaccio quoted from Hollister et al., *Medieval…*, p. 231.

3 Matilda: Boase, "Mortality…," p. 244.

4 Circulatory system: Mason, *Main…*, p. 87.

5 Vade mecum: Riddle, "Theory…," pp. 178–179. Consilia: Crombie, *Medieval…*, p. 226.

6 *Liber de diversis…*, p. 50.

7 Herbs listed in Hughes, *Women Healers…*, pp. 148–154 passim.

8 Elizabeth: Hurd-Mead, *A History…*, p. 273.

9 Medicinal uses of gems cited from Kunz, *Curious…*: diamonds, p. 70; agates, pp. 51–52; jacinth, pp. 81–82; topaz, p. 389.

10 Bullough, "Medieval Medical…," pp. 487–493 passim. For the *Malleus*, see Hanawalt, "Female Felon…," pp. 256–257.

11 Hildegarde's perception of the womb cited from Wood, "Doctors'...," p. 717 n18.

12 Handicapped baby: Ranke-Heinemann, *Eunuchs...*, p. 12.

13 Isidore: Anderson and Zinsser, *A History...*, p. 80. Florence: Trexler, "Measures...," p. 455. Beatrice: Ladurie, *Montaillou...*, p. 32.

14 Colette: Bynum, *Holy Feast...*, p. 138.

15 Trotula: O'Faolain, *Not in...*, pp. 142–143. Pomade: Braunstein, "Toward...," p. 599.

16 Aquinas, *Summa Theologica*, p. 466.

17 *Liber de diversis...*, p. 56.

18 Bullough, "Medieval Medical...," pp. 493–494.

19 Trotula: Ibid., p. 495.

20 Insanity and therapies: Neaman, *Suggestion...*, especially pp. 22, 25–26, & 133.

21 Hostiensis: Brundage, "Prostitution...," p. 87. For more about female life spans, see Herlihy, "Life...," p. 11.

22 For contraception and abortion, see Lucas, *Women...*, p. 110; Noonan, *Contraception...*, p. 211; Shahar, *Fourth...*, pp. 119–124; and Anderson and Zinsser, *A History...*, p. 137.

23 Marguerite: Valous, *Le Patriciat...*, pp. 87–88.

24 *Liber de diversis...*, p. 39. For more about leprosaries, see Gwin, "Life...," pp. 225, 229, 231.

25 Crombie, *Medieval Science...*, pp. 236, 254, 274.

26 Bertrande: Hughes, *Women Healers...*, p. 142.

27 Crombie, *Medieval Science...*: opthalmology, p. 230; dentistry, p. 234; anesthesia, p. 225; surgery, p. 233.

28 Thomasia and Maria: Lipinska, *Histoire...*, p. 148.

29 Leonard: Hurd-Mead, *History...*, p. 307.

30 King Edward's barber: Kendall, *Yorkist...*, p. 182.

31 For barbering guilds: Bullough, "Development...," pp. 38–39.

32 Ibid., p. 39.

33 Anne's purchases from Valous, *Le Patriciat...*, p. 194.

34 Owen, "White Annays...," p. 339.

35 Catherine and Agnes: Anderson and Zinsser, *A History...*, p. 420.

36 Quoted from Hurd-Mead, *History...*, p. 148.

37 Isabelle: *Fifty Earliest...*, p. 118.

38 Lemay, "Anthonius Guainerius...," p. 327.

39 Stephanie is cited from Hughes, *Women Healers...*, p. 141.

40 Antoinette and Jeannette: Ibid., p. 145.

Chapter Four — Women at Work

1 Frankfurt: Ennen, *Medieval…*, p. 206. Goda: *London…1244*, pp. 126–127. Jewish women: Jordan, "Jews…," p. 51.

2 Alice: *Calendar of Plea…*, II, p. 114. Mabilia: Anderson and Zinsser, *A History…*, p. 427; and Uitz, *Legend…*, pp. 24–25.

3 Joanna: Power and Postan, *Studies…*, p. 242. Margery: Power, "Position…," p. 427.

4 Cologne: Uitz, *Legend…*, p. 98. Frankfurt: Boulding, *Underside…*, p. 493.

5 Guillemette: O'Faolain, *Not in…*, pp. 158–159.

6 London saddlers: *Calendar of Letter…*, L, p. 275.

7 O'Faolain, *Not in…*, p. 156.

8 Harksen, *Women…*, p. 24.

9 Kendall, *Yorkist…*, p. 340; and Thrupp, *Merchant…*, p. 139 n116.

10 Frankfurt: Ennen, *Medieval…*, p. 206.

11 Mariotta: Lacey, "Women and…," pp. 52–53. Agnes: *Calendar of Letter…*, L, p. 1. Petronilla: Hutton, "Women…," p. 93.

12 Agnes: *Calendar of Plea…*, I, p. 213. Mariot: Abram, "Women…," pp. 276–277. Karyssa: Uitz, *Legend…*, p. 39.

13 Emma cited from *Calendar of Plea…*, II, pp. 128 & 158–159.

14 Salzman, *Industries…*, p. 55.

15 Géraud, *Paris sous…*: Anès, p. 43; Juliane, p. 52; Pérronnele, p. 59; Edeline, p. 38.

16 Marote: Lehmann, *Le Rôle…*, p. 435. Jehanne: *Comptes du…*, pp. 21, 26, 62, …, 178.

17 Asceline: Géraud, *Paris sous…*, p. 165.

18 Colette: Hughes, "The Library…," p. 167.

19 Maroie: Bell, "Medieval…," p. 154. Alice: Lacey, "Women and…," p. 52.

20 Marguerite: Géraud, *Paris sous…*, p. 160. Elisabeth: Greer, *Obstacle…*, p. 164; and Uitz, *Legend…*, p. 100.

21 San Giacomo: Greer, *Obstacle…*, p. 161.

22 Harksen, *Women…*, p. 47.

23 Géraud, *Paris sous…*: Hodierne, p. 37; Lorence, p. 39. Anees: Nicholas, *Domestic Life…*, p. 101.

24 Alice: Hutton, "Women…," p. 91. Antonia: Anderson and Zinsser, *A History…*, p. 409.

25 Isabella: Hutton, "Women…," p. 92.

26 Géraud, *Paris sous…*: Aaliz, p. 25; Maheut, p. 88; Marguerite, p. 21. Margaret Croke: Lacey, "Women…," p. 54.

27 Agnes and Margaret: Lacey, "Women…," p. 53.

28 Géraud, *Paris sous…*: Ameline, p. 10; Pérronnele, p. 52; Susane, p. 13. Guiote: Favier, *Les Contribuables…*, p. 137.

29 Maheut: Géraud, *Paris sous…*, p. 56. Genoa: Bonds, "Genoese…," p. 80.

30 Géraud, *Paris sous…*: Pérronnele, p. 80; Ameline, p. 59.

31 Tryngen: Wensky, "Women's…," pp. 642–645.

32 Elizabeth: Kendall, *Yorkist…*, p. 405; and Thrupp, *Merchant…*, pp. 170 & 368. Isabel: Dale, "London…," p. 329.

33 Coventry: Hilton, "Women…," p. 150. *Calendar of Plea…*, II: Emma, pp. 145–6; Agnes, p. 252; Juliana, p. 139. *Calendar of Letter…*, L: Agnes Deyntee, p. 141.

34 Géraud, *Paris sous…*: Berte, p. 97; Félise, p. 162; Emeline, p. 148; Edelot, p. 7; Phelipote, p. 43; Pérronnele & Florie, p. 5; Pentecouste, p. 77; Mabile, p. 5; Béatriz, p. 162.

35 Emma: *London...Nuisance*, p. 142.

36 Ross, "The Assize…," pp. 333–336.

37 Géraud, *Paris sous…*: Sédile, p. 53; Thomasse, p. 109; Jehanne, p. 28.

38 Coventry and Kings Lynn: Hilton, "Women…," p. 148. Géraud, *Paris sous…*: Pérronnele, p. 26; Anès, p. 61. Roysia and shop: *Calendar of Letter…*, L, pp. 175 & 232. London brewersin 1420: Thrupp, *Merchant…*, p. 42.

39 Joan: McCall, *Underworld…*, p. 153.

40 Traveler's records cited from: Jusserand, *English…*, pp. 125–126.

41 Dorothea: Uitz, *Legend…*, pp. 65–66. Isabella: *Calendar of Plea…*, I, p. 233. Quintine: Nicholas, *Domestic…*, p. 87. Géraud, *Paris sous…*: Denyse, p. 24; Ysabel, p. 147; Dame de Viane, p. 87.

Chapter Five — Personal Relationships

1 Caterina: Chamberlin, *World…*, p. 46. Contessina: Maguire, *Women…*, p. 25.

2 Mary: Jenkinson, "Mary…," p. 411. Anne: *Anglo-Norman…*, p. 91 (#43).

3 Kraft, "The German…," p. 111.

4 Power, *Medieval People*. Her translation is from *Le Ménagier de Paris, Traité de Morale et d'Economie Domestique composé vers 1393 par un Bourgeois Parisien* (1846), 2 vols., ed. and intro. by Jerome Pichon, v. 1, pp. 13–15.

5 Letter from Maguire, *Women...*, p. 43.

6 Isabel's will from *Fifty Earliest...*, p. 103.

7 St. Dominic: Fossier, *Peasant...*, p. 32.

8 Alessandra: Roncière, "Tuscan Notables...," p. 245.

9 Childlove and Lucas: Warren, *Anchorites...*, p. 257.

10 Uitz, *Legand*, p. 11.

11 Matthew Paris quoted from Hallam (ed.), *Four...*, p. 78.

12 Dati's ledger cited from O'Faolain, *Not in...*, p. 170.

13 Agnes Cook's dowry from *Calendar of Wills...*, I, p. 243.

14 Bennett, *Women in...*, p. 91.

15 Avis: Homans, *English...*, pp. 140–141.

16 For more about Alice's abduction, see *Calendar of Plea...*, I, pp. 205–206.

17 Christine: Willard, "A Fifteenth-century...," p. 108.

18 Mother's letter cited from Lungo, *Women...*, pp. 102–110.

19 O'Faolain, *Not in...*, pp. 168–169.

20 Tuchman, *A Distant...*, pp. 442–443. Presumably for the benefit of his much younger wife, De Coucy added a whole new wing including two huge halls, a lady's boudoir, and a water tank. Chimneys and windows were also added or enlarged in the castle.

21 Margery: *Cely Letters...*, #222.

22 Dorothy: Bynum, *Holy Feast...*, p. 136.

23 December/May marriages in towns: Uitz, *Legend...*, p. 171. Elizabeth and John Bridge: Kendall, *Yorkist...*, p. 365.

24 Marjorie and Robert Bruce: Duncan, *Scotland...*, pp. 400 & 585.

25 Florentine widows: Klapisch-Zuber, "The `Cruel Mother'...," pp. 128–131.

26 A variety of sources and studies about children, abandonment, and infanticide are becoming available, including: Trexler, "Infanticide...," pp. 98–116; Boswell, *The Kindness...*; Kellum, "Infanticide...," pp. 367–388; Hanawalt sees little evidence of infanticide in later medieval England, see *The Ties...*, and "Childrearing...," pp. 1–22.

27 Jeanne: Commynes, *Memoirs...*, p. 380.

28 Fossier, *Peasant...*, p. 10.

29 Accidental deaths among young children, see Hanawalt, "Childrearing...," pp. 16–17, and *The Ties...*, especially pp. 177–184.

30 Pastons: Barron, "Lords...," pp. 203–204.

31 Hanawalt, *The Ties...*, pp. 177, 183, 185.

32 Yolande quoted from Coryn, *House...*, p. 197. For more about placing out noble children, see Boswell, *Kindness...*, pp. 358–360.

33 Dwarf trade: Jacob, *Cures...*, p. 84.

34 Herlihy, "Children...," p. 120.

35 Bernard: Sommerville, *Rise...*, pp. 67–68. For these and other religious women, see Herlihy, "Children...," p. 129, and *Households...*, p. 120; also Bynum, *Holy Feast...*, p. 63, and *Jesus as...*, p. 112.

36 Rose: Valous, *Le Patriciat...*, p. 88; Frankfurt: Ennen, *Medieval...*, p. 206; Rome and Paris: Herlihy, "Children...," pp. 122–123; Florence: Trexler, "Infanticide...," pp. 98–116.

37 Vincent: Anderson and Zinsser, *A History...*, p. 346. Dante quoted from Herlihy, "Life Expectancies...," p. 12.

38 "Natural" mothers cited from Owen, "White Annays...," pp. 338–339.

39 Bianca is quoted from Maguire, *Women...*, p. 117.

40 Sermons: Thrupp, *Merchant...*, p. 200.

Chapter Six — Sexual Mores and Behavior

1 Quoted from Payer, "Early...," pp. 363 & 370–371. For more about penitentials, also see Flandrin, "Contraception...," pp. 23–47; Tannahill, *Sex...*, pp. 146 & 161; Brundage, *Law...*, especially p. 162 (chart).

2 Degrees of lechery: Braswell, *Sinner...*, pp. 43–48.

3 Schimmelpfennig, "*Ex Fornicatione...*," p. 32.

4 Vicar: Ewen, *Witchcraft...*, pp. 65–66. Dijon statistics: Rossiaud, *Prostitution...*, p. 41.

5 Nachine: Johnson, *Borgias...*, p. 65. Guilia: Chamberlin, *Fall...*, p. 100.

6 Aquinas: Boswell, *Christianity...*, pp. 326–328. For more about medieval attitudes: Richards, *Sex...*, especially p. 141.

7 Pope Gregory IX quoted from Boswell, *Christianity...*, pp. 294–295.

8 Rossiaud, *Prostitution...*, pp. 88–92.

9 Matthew Paris: Hallam (ed.), *Four...*, p. 64.

10 This girl cited from Crompton, "The Myth...," pp. 13–17; he believes the death penalty was not so rare. For clerical views, see

Brundage, *Law...*, pp. 167, 213, & 400. Also see Monter, "Sodomy...," pp. 41–53; and Goodich, *Unmentionable....*

11 Poem quoted from Southern, *The Making...*, p. 24.

12 Cleric quoted from Robinson, *Readings...*, I, p. 383.

13 Philip *the Good*: Cartellieri, *Court...*, p. 252.

14 Colette: Champion, *François...*, v.2, p. 304.

15 Villages cited from Hogan, "Medieval Villany...," p. 165. Infanticide: Shahar, *Fourth...*, p. 120.

16 Eleanora: Brundage, *Law...*, p. 519. Roger: Hallam (ed.), *Four...*, p. 56.

17 Elizabeth's hasty wedding: Armitage-Smith, *John...*, pp. 310 & 460.

18 Francesca's lament: Phillips (trans.), *Dante's...*, pp. 46–47.

19 Dijon cited from Rossiaud, *Prostitution...*, p. 10 n13. Numbers of prostitutes in other cities listed in Tannahill, *Sex...*, pp. 279–280.

20 Fulk: Otis, *Prostitution...*, p. 72.

21 Repentant Sisters of St. Catherine: Otis, *Prostitution...*, p. 74.

22 Rape laws and prostitutes: Brundage, *Law...*, p. 466.

23 Benefits of prostitution: Rossiaud, *Prostitution...*, p. 43.

24 Brundage, *Law...*, p. 463.

25 Queen Margaret: Champion, *François...*, p. 90.

26 English chronicler quoted from Hallam (ed.), *Four...*, p. 264. For more about prostitutes' clothing, see Bullough, *Prostitution...*, p. 122.

27 Dijon, Lyons, and Avignon: Rossiaud, *Prostitution...*, p. 65.

28 Dulcia: *London...1276*, p. 49. Jehannetta: Favier, *Les Contribuables...*, p. 142.

29 London council: *Calendar of Letter...*, L, p. 206.

30 Joan: *Calendar of Plea...*, II, p. 7.

31 *London...1276*: Richolda, p. 63; Beatrice, p. 37.

32 Brothel farms: Otis, *Prostitution...*, pp. 55–61 passim.

33 Gabrieli, *Arab...*, pp. 205–207.

34 Alison: O'Faolain, *Not in...*, p. 159.

35 Jeanne and Casotte: Rossiaud, *Prostitution...*, p. 45.

36 Marginalia depicting baths cited from Verdier, "Women...," p. 132.

37 Spanish miscreants: Dillard, *Daughters...*, p. 175. Valencienne: Kendall, *Yorkist...*, pp. 339–340.

38 Prostitutes' wages: Rossiaud, *Prostitution...*, pp. 34–35.

39 Prague: Klassen, The *Nobility...*, p. 20.

40 Simone: Rossiaud, *Prostitution...*, p. 34 n15.

Chapter Seven — Women in Church

1 Noble households: Mertes, *English…*, p. 148.
2 London: Gray, *A History…*, p. 90.
3 Bynum, *Holy Feast…*, pp. 123–124, 129, 139, & 228–233 passim.
4 Cecily's daily regimen cited from Rosenthal, *Nobles…*, p. 181.
5 Hens and pigs: Davis, *First…*, pp. 253–254.
6 French statistic: Schulenburg, "Sexism…," p. 130 n7.
7 Agnes: Johnson, *Prayer…*, pp. 11–12.
8 Spence, *Cathedrals…*, p. 161.
9 Katherine's will: *Calendar of Wills…*, I, p. 642.
10 Aleydis: Phillips, *Beguines…*, p. 137.
11 Elizabeth: Rosenthal, *Nobles…*, pp. 187–188. Isabelle: *Fifty Earliest…*, pp. 116–117.
12 Guyette: Valous, *Le Patriciat…*, p. 87. Alice: *Calendar of Wills…*, I, p. 175.
13 Holy Trinity fraternity: Thrupp, *Merchant…*, p. 36. Confraternity of Lyons: Valous, *Le Patriciat…*, p. 433.
14 Guyette: Valous, *Le Patriciat…*, p. 88. Nuremburg: Wiesner, *Working Women…*, p. 78. Joan: Johnstone, "Poor-Relief…," pp. 165–166.
15 Bolton, "*Vitae Matrum…*," p. 260.
16 Juliana: Goodich, "Contours…," p. 30.
17 Bertsenda: Vitalis, *Ecclesiastical…*, II, p. 161.
18 Holy Vernicle cited from Rowling, *Everyday…*, p. 104.
19 Statistics on pilgrims cited from Finucane, *Miracles…*, pp. 143 & 147.
20 Badges and women: Cohen, "Pilgrim…," p. 202.
21 Matilda's letter quoted from Thièbaux, *The Writings…*, p. 176.
22 Petrarch: Hollister et al., *Medieval…*, p. 225.
23 Bridget's vision: Heer, *Medieval…*, p. 278.
24 Eleanor: Paris, *Chronicles…*, p. 129.
25 Isabella: Jordan, *Louis…*, p. 68. Agnes: Tyerman, *England…*, p. 260.
26 Quoted from Paris, *Chronicles…*, p. 197.
27 Crusading women: Lehmann, *Le Rôle de la…*, pp. 374–381 passim.
28 Hildegarde and Mechtild: Boulding, *Underside…*, p. 424.
29 Margaret, Jeanne, and Isabel: Lehmann, *Le Rôle de la…*, p. 388.

30 Richilde: Harksen, *Women...*, p. 16.

31 Arabic accounts of Crusades: Gabrieli, *Arab...*, pp. 205–207.

Chapter Eight — Female Saints and Religious

1 For more about the significance of such eating habits, see Bynum, *Holy Feast...*, especially Chapter Six.

2 Heloise's letters have been edited and translated in *Letters of Abelard...*, see pages 112–116. Also see Radice, "The French...," pp. 101, 103, & 106. Some people believe Abelard, or some third party, actually wrote these letters, but most think the missives were composed by Heloise.

3 Convent at Coldstream: Warren, *Anchorites...*, pp. 83–84.

4 Cecilia: Brown, *Normans...*, p. 146. Peckham: Power, *Nunneries...*, p. 27.

5 Quoted from *Exercises...*, pp. 15, 16, 85, 137, 196, 197.

6 *Chansons de nonne* quoted from Daichman, *Wayward...*, pp. 71 & 74. Margaret cited from Power, *Nunneries...*, p. 36.

7 London merchants' daughters: Thrupp, *Merchant...*, p. 189. *Chansons de nonne*: Daichman, *Wayward...*, p. 98.

8 McLaughlin, "Women, Power...," p. 108.

9 This petition quoted from Warren, *Anchorites...*, pp. 115, 119, & 120.

10 *St. Catherine of Siena...*, p. 151.

11 Bennett et al. (ed.), *Sisters...*, p. 5.

12 *Revelations of Mechtild...*, pp. 11–12.

13 Beatrice quoted from Colledge, *Medieval Netherlands...*, p. 23.

14 Cluny: Schulenburg, "Sexism...," p. 124.

15 Premonstratensians: Eckenstein, *Woman under...*, p. 194.

16 Cistercian limits: Thompson, "The Problem...," p. 233. England: Graves, "*English...*," p. 499.

17 Quoted from Hallam (ed.), *Four...*, p. 64.

18 Amica: McDonnell, *Beguines...*, pp. 191–193, and Goodich, "Contours...," p. 27 (called Amica of Oigny here).

19 Warren, *Anchorites...*, pp. 19–21.

20 John Emlyn: *Calendar of Plea...*, VI, p. 135.

21 Essen: Kashnitz, "Gospel Book...," pp. 122–166.

22 Eckenstein, *Woman under...*, pp. 217–218.

23 Elkins, *Holy Women...*, p. 106.

24 St. Bernard quoted from Robbins, *Encyclopedia…*, p. 65.

25 Schulenburg, "Women's…," pp. 208–209.

26 Agnes: Power, *Nunneries…*, pp. 443–445, and Daichman, *Wayward…*, p. 12.

27 Archbishop of Rouen cited from Robinson, *Readings…*, I, pp. 378–379.

28 Lutgard's fasts cited from Bynum, *Holy Feast…*, p. 121.

29 Quoted from O'Faolain, *Not in…*, p. 140.

30 Information on these individualistic forms of religious expression can be found in many sources, including: McDonnell, *Beguines…*; Bolton, "*Vitae Matrum…*," and "*Mulieres Sanctae…*,"; Phillips, *Beguines…*; and Neel, "Origins…,".

Chapter Nine — Heretics

1 Church council cited from Anderson and Zinsser, *A History…*, p. 226.

2 Shahar, *Fourth…*, p. 257.

3 Sancia: Musto, "Queen Sancia…," pp. 179–214.

4 Shahar, *Fourth…*, p. 255.

5 Abels and Harrison, "Participation…," pp. 218–219. Also see Strayer, *Albigensian…*, especially p. 28.

6 Willelma: Abels and Harrison, "Participation…," pp. 238 & 250–251.

7 Eleanor's service: Heer, *Medieval…*, pp. 168 & 171.

8 For de Montfort's tactics, see Strayer, *Albigensian…*, pp. 71, 79–80.

9 Strayer, *Albigensian…*, pp. 36 & 155.

10 Quoted from Shahar, *Fourth…*, pp. 255–256.

11 Antinomianism, Adamites, and Luciferans: Russell, *Witchcraft…*, pp. 138 & 178–179.

12 Joan: Thrupp, *Merchant…*, p. 182. Other women from Cross, "Great...": Anna, p. 361 and Matilda, p. 360. Also see Warren, *Anchorites…*, Anna, p. 81 and Matilda, pp. 79–80 & 87.

13 Leff, *Heresy…*, II, p. 608.

14 Catherine: Klassen, The *Nobility…*, p. 87.

15 Barstow, *Joan…*, p. 86.

16 Hussite women: Harksen, *Women…*, p. 38; Leff, *Heresy…*, II, pp. 607–620; von Lutzow, *Hussite…*; and Klassen, *The Nobility….*

17 McDonnell, *Beguines…*, p. 385.

Chapter Ten — Superstitions and Witchcraft

1 Birds: Ladurie, *Montaillou…*, p. 42. Rubies: Kunz, *Curious…*, p. 103.

2 Dangers to sailors: Brundage, *Law…*, p. 467. *Malleus* cited from Wolf, *Bluebeard…*, p. 39.

3 For more about wild women, see Bernheimer, *Wild….*

4 Hartdyfa: Coulton, *Life…*, I, p. 72.

5 Coral: Jacob, *Cures…*, p. 70. Beatrice: Ladurie, *Montaillou…*, p. 32.

6 Tuscany ritual cited from Origo, "The Domestic Enemy…," p. 345.

7 Anna: Ennen, *Medieval…*, pp. 242–247.

8 Quoted from Klaits, *Servants…*, p. 36.

9 Bedford's report: Ewen, *Witchcraft…*, p. 36.

10 For Joan, see Pernoud, *Joan...* and *The Retrial…*; and Barstow, *Joan…*, especially p. 100 for links between superstition and witchcraft.

11 Quoted from Ennen, *Medieval…*, p. 251.

12 See Barstow, *Joan…*, p. 113 and Monter, "Pedestal…," pp. 133–134.

13 These four characteristics cited from Russell, *Witchcraft…*, p. 232.

14 Quoted from Richards, *Sex…*, p. 75.

15 This 1493 case from Kieckhefer, *European…*, pp. 134–135, 138, & 145.

16 Russell, *Witchcraft…*, pp. 42–43.

17 Else: Kieckhefer, *European…*, p. 129.

18 Langendorf in 1492: Ibid., p. 145.

19 For examples of this belief, see Kieckhefer, *European…*; Richards, *Sex…*; and Cohn, *Europe's….*

Chapter Eleven — Legal Systems

1 Felonious pig: Coulton, *Life…*, III, pp. 152–153.

2 Village customs: Olmert, "Points…," pp. 32 & 34.

3 Juetta: Bellamy, *Crime…*, p. 188.

4 *London...1276*: Emma, p. 33; Agnes, p. 12.

5 Levels of "honesty": Rossiaud, *Prostitution…*, p. 28. Different German legal codes cited from Vinogradoff, "Customary…," p. 291.

6 This case cited from Bennett, *Women in…*, p. 108.

7 Elizabeth's case: Post, "King's…," p. 161.

8 *Customs of Beauvais* cited from Shahar, *Fourth…*, pp. 89–92. Also see Beaumanoir, *Coutumes…*, I, p. 484, and II, p. 1054.

9 *Mundualdus*: Kuehn, "*Cum Consensu…*," p. 310. Sienese women: Riemer, "Women…," p. 68.

10 Florentine women: Kirshner, "Wives…," pp. 278–279 & 299.

11 Germany: Harksen, *Women…*, pp. 10–11; and Shahar, *Fourth…*, p. 14.

12 For Spanish practices, see O'Faolain, *Not in…*, pp. 150–151.

13 For England and this poetic comparison, see Ibid., p. 149.

14 Kittel, *Married…*, p. 124.

15 Christina Rudd cited from Bennett, *Life…*, p. 313.

16 Proof-of-age cases cited from Walker, "Proof…," pp. 307–312 passim. Olive's case can be found in *Calendar of Wills…*, I, pp. 63–64.

17 Callekin cited from Nicholas, *Domestic Life…*, p. 64.

18 Avice: *Calendar of Letter…*, A, p. 31. Clare: Anderson and Zinsser, *A History…*, p. 377. Checa: Kuehn, "*Cum Consensu…*," p. 322.

19 Idonea: *Calendar of Plea…*, I, p. 158. Isabella: *Calendar of Plea…*, II, p. 165.

20 Emma: *Calendar of Plea…*, II, pp. 90–91.

21 Alianore cited from *Calendar of Plea…*, I, p. 52.

22 Johanna: Bellamy, *Crime…*, p. 63.

23 Wenthiliana: *Select Cases...Edward I*, I, pp. 82–83. Cecilia: Bellamy, *Crime…*, p. 20.

24 Gang rapes cited from Rossiaud, *Prostitution…*, pp. 11–26 passim.

25 Rose: *Select Cases...Edward I*, I, pp. 101–102. Three London cases can be found in *London...1276*, on pages 21, 25, & 116.

26 Bennett, *Women in…*, pp. 26–27.

27 Warboys information culled from Hogan, "Medieval Villany…," pp. 159–161 & 210.

28 Alice: Homans, *English…*, p. 179.

29 Angareta: Ibid., pp. 224–227.

30 Jeanne: Belleval, *Les fiefs…*, pp. 82, 150, 161.

31 Borgine's case cited from Benton, "Philip…," pp. 312, 317, 325, & 328.

32 Lady Christine's case cited from Ibid., p. 323.

33 Hair, *Bawdy…*: Nicholas, p. 65 (#102); Isabella and Catherine, p. 177 (445).

34 Iceland: Frank, "Marriage…," p. 477.

35 Edmund's request cited from Rosenthal, *Nobles...*, pp. 173–174.
36 Catherine McKesky cited from Hair, *Bawdy...*, p. 153 (#373).
37 French court: O'Faolain, *Not in...*, p. 151.
38 Sheehan, "Influence...," pp. 110–111 & 116.
39 Hostiensis: Brundage, "Prostitution...," p. 86.
40 For conjugal debt, see Makowski, "Conjugal...," pp. 106–111, and Ranke-Heinemann, *Eunuchs...*, pp. 138–140. Margaret's complaint is cited from Hair, *Bawdy...*, p. 117 (#270).
41 Among the many available sources, one of the most detailed accounts of the trials themselves can be found in Pernoud, *Retrial...*.

Chapter Twelve — Feudal Landholders and Politicians

1 *Cambridge...*, II, pp. 639 & 654.
2 Statistic cited from Wood, *Age...*, p. 35.
3 Herlihy, *Women...*, p. 8.
4 Aelis: Belleval, *Les fiefs...*, p. 48.
5 Elizabeth: Fryde, *Tyranny...*, pp. 114–115, 230, 255.
6 Guidinild: Shahar, *Fourth...*, p. 149, and McLaughlin, "Woman...," p. 203.
7 McLaughlin, "Woman...," pp. 203–204.
8 Sophia and Agnes are cited from *Cambridge...*, V, p. 339.
9 Ennen, *Medieval...*, pp. 268–269.
10 McLaughlin, "Women...," p. 196.
11 Blanche: Robinson, *Readings...*, I, pp. 178–179, and Davis, *Life...*, p. 29.
12 Molecous: Searle, "Seigneurial...," p. 30.
13 Agnes: Ibid., pp. 21–22, 209, 245, & 247.
14 Juliana: Muir, *English...*, p. 68.
15 Alice: Muir, *English...*, p. 68. Agnes Chilyonge: O'Faolain, *Not in...*, p. 161. Agnes de Broughton: Britton, *Community...*, pp. 33, 72, 247.
16 Petronilla's sow and piglets cited from Johnson, *Prayer...*, p. 77.
17 Isabelle's letter quoted from Green, *Letters of Royal...*, I, pp. 29–30.
18 Joanna's letter quoted from Ibid., pp. 82–84. Alyne's petition cited from Warren, *Anchorites...*, p. 73.
19 Ava of Auvergne cited from Lewis, *Development...*, p. 275.

Chapter Thirteen — Consorts, Rulers, and Regents

1 Adelaide: Facinger, "Study…," pp. 27, 29, & 30.

2 Tamara: Vernadsky, *Kievan…*, pp. 357–360.

Chapter Fourteen — Games, Entertainment, Ceremonies

1 Elizabeth's bowling set cited from Kendall, *Yorkist…*, p. 179.

2 Chess in marginalia: Verdier, "Woman…," p. 139. Juliana: *London...1276*, p. 42. Caxton's book: Hindley, *England…*, p. 240.

3 Gamblers: Chaney, "A Glimpse of…," p. 356.

4 London hunters: Thrupp, *Merchant…*, pp. 145 & n136.

5 Hunting codes: Savage, "Hunting…," pp. 30–41.

6 John of Salisbury: Bedos Rezak, "Women…," p. 76.

7 Tournament themes: Cartellieri, *Court…*, pp. 123–124. For more about tournaments, see Barber and Barker, *Tournaments…*, pp. 121–125.

8 Chronicler cited from Coulton, *Life…*, II, pp. 93–94.

9 Ferrara: Barber and Barker, *Tournaments…*, p. 207.

10 Hartnoll, *Concise…*, pp. 47–48.

11 Margaret and Isabella: Lewis, *King Spider…*, pp. 179–180. Lucrezia's wedding festivities are cited from Fusero, *Borgias…*, p. 162.

12 Frankfurt female musicians cited from Ennen, *Medieval…*, p. 205. Mahaut's hirings are cited from Rokseth, "Les femmes…," p. 474.

13 Mechtild quoted from Howard, "The German Mystic…," p. 175.

14 Parisian minstrels: Anderson and Zinsser, *A History…*, p. 371. Feuds between entertainers: Boulding, *Underside…*, p. 495.

15 Christmas: Cosman, *Medieval Holidays…*: "humble pie," p. 100; Del Re, *Christmas…*: mistletoe, pp. 107–109; Yule log, p. 163; banquet, p. 19. For "Feasts of Fools," see Chambers, *Mediaeval…*, I, pp. 286–287, 294, & 361; also see Henshaw, "Attitude…," pp. 12–13 & 17.

16 Valentine's Day celebrations: Cosman, *Medieval Holidays…*, pp. 34–37.

17 Easter and Hocktide: Baskervill, "Dramatic…," p. 42, and Cosman, *Medieval Holidays…*, pp. 43 & 46.
18 Summer and fall: Cosman, *Medieval Holidays…*, pp. 59–62 & 87.
19 Edward III: Baskervill, "Dramatic…," p. 70. Duties of godparents: Bishop, *Middle…*, p. 120.
20 Sanchia's wedding cited from Labarge, *Simon…*, pp. 67–68.
21 Elizabeth's coronation: *Coronation…*, pp. 14–17.
22 Warren, *Anchorites…*, pp. 97–99.
23 Wakes and vigils: Baskervill, "Dramatic…," pp. 73–74.
24 Margaret's chantry: Anderson and Zinsser, *A History…*, p. 292.
25 Gaunt: Lewis, "Anniversary…," pp. 176–180.
26 Ellen quoted from Bynum, *Holy Feast…*, p. 215.

Chapter Fifteen — Learning and Literacy

1 Kamar quoted from Bendiner, *Rise…*, p. 139.
2 Bertrand: Jamison, *Life…*, p. 143. Virgil: St. Aubyn, *Year…*, p. 193.
3 Ennen, *Medieval…*, p. 191.
4 Machaut quoted from Duby, Private *Life…*, p. 378.
5 For more about silent reading, see Saenger, "Silent…," pp. 367–414.
6 Guibert quoted from Herlihy, "Children…," p. 122.
7 Margery: Orme, *English Schools…*, p. 192.
8 Gardiner, *English Girlhood…*, pp. 151–153.
9 Cracow: Shank, "Female…," pp. 373–380.
10 Heinrich, *Canonesses…*, p. 207.
11 Cecilia: Jourdain, "Memoire sur…," p. 483.
12 Manuscripts: Warren, *Anchorites…*, pp. 294–298.
13 Marguerite: Lejeune, "La femme dans…," p. 202.
14 Elizabeth: Gardiner, *English Girlhood…*, pp. 12 & 77.
15 London schoolmistresses: Orme, *English Schools…*, p. 55.
16 Twenty-one schoolmistresses: Decaux, *Histoire des…*, I, p. 355.
17 Florentine statistics: Herlihy, "Children…," p. 122. Clementia cited from Rashdall, *Universities…*, II, p. 47 n1.
18 Cologne: Ennen, *Medieval…*, p. 199. Brussels: Uitz, *Legend…*, p. 97. German female teachers: Wiesner, *Working Women…*, pp. 79–80.

19 *Sachenspiegel*: Harksen, *Women...*, p. 13.
20 Cecily's books cited from *Oxford...Prose*, p. 94.

Chapter Sixteen — Women Writers and Artists

1 Castelloza: Bogin, *Women...*, pp. 121, 127, & 129, and Dronke, "Provençal...," pp. 147 & 151.
2 Anonymous poet: Bogin, *Women...*, p. 147. Azalais: Bogin, *Women...*, p. 95, and Anderson and Zinsser, *A History...*, p. 309.
3 Snow, "Spanish...," p. 329.
4 This translation is a composite based on several editions of Dhouda's work, especially Dhuoda, *Le Manuel...* and Dhuoda, *Manuel...*
5 Sister Illuminato: Ragg, *Women...*, pp. 71, 112, 132, 144, 148, & 151.
6 Mechtild quoted from *Oxford...Prose*, pp. 101–102.
7 Marguerite: Muir, *Literature...*, pp. 160 & 171.
8 Gertrude: *Exercises...*, pp. 9, 14, 16, 36, 85, 100, & 136.
9 Margery quoted from Provost, "The English...," p. 306.
10 Comnena, *Alexiad*, pp. 511–512; also see Buckler, *Anna...*, pp. 117–119.
11 Jourdain, "Memoire sur...," pp. 482–483.
12 Jeanne: Heer, *Medieval...*, p. 121. Isabeau: Barber, *Guide...*, p. 233.
13 Marguerite: Dunlop, *Châteaux...*, pp. 25–29.
14 Sabina: Petersen and Wilson, *Women...*, p. 21.
15 Monks: Greer, *Obstacle...*, p. 162.
16 Ende: Petersen and Wilson, *Women...*, pp. 13–14.
17 Tomassina cited from Greer, *Obstacle...*, pp. 166–167.
18 Nuns of Nuremburg cited from Ibid., pp. 161–162.
19 Juttchen cited from Ennen, *Medieval...*, p. 205.
20 Parker and Pollack, *Old...*, p. 16.
21 Berthe: Jourdain, "Memoire sur...," p. 473.
22 Joanna: Carr, "Women...," p. 8.
23 Joanna: Zarnecki, "Contributions...," p. 79. Jehannette: Géraud, *Paris sous...*, p. 30.
24 Seams: Heinrich, *Canonesses...*, p. 185.
25 *Opus Anglicanum*: Parker and Pollack, *Old...*, pp. 16–17.
26 Decreasing feminine role: Ibid., p. 61.

Appendix I — Class Structure

1 Boswell, *The Kindness...*, p. 273.

Appendix II — Money

1 Miskimin, "Legacies...," pp. 223–224.
2 London wills: Thrupp, *Merchant...*, pp. 116 & 143.
3 Hallam (ed.), *Plantagenet Chronicles...*, p. 301.
4 Sir John's records cited from *Manners and Household...*, pp. 150 & 201.

Appendix III — Life Expectancy

1 Information on Carolingian and Merovingian women's mortality is cited from Herlihy, *Women in...*, p. 5.
2 Increases in female population cited from Ibid., p. 6.
3 Bologna and Nuremburg: Ibid.

SELECTED BIBLIOGRAPHY

For a more complete bibliography, see Echols and Williams, *An Annotated Index of Medieval Women.*

Abels, Richard, and Ellen Harrison. "The Participation of Women in Languedocian Catharism." *Mediaeval Studies* 41 (1979), 215–251.

Abram, A. *English Life and Manners in the Later Middle Ages.* New York, 1913.

_____. "Women Traders in Medieval London." *Economic Journal* (June 1916), 276–285.

Adamson, J. W. "Education." *The Legacy of the Middle Ages,* ed. by C. G. Crump and E. F. Jacob, 255–285. Oxford, 1962 (orig. pub. 1926).

Alexandre-Bidon, Daniele, and Monique Closson. *L'Enfant à l'ombre des cathédrales.* Lyon, 1985.

Anderson, Bonnie S., and Judith P. Zinsser. *A History of Their Own: Women in Europe from Prehistory to the Present,* vol. 1. New York, 1988.

Anglo-Norman Letters and Petitions, ed. by M. Dominica Legge. Oxford, 1941.

Aquinas, St. Thomas. *Summa Theologica.* Trans. by the Fathers of the English Dominican Province. Westminster, MD. Reprinted 1981.

_____. *Summa Theologiae,* ed. by August Borgnet. Paris, 1895.

Armitage-Smith, Sydney. *John of Gaunt.* London, 1964 (orig. ed. 1904).

Artur, Michel. "The Earliest Dance Manuals." *Medievalia et Humanistica* 3 (1945), 117–131.

Aston, Margaret. *The Fifteenth Century: The Prospect of Europe.* New York, 1968.

Atkinson, Clarissa W. *Mystic and Pilgrim: The Book and the World of Margery Kempe.* Ithaca and London, 1983.

_____. "Precious Balsam in a Fragile Glass: The Ideology of Virginity in the Later Middle Ages." *Journal of Family History* 8 (Summer 1983), 131–143.

Attwater, Donald. *A Dictionary of Saints*. New York, 1938.

Aubert, Marcel. "The Decorative and Industrial Arts." *The Legacy of the Middle Ages*, ed. by C. G. Crump and E. F. Jacob (1962), 123–145.

Ault, Warren O. "The Village Church and the Village Community in Medieval England." *Speculum* 45, #2 (April 1970), 197–215.

Ayerbe-Chaux, Reinaldo. "Las Memorias de Dona Leonor Lopez de Cordoba." *Journal of Hispanic Philology* 2, #1 (Autumn, 1977), 11–33.

Baker, Derek, ed. *Medieval Women*. Oxford, 1978.

_____. "A Nursery of Saints: St. Margaret of Scotland Reconsidered." *Medieval Women*, ed. by Derek Baker (1978), 119–142.

Baldwin, John W. *The Government of Philip Augustus: Foundations of French Royal Power in the Middle Ages*. Berkeley, Los Angeles, London, 1986.

Barber, Richard, and Juliet Barker. *Tournaments: Jousts, Chivalry, and Pageants in the Middle Ages*. New York, 1989.

Barber, Richard. *Penguin Guide to Medieval Europe*. New York, 1984.

Barlow, Frank. *Edward the Confessor*. Berkeley and Los Angeles, 1970.

Barraclough, Geoffrey. *The Origins of Modern Germany*. Oxford, 1966.

Barron, Caroline. "The Lords of the Manor." *The Making of Britain*, ed. by L. M. Smith (1985), 101–117.

Barstow, Anne L. *Joan of Arc: Heretic, Mystic, Shaman*. Lewiston, NY, 1986.

_____. *Married Priests and the Reforming Papacy: The Eleventh Century Debates*. New York and Toronto, 1982.

Barthélemy, Dominique. "Civilizing the Fortress: The Eleventh to Thirteenth Century." *A History of Private Life*, vol. 2, ed. by G. Duby (1988), 397–423.

_____. "Kinship." *A History of Private Life*, vol. 2, ed. by G. Duby (1988), 85–155.

Baskervill, Charles K. "Dramatic Aspects of Medieval Folk Festivals in England." *Studies in Philology* 17 (January 1920), 19–87.

Baskin, Judith R., ed. *Jewish Women in Historical Perspective*. Detroit, 1991.

_____. "Jewish Women in the Middle Ages." *Jewish Women in Historical Perspective*, ed. by Judith Baskin (1991), 94–114.

Bates, David. *Normandy Before 1066*. New York, 1982.

Baugh, Albert C., ed. *Chaucer's Major Poetry*. New York, 1963.

Bauml, Franz H. "Varieties and Consequences of Medieval Literacy and Illiteracy." *Speculum* 55, #2 (1980), 237–265.

Beaumanoir, Philippe de. *Coutumes de Beauvaisis*, 2 vol., ed. by A. Salmon. Paris, 1899–1974.

Becker, Marvin B. "Some Common Features of Italian Urban Experience (c. 1200–1500)." *Medievalia et Humanistica*, n.s., #1 (1970), 175–202.

Bedos Rezak, Brigitte. "Women, Seals and Power in Medieval France, 1150–1350." *Women and Power in the Middle Ages,* ed. by M. Erler and M. Kowaleski (1988), 61–82.

Bell, Susan Groag. "Medieval Women Book Owners: Arbiters of Lay Piety and Ambassadors of Culture." *Women and Power in the Middle Ages,* ed. by M. Erler and M. Kowaleski (1988), 149–187.

Bellamy, John. *Crime and Public Order in England in the Later Middle Ages.* London and Toronto, 1973.

Belleval, René de. *Les Fiefs et les seigneuries du Ponthieu et du Vimeu.* Paris and Brionne, 1975.

Bendiner, Elmer. *The Rise and Fall of Paradise.* New York, 1983.

Bennett, Henry S. *Life on the English Manor: A Study of Peasant Conditions, 1150–1400.* Cambridge, 1967.

_____. *The Pastons and Their England.* 2nd ed. Cambridge, England, 1932.

Bennett, Judith M. "Public Power and Authority in the Medieval English Countryside." *Women and Power in the Middle Ages,* ed. by M. Erler and M. Kowaleski (1988), 18–36.

_____, et al. *Sisters and Workers in the Middle Ages.* Chicago, 1989.

_____. "The Tie That Binds: Peasant Marriages and Families in Late Medieval England." *Journal of Interdisciplinary History* 15, #1 (Summer 1984), 111–129.

_____. *Women in the Medieval English Countryside.* New York and Oxford, 1987.

Benton, John F. "The Court of Champagne as a Literary Center." *Speculum* 36, #4 (1961), 551–591.

_____. "Philip the Fair and the Jour of Troyes." *Studies in Medieval and Renaissance History* 6 (1969), 279–344.

Bernardo, Aldo. "Petrarch's Laura: The Convolutions of a Humanistic Mind." *The Role of Women in the Middle Ages,* ed. by R. T. Morewedge (1975), 65–89.

Berners, Dame Juliana. *The Book of St. Albans.* First printed 1496. Facsimile reprint: New York, 1966.

Bernheimer, Richard. *Wild Men in the Middle Ages.* Cambridge, MA, 1952.

Berrigan, Joseph. "The Tuscan Visionary: Saint Catherine of Siena." *Medieval Women Writers,* ed. by K. Wilson (1984), 252–268.

Biller, P. P. A. "Birth Control in the West in the Thirteenth and Early Fourteenth Centuries." *Past and Present* 94 (1982), 3–26.

Bingham, Caroline. *The Crowned Lions: The Early Plantagenet Kings.* London, 1978.

Binns, A. L. "A Manuscript Source of the Book of St. Albans." *Bulletin of the John Rylands Library* 33, #1 (Sept. 1950), 15–24.

Bishop, Morris. *The Middle Ages*. New York, 1970.

Bisson, Thomas N. *The Medieval Crown of Aragon: A Short History*. Oxford, 1986.

Bloch, Marc. *Feudal Society*. Chicago, 1961.

Blumenfeld-Kosinski, Renate. "Christine de Pizan and the Misogynistic Tradition." *Romanic Review* 82, #3 (May 1990), 279–292.

Boase, T. S. R. "Mortality, Judgment, and Remembrance." *The Flowering of the Middle Ages*, ed. by Joan Evans (1976), 203–244.

Bogin, Meg. *The Women Troubadours*. New York, 1976.

Bolton, Brenda M. "Mulieres Sanctae." *Women in Medieval Society*, ed. by Susan Stuard (1976), 141–158.

_____. "Vitae Matrum: A Further Aspect of the Frauenfrage." *Medieval Women*, ed. by Derek Baker (1978), 253–273.

Bonds, William N. "Genoese Noblewomen and Gold Thread Manufacturing." *Medievalia et Humanistica* 17 (1966), 79–81.

Bonner, Anthony, trans. *The Complete Works of François Villon*. New York, 1960.

_____, ed. *Songs of the Troubadours*. New York, 1972.

Bornstein, Diane. "Military Manuals in Fifteenth Century England." *Mediaeval Studies* 37 (1975), 469–477.

Boswell, John. *Christianity, Social Tolerance and Homosexuality*. Chicago and London, 1980.

_____. *The Kindness of Strangers: The Abandonment of Children in Western Europe from Late Antiquity to the Renaissance*. New York, 1988.

Boulding, Elise. *The Underside of History: A View of Women Through Time*. Boulder, CO, 1976.

Bourchier, Sir John, trans. *The Chronicle of Froissart*. London, 1901–1903.

Bowden, Betsy. "The Art of Courtly Copulation." *Medievalia et Humanistica* n.s. #9 (1979), 67–85.

Boyd, Catherine E. *A Cistercian Nunnery in Medieval Italy*. Cambridge, MA, 1943.

Braddy, Haldeen. "Chaucer, Alice Perrers and Cecily Chaumpaigne." *Speculum* 52, #4 (October 1977), 906–911.

Bradley, Ritamary. "Julian of Norwich: Writer and Mystic." *An Introduction to the Medieval Mystics of Europe*, ed. by P. E. Szarmach. Albany, NY, 1984, 195–216.

Branner, Robert. "Manuscript-Makers in Mid-Thirteenth Century Paris." *Art Bulletin* XLVIII (1966), 65–67.

Braswell, Mary Flowers. *The Medieval Sinner: Characterization and Confession in the Literature of the English Middle Ages*. London and Toronto, 1983.

_____. "Sin, the Lady, and the Law: The English Noblewoman in the Late Middle Ages." *Medievalia et Humanistica* n.s. #14 (1986), 81–100.

Braunstein, Philippe. "Toward Intimacy: The Fourteenth and Fifteenth Centuries." *A History of Private Life*, vol. 2, ed. by G. Duby (1988), 535–630.

Bridenthal, Renate, and Claudia Koonz, eds. *Becoming Visible: Women in European History*. Boston, 1977.

Bridge, Antony. *The Crusades*. New York, 1982.

Brion, Marcel. *The Medici: A Great Florentine Family*. Trans. by Heather and Gilles Cremonesi. New York, 1969.

Britton, Edward. *The Community of the Vill*. Toronto, 1977.

Brooke, Rosalind B., and Christopher N. L. Brooke. "St. Clare." *Medieval Women*, ed. by Derek Baker (1978), 275–287.

Brooke, Christopher. *The Twelfth Century Renaissance*. New York, 1969.

Brooke, Iris. *English Costume of the Early Middle Ages*. London, 1956 (orig. pub. 1936).

_____. *English Costume of the Later Middle Ages*. London, 1956 (orig. pub. 1935).

Brown, Elizabeth A. R. "Eleanor of Aquitaine: Parent, Queen, and Duchess." *Eleanor of Aquitaine, Patron and Politician*, ed. by William W. Kibler (1976), 9–39.

Brown, R. Allen. *The Normans and the Norman Conquest*. New York, 1969.

Brucker, Gene A. *Renaissance Florence*. Berkeley and Los Angeles, 1983.

Brundage, James A. *Law, Sex and Christian Society in Medieval Europe*. Chicago, 1987.

_____. "Prostitution in Medieval Canon Law." *Sisters and Workers in the Middle Ages*, ed. by J.M. Bennett et al. (1989), 79–99.

Bryant, Arthur. *The Age of Chivalry*. Garden City, NY, 1963.

Bryant, Gwendolyn. "The French Heretic Beguine: Marguerite Porete." *Medieval Women Writers*, ed. by K. Wilson (1984), 204–226.

Bryce, James. *The Holy Roman Empire*. New York, 1961.

Buckler, Georgina. *Anna Comnena: A Study*. London, 1968.

Bullough, Vern L. "The Development of the Medical Guilds at Paris." *Medievalia et Humanistica* 12 (1958), 33–40.

_____, and Cameron Campbell. "Female Longevity and Diet in the Middle Ages." *Speculum* 55, #2 (1980), 317–325.

_____. "Medieval Medical and Scientific Views of Women." *Viator: Medieval and Renaissance Studies* 4 (1973), 485–501.

_____. "The Prostitute in the Middle Ages." *Studies in Medieval Culture* 10 (1977), 9–17.

_____, and Bonnie Bullough. *Prostitution: An Illustrated Social History.* New York, 1978.

Burnham, Philip E., Jr. "The Patronage of Clement VI." *History Today* 28, #6 (June 1978), 372–381.

Butt, Ronald. *A History of Parliament: The Middle Ages.* London, 1989.

Bynum, Caroline Walker. *Holy Feast and Holy Fast: The Religious Significance of Food to Medieval Women.* Berkeley, 1987.

_____. *Jesus as Mother: Studies in the Spirituality of the High Middle Ages.* Berkeley, 1982.

Calendar of Letter-Books of the City of London: A, C, and L, ed. by R. R. Sharpe. London, 1899 (A), 1901 (C), 1912 (L).

Calendar of Plea and Memoranda Rolls, 1323–1364, vol. I, ed. by A. H. Thomas. Cambridge, England 1926.

Calendar of Plea and Memoranda Rolls, 1364–1381, vol. II, ed. by A. H. Thomas. Cambridge, England 1929.

Calendar of Plea and Memoranda Rolls, 1458–1482, vol. VI, ed. by A. H. Thomas. Cambridge, England 1951.

Calendar of Wills Proved and Enrolled in the Court of Husting, London, 2 vols. (A.D. 1258–1688), ed. by R. R. Sharpe. London, 1889 and 1890.

Calmette, Joseph. *The Golden Age of Burgundy.* Trans. by Doreen Weightman. New York, 1963.

Cambridge Medieval History, vols. II–V and VII, ed. by H. M. Gwatkin, J. R. Tanner, et al. Cambridge and London, 1913–1936.

Carpenter, David. "Working the Land." *The Making of Britain,* ed. by Leslie M. Smith (1985), 87–100.

Carr, Anne Marie Weyl. "Women Artists in the Middle Ages." *Feminist Art Journal* 5, #1 (Spring 1976), 5–9.

Carroll, Berenice A., ed. *Liberating Women's History: Theoretical and Critical Essays.* Urbana, Chicago, and London, 1976.

Cartellieri, Otto. *The Court of Burgundy.* New York, 1972 (orig. pub. 1929).

Carter, John M. "Rape in Medieval England: The Evidence of Yorkshire, Wiltshire and London, 1218–76." *Comitatus* 13 (1982), 33–63.

Carus-Wilson, E.M. "The English Cloth Industry in the Late Twelfth and Early Thirteenth Centuries." *Economic History Review* 14 (1941), 32–50.

_____. "The Overseas Trade of Bristol." *Studies in English Trade in the Fifteenth Century,* ed. by E. Power and M. Postan (1933), 183–246.

Casey, Kathleen. "The Cheshire Cat: Reconstructing the Experience of Medieval Women." *Liberating Women's History: Theoretical and Critical Essays,* ed. by Berenice A. Carroll (1976), 224–249.

Cely Letters, 1472–1488, ed. by Alison Hanham. Early English Text Society, #273. London and Toronto, 1975.

Chamberlin, E. R. *The Fall of the House of Borgia*. New York, 1974.

_____. *The World of the Italian Renaissance: Italy c. 1268–1559*. London, 1982.

Chambers, E. K. *The Mediaeval Stage*, 2 vols. London, 1967 (orig. pub. 1903).

Champion, Pierre. *François Villon, sa vie et son temps*. 2 vols. Paris, 1913. 2nd ed., 1933.

_____. *Louis XI*. Trans. by Winifred Stephens Whales. Freeport, NY, 1970 (Orig. pub.1929).

_____. *Procès de condemnation de Jeanne d'Arc, texte, traduction et notes*. Paris, 1920.

Chaney, E. F. "A Glimpse of Villon's Paris." *Bulletin of the John Rylands Library* 28, #2 (December 1944), 340–357.

Charles, Lindsey, and Lorna Duffin, eds. *Women and Work in Pre-Industrial England*. Dover, NH, 1985.

Chaucer, Geoffrey. *The Canterbury Tales*. Oxford, 1985.

_____. *The Tales of Canterbury Complete*, ed. by Robert A. Pratt. Boston, 1974.

Chojnacki, Stanley. "The Power of Love: Wives and Husbands in Late Medieval Venice." *Women and Power in the Middle Ages*, ed. by M. Erler and M. Kowaleski (1988), 126–148.

Clark, Cecily, and Elizabeth Williams. "The Impact of 1066. " *Women of Anglo-Saxon England*, by Christine Fell (1984), 148–193.

Clarke, Helen. *The Archaeology of Medieval England*. London, 1984.

Clay, Rotha M. *The Hermits and Anchorites of England*. London, 1914.

Cohen, Esther. "The Pilgrim Badge Trade." *Journal of Medieval History* 2, #3 (September 1976), 193–214.

Cohn, Norman. *Europe's Inner Demon*. London, 1975.

_____. *The Pursuit of the Milennium*. New York, 1970.

Colledge, Eric. *Medieval Netherlands Religious Literature*. New York, 1965.

Collison-Morley, Lacy. *The Story of the Sforzas*. New York, 1934.

Colman, Rebecca V. "Reason and Unreason in Early Medieval Law." *Journal of Interdisciplinary History* 4, #4 (Spring, 1974), 571–591.

Commynes, Philippe de. *The Memoirs of Philippe de Commynes*, 2 vols., ed. by Samuel Kinser; trans. by Isabelle Cazeaux. New York, 1969.

Comnena, Anna. *The Alexiad*. Trans. by E. R. A. Sewter. New York, 1969 (reprinted 1979).

Comptes du domaine de la ville de Paris, 1424–1457. Histoire Générale de Paris Series, vol. I, ed. by A. Vidier, L. le Grand, and P. Dupieux. Paris, 1948.

Contamine, Philippe. "Peasant Hearth to Papal Palace: The Fourteenth and Fifteenth Centuries." *A History of Private Life*, vol. 2, ed. by G. Duby (1988), 425–505.

Contini, Mila. *Fashion: From Ancient Egypt to the Present Day.* New York, 1965.

Coronation of Elizabeth Wydeville. Set forth from a 15th Century Manuscript by George Smith. London, 1935.

Coryn, Marjorie. *House of Orléans.* New York, 1936.

Cosman, Madeleine Pelner. *Fabulous Feasts: Medieval Cookery and Ceremony.* New York, 1976.

_____. *Medieval Holidays and Festivals.* New York, 1981.

Cotton, Nancy. *Women Playwrights in England, c.1363–1750.* London and Toronto, 1980.

Coulton, G. G. *Life in the Middle Ages,* 4 vols. Cambridge, England, 1930 (orig. pub. 1910).

Craig, Hardin. *English Religious Drama of the Middle Ages.* Oxford, 1955.

Crombie, A. C. *Medieval and Early Modern Science.* New York, 1959.

Cromptin, J. "Leicestershire Lollards." *Transactions of the Leicester Archaeological and Historical Society* 44 (Leicester, 1968–1969).

Crompton, Louis. "The Myth of Lesbian Impunity: Capital Laws from 1270 to 1791." *The Gay Past,* ed. by S. Licata and R. Petersen (1985), 11–26.

Cross, Claire. "'Great Reasoners in Scripture': The Activities of Women Lollards 1380–1530." *Medieval Women,* ed. by Derek Baker (1978), 359–379.

Crump, C. G., and E. F. Jacob, eds. *The Legacy of the Middle Ages.* Oxford, 1962 (orig. pub. 1926).

Curtis, Edmund. *A History of Ireland.* London, 1936 (reprinted 1968).

Dahmus, Joseph. *Seven Medieval Queens: Vignettes of Seven Outstanding Women of the Middle Ages.* Garden City, NY, 1972.

Daichman, Graciela S. *Wayward Nuns in Medieval Literature.* Syracuse, NY, 1986.

Dale, Marion K. "The London Silkwomen of the Fifteenth Century." *Economic History Review* 4 (1933), 324–335.

Davis, William Stearns. *Life on a Medieval Barony.* New York, 1923.

Day, John. "On the Status of Women in Medieval Sardinia." *Women of the Medieval World,* ed. by J. Kirshner and S. Wemple (1985), 304–316.

Deanesly, Margaret. *A History of the Medieval Church, 590–1500.* London, reprinted 1962.

Decaux, Alain. *Histoire des Françaises I: La Soumission.* Paris, 1972.

Del Re, Gerard, and Patricia Del Re. *The Christmas Almanack.* New York, 1979.

Denholm-Young, Noel. "The Yorkshire Estates of Isabella de Fortibus." *Yorkshire Archaeological Journal* 31 (1934), 389–420.

Dent, Anthony. "King Edward's Vineyards: Aquitaine under the Plantagenet Crown." *History Today* 29 (July 1979), 464–470.

Dhuoda. *Le Manuel de Dhuoda* (843): *L'Éducation Carolingienne*. Paris, 1887.

_____. *Manuel pour mon fils*, ed. and trans. by P. Riché. Paris, 1975.

Diehl, Charles. *Byzantine Empresses*. Trans. by Harold Bell and Theresa de Kerpely. New York, 1963.

Dillard, Heath. *Daughters of the Reconquest: Women in Castilian Town Society, 1100–1300*. Cambridge, 1984.

Dixon, E. "Craftswomen in the 'Livre des Métiers'." *Economic Journal* 5 (1895), 209–228.

Douglas, David C. *William the Conqueror: The Norman Impact Upon England*. Berkeley and Los Angeles, 1966.

Dresbeck, Le Roy. "Techne, Labor, et Natura: Ideas and Active Life in the Medieval Winter." *Studies in Medieval and Renaissance History* 2 (1979), 81–120.

Drinker, Sophie. *Music and Women: The Story of Women in Their Relation to Music*. New York, 1948.

Dronke, Peter. "The Provençal Trobairitz: Castelloza." *Medieval Women Writers*, ed. by K. Wilson (1984), 131–152.

_____. *Women Writers of the Middle Ages*. Cambridge, MA, 1984.

Duby, Georges. *History of Medieval Art, 980–1440*. New York, 1986.

_____, ed. and author. *A History of Private Life*, vol. 2: *Revelations of the Medieval World*. Trans. by Arthur Goldhammer. Cambridge, MA, and London, 1988.

_____. *The Knight, the Lady, and the Priest: The Making of Modern Marriage in Medieval France*. Trans. by Barbara Bray. New York, 1983.

Duncan, Archibald A. M. *Scotland: The Making of the Kingdom*. Edinburgh, 1975.

Dunlop, Ian. *Châteaux of the Loire*. New York, 1969.

Durant, Will. *The Age of Faith*. New York, 1950.

DuVal, John, trans. *Cuckolds, Clerics, and Countrymen: Medieval French Fabliaux*. Fayetteville, AR, 1982.

Duvernoy, Jean. *Inquisition à Pamiers, interrogatoiries de Jacques Fournier Évêque de Pamiers* (1318–1325). Toulouse, 1966.

Eckenstein, Lina. *Woman Under Monasticism*. Cambridge, England, 1896.

Elkins, Sharon K. *Holy Women of Twelfth-Century England*. Chapel Hill and London, 1988.

Ennen, Edith. *The Medieval Woman*. Trans. by Edmund Jephcott. Oxford, 1989.

Erickson, Carolly, and K. Casey. "Women in the Middle Ages: A Working Bibliography." *Mediaeval Studies* 37 (1975), 340–359.

Erler, Mary, and Maryanne Kowaleski, eds. *Women and Power in the Middle Ages*. Athens, GA, and London, 1988.

Evans, Joan, ed. *The Flowering of the Middle Ages*. New York, 1976.

Ewen, Cecil Henry. *Witchcraft and Demonianism*. London, 1970.

Exercises of St. Gertrude, Virgin and Abbess of the Order of St. Benedict. London, 1877.

Facinger, Marion F. "A Study of Medieval Queenship: Capetian France, 987–1237." *Studies in Medieval and Renaissance History* 5 (1968), 3–48.

Farmer, Sharon. "Persuasive Voices: Clerical Images of Medieval Wives." *Speculum* 61, #3 (1986), 517–543.

Favier, Jean. *Les Contribuables Parisiens à la fin de la Guerre de Cent Ans: Les Rôles d'impôt de 1421, 1423, and 1438*. Geneva, 1970.

Fell, Christine, with C. Clark and E. Williams. *Women in Anglo-Saxon England and the Impact of 1066*. Bloomington, IN, 1984.

Ferguson, W. K. *Europe in Transition: 1300–1500*. Boston, 1962.

Ferrante, Joan M. "The Education of Women in the Middle Ages in Theory, Fact, and Fantasy." *Beyond Their Sex*, ed. by Patricia Labalme, (1980), 9–42.

_____. "The French Courtly Poet: Marie de France." *Medieval Women Writers*, ed. by K. Wilson (1984), 64–89.

_____, and R. W. Hannings, eds. *The Lais of Marie de France*. New York, 1978.

_____. "Public Postures and Private Manuevers: Roles Medieval Women Play." *Women and Power in the Middle Ages*, ed. by M. Erler and M. Kowaleski (1988), 213–229.

_____. *Women as Image in Medieval Literature*. New York and London, 1975.

Fifty Earliest English Wills in the Court of Probate, London, ed. by F.J. Furnivall. London, 1882.

Fine, Elsa Honig. *Women and Art: A History of Women Painters and Sculptors from the Renaissance to the Twentieth Century*. Montclair, NJ, 1962.

Finucane, Ronald C. *Miracles and Pilgrims: Popular Beliefs in Medieval England*. London, 1977.

Flandrin, Jean-Louis. "Contraception, Marriage and Sexual Relationships in the Christian West." *Biology of Man in History*, ed. by Robert Forster and Orest Ranum (1975), 23–47.

Forster, Robert, and Orest A. Ranum, eds. *Biology of Man in History. Selections from the Annales, Économies, Sociétés, Civilisations*. Baltimore, 1975.

Fossier, Robert. *Peasant Life in the Medieval West*. Trans. by Juliet Vale. Oxford and New York, 1988.

Fox, John. *A Literary History of France: The Middle Ages*. London and New York, 1974.

Frank, Roberta. "Marriage in Twelfth and Thirteenth Century Iceland." *Viator: Medieval and Renaissance Studies* 4 (1973), 473–484.

Freeman, Margaret. *Herbs for the Medieval Household.* New York, 1943.

Freeman, Michelle. "The Power of Sisterhood: Marie de France's 'Le Fresne'." *Women and Power in the Middle Ages,* ed. by M. Erler and M. Kowaleski (1988), 250–264.

Friedenwald, Harry. "Jewish Doctoresses in the Middle Ages." *The Jews and Medicine: Essays.* Baltimore, 1944. Chap. 13, 217–220.

_____. *The Jews and Medicine: Essays.* Baltimore, 1944.

Fries, Maureen. "Margery Kempe." *An Introduction to the Medieval Mystics of Europe,* ed. by P. E. Szarmach. Albany, NY, 1984, 217–235.

Froissart, Sir John. *Chronicles of England, France, Spain.* Trans. by Thomas Johnes. Revised ed., 2 vols. New York and London, 1901.

Fryde, Natalie. *The Tyranny and Fall of Edward II, 1321–1326.* Cambridge, England, 1979.

Fuhrmann, Horst. *Germany in the High Middle Ages, c. 1050–1200.* Trans. by Timothy Reuter. Cambridge, 1986.

Fusero, Clemente. *The Borgias.* Trans. by Peter Green. New York, 1972. (orig. pub. Italy, 1966).

Gabrieli, Francesco. *Arab Historians of the Crusades.* Berkeley, 1969.

Gardiner, Dorothy K. *English Girlhood at School: A Study of Women's Education through Twelve Centuries.* London, 1929.

Géraud, Hercule. *Paris sous Phillippe le Bel. Le Rôle de la taille.* Paris, 1837.

Gies, Frances and Joseph. *Marriage and the Family in the Middle Ages.* New York, 1987.

_____. *Merchants and Moneymen: The Commercial Revolution, 1000–1500.* New York, 1972.

_____. *Women in the Middle Ages.* New York, 1978.

Gillingham, John Bennett. *Richard the Lionheart.* New York, 1978.

Glasser, Marc. "Marriage in Medieval Hagiography." *Studies in Medieval and Renaissance History* 4 (1981), 3–34.

Gold, Penny Schine. *The Lady and the Virgin.* Chicago, 1985.

Goodich, Michael. "The Contours of Female Piety in Later Medieval Hagiography." *Church History* 50, #1 (1981), 20–32.

_____. *The Unmentionable Vice: Homosexuality in the Later Medieval Period.* Santa Barbara, CA, 1979.

Goodman, A. E. "The Piety of John Brunham's Daughter, of Lynn." *Medieval Women,* ed. by Derek Baker (1978), 347–358.

Goulianos, Joan, ed. *By a Woman Writt; Literature from Six Centuries by and about Women.* Indianapolis, IN, 1973.

Gras, N. S. B. "The Economic Activity of Towns." *The Legacy of the Middle Ages*, ed. by C. G. Crump and E. F. Jacob (1962), 435–464.

Graves, Coburn V. "English Cistercian Nuns in Lincolnshire." *Speculum* 54 (1979), 492–499.

Gray, Robert. *A History of London*. New York, 1979.

Green, M. A. E. *Letters of Royal and Illustrious Ladies of Great Britain*, vol. I. London, 1846.

Greer, Germaine. *The Obstacle Race: The Fortune of Women Painters and their Work*. New York, 1979.

Griffiths, Ralph A., and Roger S. Thomas. *The Making of the Tudor Dynasty*. New York, 1985.

Gundersheimer, Werner L. "Women, Learning, and Power: Eleonora of Aragon and the Court of Ferrara." *Beyond Their Sex*, ed. by Patricia Labalme (1980), 43–65.

Gwin, Howell H. Jr. "Life in the Medieval Leprosary." *Studies in Medieval Culture* 4, #2 (1974), 225–232.

Hair, P. E. H., comp. *Before the Bawdy Court*. London and New York, 1972.

Hallam, Elizabeth M. *Capetian France, 987–1328*. London and New York, 1980.

_____, ed. *Four Gothic Kings*. New York, 1987.

_____, ed. *The Plantagenet Chronicles*. New York, 1986.

Halligan, Theresa A., ed. *Booke of Gostlye Grace of Mechtild of Hackeborn*. Toronto, 1979.

Halperin, Charles J. *Russia and the Golden Horde*. Bloomington, IN, 1985.

Hamilton, Bernard. "Women in the Crusader States: The Queens of Jerusalem, 1100–1190." *Medieval Women*, ed. by Derek Baker (1978), 143–174.

Hanawalt, Barbara A. "Childrearing Among the Lower Classes of Late Medieval England." *Journal of Interdisciplinary History* 8, #1 (Summer 1977), 1–22.

_____. "The Female Felon in Fourteenth Century England." *Viator: Medieval and Renaissance Studies* 5 (1974), 253–268.

_____. "The Female Felon in Fourteenth Century England." *Women in Medieval Society*, ed. by Susan M. Stuard (1976), 143–174.

_____. "Fur Collar Crime: The Pattern of Crime among the Fourteenth Century English Nobility." *Journal of Social History* 8 (Summer 1975), 1–17.

_____. "Golden Ages for the History of Medieval English Women." *Women in Medieval History and Historiography*, ed. by S. M. Stuard (1987), 1–24.

_____. "Peasant Women's Contribution to the Home Economy in Late Medieval England." *Women and Work in Pre-Industrial Europe,* ed. by Barbara Hanawalt (1986), 3–19.

_____. *The Ties That Bound: Peasant Families in Medieval England.* New York and Oxford, 1986.

_____, ed. *Women and Work in Pre-Industrial Europe.* Bloomington, IN, 1986.

Hansen, Elaine Tuttle. "The Powers of Silence: The Case of the Clerk's Griselda." *Women and Power in the Middle Ages,* ed. by M. Erler and M. Kowaleski (1988), 230–249.

Hardy, Blanche Christabel. *Philippa of Hainault and Her Times.* London, 1910.

Harksen, Sibylle. *Women in the Middle Ages.* New York, 1975.

Hartley, Dorothy. *Medieval Costume and Life.* London, 1931.

Hartnoll, Phyllis. *The Concise History of the Theatre.* New York, 1968.

Haskell, Ann S. "The Paston Women on Marriage in Fifteenth-Century England." *Viator: Medieval and Renaissance Studies* 4 (1973), 459–471.

Haverkamp, Alfred. *Medieval Germany 1056–1273.* Trans. by Helga Braun and Richard Mortimer. Oxford, 1988.

Hazlitt, W. Carew. *The Coinage of the European Continent.* Chicago, 1974.

Heer, Frederick. *The Holy Roman Empire.* Trans. by J. Sondheimer. New York, 1968.

_____. *The Medieval World: Europe, 1100–1500.* New York, 1962.

Heinrich, Sister Mary Pia. *The Canonesses and Education in the Early Middle Ages.* Washington, DC, 1924.

_____. "The Industrial Position of Women in the Middle Ages." *Catholic Historical Review,* n.s. 4, #4 (January 1925), 556–560.

Henshaw, Millet. "The Attitude of the Church Toward the Stage at the End of the Middle Ages." *Medievalia et Humanistica* 7 (1952), 3–17.

Herlihy, David. "Life Expectancies for Women in Medieval Society." *The Role of Women in the Middle Ages,* ed. by R. T. Morewedge (1975), 1–22.

_____. "Medieval Children." *Essays on Medieval Civilization,* ed. by B. K. Lackner and K. R. Philp (1978), 109–142.

_____. *Medieval Households.* Cambridge, MA, and London, 1985.

_____. *Women in Medieval Society.* Austin, TX, 1971.

Heymann, Frederick G. "The Hussite Revolution and the German Peasants' War: An Historical Comparison." *Medievalia et Humanistica,* n.s. #1 (1970), 141–160.

Hieatt, Constance B., and Butler, Sharon. *Plen Delit: Medieval Cookery for Modern Cooks.* Toronto and Buffalo, NY, 1976.

Hilton, Rodney H. *The English Peasantry in the Later Middle Ages.* Oxford, 1975.

_____. "Women Traders in Medieval England." *Women's Studies* 11 (1984), 139–155.

Hindley, Geoffrey. *England in the Age of Caxton*. New York, 1979.

Hogan, M. Patricia. "Medieval Villany: A Study in the Meaning and Control of Crime in an English Village." *Studies in Medieval and Renaissance History*, n.s. vol. 2 (1979), 121–215.

Holdsworth, Christopher J. "Christina of Markyate." *Medieval Women*, ed. by Derek Baker (1978), 185–204.

Hollister, C. Warren, et al. *Medieval Europe: A Short History*. Sixth Edition. New York, 1990.

Holmes, George. *Florence, Rome, and the Origins of the Renaissance*. Oxford, 1986.

_____. *The Later Middle Ages, 1272–1485*. New York, 1962.

Homans, George C. *English Villages of the Thirteenth Century*. Cambridge, MA, 1941.

Horizon Cookbook and Illustrated History of Eating and Drinking Through the Ages. New York, 1968.

Household Book of Dame Alice de Bryene of Action Hall, Suffolk, Sept. 1412–Sept. 1413. Trans. by M.K. Dale and ed. by V.B. Redstone. Ipswich, England, 1931.

Howard, John. "The German Mystic: Mechtild of Magdeburg." *Medieval Women Writers*, ed. by K. Wilson (1984), 153–185.

Howell, Martha C. "Citizenship and Gender: Women's Political Status in Northern Medieval Cities." *Women and Power in the Middle Ages*, ed. by M. Erler and M. Kowaleski (1988), 37–60.

_____, with S. Wemple and D. Kaiser. "A Documented Presence: Medieval Women in Germanic Historiography." *Women in Medieval History and Historiography*, ed. by S. M. Stuard (1987), 101–131.

_____. "Women, the Family Economy and the Structure of Market Production in the Cities of Northern Europe during the Late Middle Ages." *Women and Work in Pre-Industrial Europe*, ed. by B. Hanawalt (1986), 198–222.

Hughes, Diane Owen. "Earrings for Circumcision: Distinction and Purification in the Italian Renaissance City." *Persons in Groups*, ed. by R. C. Trexler (1985), 155–177.

_____. "From Bridespiece to Dowry in Mediterranean Europe." *Journal of Family History* 3 (1978), 262–296.

_____. "Invisible Madonnas? The Italian Historiographical Tradition and the Women of Medieval Italy." *Women in Medieval History and Historiography*, ed. by S. M. Stuard (1987), 25–57.

_____. "Urban Growth and Family Structure in Medieval Genoa." *Past and Present* #66 (February 1975), 3–28.

Hughes, Muriel J. "The Library of Philip the Bold." *Journal of Medieval History* 4, #2 (June 1978), 145–188.

_____. *Women Healers in Medieval Life and Literature*. New York, 1968.

Hurd-Mead, Kate Campbell. *A History of Women in Medicine*. Haddam, CT, 1938.

Hutton, Diane. "Women in Fourteenth Century Shrewsbury." *Women and Work in Pre-Industrial England*, ed. by L. Charles and L. Duffin (1985), 83–99.

Hyatte, Reginald, trans. *Laughter for the Devil: The Trials of Gilles de Rais, Companion-in-arms of Joan of Arc*. Cranbury, NJ, 1984.

Ide, Arthur Frederick. *Women: A Synopsis*. Mesquite, TX, 1983.

Jacob, Dorothy. *Cures and Curses*. New York, 1967.

James, Edward. *The Origins of France: From Clovis to the Capetians, 500–1000*. New York, 1982.

Jamison, D. F. *The Life and Times of Bertrand du Guesclin: A History of the Fourteenth Century*. 2 vols. Charleston, SC, 1864.

Jamison, Evelyn M. "The Abbess Bethlem of Santa Maria di Porta Somma and the Barons of the Terra Beneventana." *Oxford Essays in Medieval History*, Presented to H. E. Salter. New York, 1968 (orig. pub. 1934).

Jenkinson, Hilary. "Mary de Sancto Paulo, Foundress of Pembroke College, Cambridge." *Archaeologia* LXVI (1915), 401–446.

Jennings, J.M. "London and the Statute of Mortmain: Doubts and Anxieties Among Fifteenth Century London Testators." *Mediaeval Studies* 36 (1974), 174–177.

Johnson, Marion. *The Borgias*. New York, 1981.

Johnson, P. A. *Duke Richard of York: 1411–1460*. Oxford, 1988.

Johnson, Penelope D. *Equal in Monastic Profession: Religious Women in Medieval France*. Chicago, 1991.

_____. *Prayer, Patronage and Power: The Abbey of la Trinité, Vendôme, 1032–1187*. New York and London, 1981.

Johnstone, Hilda. "Poor-Relief in the Royal Households of Thirteenth Century England." *Speculum* 4 (1929), 149–167.

Jones, Catherine. "The English Mystic: Julian of Norwich." *Medieval Women Writers*, ed. by K. Wilson (1984), 269–296.

Jones, Gwyn. *A History of the Vikings*. London, 1968.

Jones, Michael. *The Creation of Brittany: A Late Medieval State*. London and Ronceverte, WV, 1988.

_____. *Ducal Brittany, 1364–1399: Relations with England and France During the Reign of Duke John IV*. London, 1970.

Jordan, W., B. McNab, and T. Ruiz, eds. *Order and Innovation in the Middle Ages: Essays in Honor of Joseph R. Strayer*. Princeton, NJ, 1976.

Jordan, William Chester. "Jews on Top: Women and the Availibility of Consumption Loans in Northern France in the Mid-Thirteenth Century." *Journal of Jewish Studies* 29, #1 (Spring 1978), 39–56.

_____. *Louis IX and the Challenge of the Crusade: A Study in Rulership*. Princeton, NJ, 1979.

Jourdain, Charles. "Memoire sur l'éducation des femmes au Moyen Âge." *Excursions historiques et philosophiques à travers le Moyen Âge*. Paris, 1888; Frankfurt, 1966. 463–510.

Julian of Norwich: Showings. Ed. and trans. by Edmund Colledge and James Walsh. New York, 1978.

Jusserand, J. J. *English Wayfaring Life in the Middle Ages*. Trans. by L.T. Smith. New York, 1950 (orig. pub. 1929).

Kanner, Barbara, ed. *The Women of England from Anglo-Saxon Times to the Present*. Hamden, CT, 1979.

Kashnitz, Rainer. "The Gospel Book of Abbess Svanhild of Essen in the John Rylands Library." *Bulletin of the John Rylands Library* 53, #1 (Autumn 1970), 122–166.

Kellum, Barbara A. "Infanticide in England in the Later Middle Ages." *History of Childhood Quarterly* 1 (1974), 367–388.

Kelly, Amy. *Eleanor of Aquitaine and the Four Kings*. Cambridge, MA, 1950.

Kelly, H. A. "Canonical Implications of Richard III's Plan to Marry his Niece." *Traditio* 23 (1967), 269–311.

Kelly-Gadol, Joan. "Did Women Have a Renaissance?" *Becoming Visible: Women in European History*, ed. by R. Bridenthal and C. Koonz (1977), 137–164.

Kempe, Margery. *The Book of Margery Kempe*. Trans. by W. Butler Bowdon. London, 1936.

Kendall, Paul Murray. *Yorkist Age*. New York, 1962.

Kennan, Elizabeth. "Innocent III and the First Political Crusade: A Comment on the Limitations of Papal Power." *Traditio* 27 (1971), 231–249.

Kibler, William, W., ed. *Eleanor of Aquitaine, Patron and Politician*. Austin, TX, 1976.

Kieckhefer, Richard. *European Witch Trials; Their Foundation in Popular and Learned Culture, 1300–1500*. Berkeley and Los Angeles, 1976.

King, Donald. "Industries, Merchants, and Money." *The Flowering of the Middle Ages*, ed. by Joan Evans (1976), 245–280.

King, Margaret L. "Book-Lined Cells: Women and Humanism in the Early Italian Renaissance." *Beyond Their Sex: Learned Women of the European Past*, ed. by Patricia Labalme (1980), 66–90.

_____. "Goddess and Captive." *Medievalia et Humanistica*. n.s. #10 (1981), 103–127.

_____, and Albert Rabil, Jr., eds. *Her Immaculate Hand: Selected Works by and About the Women Humanists of Quattrocento Italy*. Binghamton, NY, 1983.

Kirshner, Julius. "Wives' Claims Against Insolvent Husbands in Late Medieval Italy." *Women of the Medieval World*, ed. by J. Kirshner and S. Wemple (1985), 256–303.

_____, and Suzanne Wemple, eds. *Women of the Medieval World: Essays in Honor of John H. Mundy*. Oxford and New York, 1985.

Kittel, Margaret Ruth. *Married Women in Thirteenth-Century England: A Study in Common Law*. Ph. D. Dissertation, University of California, Berkeley, 1973.

Klaits, Joseph. *Servants of Satan: The Age of the Witch Hunts*. Bloomington, IN, 1985.

Klapisch-Zuber, Christiane. "The 'Cruel Mother': Maternity, Widowhood and Dowry in Florence in the Fourteenth and Fifteenth Centuries." *Women, Family and Ritual in Renaissance Italy* (1985), 117–131.

_____. *Women, Family and Ritual in Renaissance Italy*. Chicago and London, 1985.

Klassen, John Martin. *The Nobility and the Making of the Hussite Revolution*. New York, 1978.

Kluchevsky, V. O. *A History of Russia*. Trans. by C. J. Hogarth. New York, 1960.

Kowaleski, Maryanne. "Women's Work in a Market Town: Exeter in the Late Fourteenth Century." *Women and Work in Pre-Industrial Europe*, ed. by Barbara Hanawalt (1986), 145–164.

Kraft, Kent. "The German Visionary: Hildegard of Bingen." *Medieval Women Writers*, ed. by K. Wilson (1984), 109–130.

Kristeller, Oskar. "Learned Women of Early Modern Italy: Humanists and University Scholars." *Beyond Their Sex: Learned Women of the European Past*, ed. by Patricia H. Labalme (1980), 102–114.

Kuehn, Thomas. "Cum Consensu Mundualdi: Legal Guardianship of Women in Quattrocento Florence." *Viator: Medieval and Renaissance Studies* 13 (1982), 309–333.

Kunz, George Frederick. *The Curious Lore of Precious Stones*. Philadelphia and London, 1913.

Labalme, Patricia H., ed. *Beyond Their Sex: Learned Women of the European Past*. New York, 1980.

Labande, L. H. *Histoire de Beauvais et de ses institutions communales jusqu'au commencement du xve siècle*. Reprinted Geneva, 1978.

Labarge, Margaret Wade. *A Baronial Household of the Thirteenth Century*. London, 1965.

_____. *Simon de Montfort*. London, 1962.

Lacey, Kay E. "Women and Work in Fourteenth and Fifteenth Century London." *Women and Work in Pre-Industrial England*, ed. by L. Charles and L. Duffin (1985), 24–82.

Lackner, B. K., and K. R. Philp. *Essays on Medieval Education*. Austin, TX, and London, 1978.

Ladurie, Emmanuel Le Roy. *Montaillou: The Promised Land of Error*. New York, 1978.

Lagorio, Valerie M. "The Medieval Continental Women Mystics: An Introduction." *An Introduction to the Medieval Mystics of Europe*, ed. by P. E. Szarmach. Albany, NY, 1984.

Lambert, Malcolm. *Medieval Heresy: Popular Movements from Bogomil to Hus*. New York, 1977.

Lancaster, R. Kent. "Artists, Suppliers and Clerks: The Human Factors in the Art Patronage of King Henry III." *Journal of the Warburg and Courtauld Institutes* XXXV (1972), 81–107.

Larsen, Karen. *History of Norway*. Princeton, NJ, 1948.

Lea, Henry C. *History of the Inquisition of the Middle Ages*, vols. II and III. New York, 1922.

_____. *Materials Toward a History of Witchcraft*, vol. I. Ed. by A. C. Howland. Philadelphia, 1939.

Leach, Maria. *The Soup Stone: The Magic of Familiar Things*. New York, 1954.

Lee, Patricia-Ann. "Reflections of Power: Margaret of Anjou and the Dark Side of Queenship." *Renaissance Quarterly* 39 (1986), 183–217.

Leff, Gordon. *Heresy in the Later Middle Ages*, vol. I and II. New York, 1967.

Lehmann, A. *Le Rôle de la femme dans l'histoire de France au Moyen Âge*. Paris, 1952.

Lejeune, Rita. "La Femme dans les littératures Française et Occitane du XI au XIII siècle." *Cahiers de Civilisation Médiéval* 20, #2–3 (April–September 1977), 201–217.

Lemay, Helen Rodnite. "Anthonius Guainerius and Medieval Gynecology." *Women of the Medieval World*, ed. by J. Kirshner and S. F. Wemple (1985), 317–336.

Leroy, Beatrice. *La Navarre au Moyen Âge*. Paris, 1984.

Lester, Katherine M., and Bess Viola Oerke. *Accessories of Dress*. Peoria, IL, 1940.

Letters of Abelard and Heloise. Trans. by Betty Radice. London, 1974.

Lewis, Archibald R. *The Development of Southern French and Catalan Society, 718–1050*. Austin, TX, 1965.

Lewis, D. B. Wyndham. *King Spider*. New York, 1929.

Lewis, N. B. "The Anniversary Service for Blanche, Duchess of Lancaster, 12th September 1374." *Bulletin of the John Rylands Library* 21, #1 (April 1937), 176–192.

Liber de Diversis Medicinis. Ed. by Margaret Sinclair for the Early English Text Society. London, 1938.

Licata, Salvatore, and Robert Petersen. *The Gay Past: A Collection of Historical Essays*. New York, 1985.

Lind, L. R., ed. *Lyric Poetry of the Italian Renaissance*. New Haven, CT, 1964.

Lipinska, Melanie. *Histoire des femmes médicins*. Paris, 1900.

Lister, Margot. *Costume: An Illustrated Survey from Ancient Times to the Twentieth Century*. London, 1967.

Loengard, Janet Senderowitz. "Of the Gift of Her Husband: English Dower and Its Consequences in the Year 1200." *Women of the Medieval World*, ed. by J. Kirshner and S. Wemple (1985), 215–255.

London Assize of Nuisance, 1301–1431: A Calendar. Ed. by Helena M. Chew and William Kellaway. London Record Society, 1973.

London Eyre of 1244. Ed. by Helena M. Chew and Martin Weinbaum. London Record Society, 1976.

London Eyre of 1276. Ed. by Martin Weinbaum. London Record Society, 1976.

Lucas, Angela M. *Women in the Middle Ages: Religion, Marriage and Letters*. New York, 1983.

Lungo, Isidoro del. *Women of Florence*. Trans. by M. C. Steegman. New York, 1908.

Luria, Maxwell. *A Reader's Guide to the Roman de la Rose*. Hamden, CT, 1982.

Lutzow, Count von. *The Hussite Wars*. London and New York, 1914.

Maguire, Yvonne. *Women of the Medici*. London, 1927.

Makowski, Elizabeth M. "The Conjugal Debt and Medieval Canon Law." *Journal of Medieval History* 3, #2 (June 1977), 99–114.

Manners and Household Expenses in the Thirteenth and Fifteenth Century. Ed. by H. T. Turn. London, 1841.

Mantzius, Karl. *A History of Theatrical Art in Ancient and Modern Times*. Trans. by Louise von Cossel. New York, 1937.

Marks, Claude. *Pilgrims, Heretics and Lovers: A Medieval Journey*. New York, 1975.

Martindale, Andrew. "The Changing Status of the Craftsman." *The Flowering of the Middle Ages*, ed. by Joan Evans (1976), 281–314.

Martines, Lauro. "A Way of Looking at Women in Renaissance Florence." *Journal of Medieval and Renaissance Studies* 4, #1 (Spring 1974), 15–28.

Mason, Stephen. *Main Currents of Scientific Thought: A History of the Sciences*. New York, 1953.

Mate, Mavis. "Profit and Productivity on the Estates of Isabella de Forz." *Economic History Review*, 2nd series, 33, #3 (August 1980), 326–334.

Matthew, Donald. *The Medieval European Community*. London, 1977.

May, W. "The Confessions of Prous Boneta, Heretic and Heresiarch." *Essays in Medieval Life and Thought*, ed. by J. Mundy, et al. (1965), 3–30.

McCall, Andrew. *The Medieval Underworld*. London, 1979.

McDonnell, Ernest W. *The Beguines and Beghards in Medieval Culture*. New York, 1969.

McFarlane, K. B. *The Nobility of Later Medieval England*. Oxford, 1973.

McLaughlin, Eleanor. "Women, Power, and the Pursuit of Holiness." *Women of Spirit: Female Leadership in the Jewish and Christian Traditions*, ed. by R. Ruether and E. McLaughlin (1979), 99–130.

McLaughlin, Megan. "The Woman Warrior: Gender, Warfare and Society in Medieval Europe." *Women's Studies* 17 (1990), 193–209.

McNamara, Jo Ann. "A Legacy of Miracles: Hagiography and Nunneries in Merovingian Gaul." *Women of the Medieval World*, ed. by J. Kirshner and S. Wemple (1985), 36–52.

_____, and Suzanne Wemple. "The Power of Women through the Family in Medieval Europe, 500–1100." *Women and Power in the Middle Ages*, ed. by M. Erler and M. Kowaleski (1988), 83–101.

_____, and Suzanne Wemple. "Sanctity and Power: The Dual Pursuit of Medieval Women." *Becoming Visible: Women in European History*, ed. by R. Bridenthal and C. Koonz (1977), 90–118.

Meade, Marion. *Eleanor of Aquitaine: A Biography*. New York, 1977.

Mertes, Kate. *The English Noble Household 1250–1600: Good Governance and Politic Rule*. Oxford and New York, 1988.

Michaëlsson, Karl. *Le Livre de la taille de Paris l'an de grâce 1313*. Stockholm, 1962.

Miron, E. L. *The Queens of Aragon: Their Lives and Times*. Port Washington, NY, 1970.

Miskimin, Harry A. "The Legacies of London: 1259–1330." *The Medieval City*, ed. by H. Miskimin, D. Herlihy, and A. Udovitch (1978), 209–227.

_____, David Herlihy, and A. L. Udovitch, eds. *The Medieval City*. New Haven, CT, and London, 1978.

Monter, E. William. "The Pedestal and the Stake: Courtly Love and Witchcraft." *Becoming Visible: Women in European History*, ed. by R. Bridenthal and C. Koonz (1977), 119–136.

_____. "Sodomy and Heresy in Early Modern Switzerland." *The Gay Past*, ed. by S. Licata and R. Petersen (1985), 41–53.

Morewedge, Rosemarie T., ed. *The Role of Women in the Middle Ages*. Albany, NY, 1975.

Morrall, John B. *The Medieval Imprint: The Founding of the Western European Tradition*. New York, 1967.

Moulin, Jeanine, ed. *La Poésie féminine du XII au XIX siècle*. Paris, 1966.

Mozans, H. J. *Woman in Science*. Cambridge, MA, 1974 (orig. pub. 1913).

Muchembled, Robert. *Sorcière au village* (XV–XVIII siècle). Paris, 1979.

Muir, Lynette R. *Literature and Society in Medieval France: The Mirror and the Image 1100–1500*. London, 1985.

Muir, Richard. *The English Village*. New York, 1980.

Munsterberg, Hugo. *A History of Women Artists*. New York, 1975.

Musto, Ronald G. "Queen Sancia of Naples (1286–1345) and the Spiritual Franciscans." *Women of the Medieval World*, ed by J. Kirshner and S. Wemple (1985), 179–214.

Myers, A. R. "The Captivity of a Royal Witch: The Household Account of Queen Joan of Navarre, 1419–1421." *Bulletin of the John Rylands Library* 24 (October 1940), 263–284.

_____. "The Household of Queen Elizabeth Woodville, 1466–1467." *Bulletin of the John Rylands Library* 50 (1967–1968), 207–235.

_____. "The Household of Queen Margaret of Anjou, 1452–1453." *Bulletin of the John Rylands Library* 40, #1 (September 1957), 79–113.

_____. "Some Household Ordinances of Henry VI." *Bulletin of the John Rylands Library* 36, #2 (March 1954), 449–467.

Neaman, Judith S. *Suggestion of the Devil: The Origins of Madness*. Garden City, NY, 1975.

Neel, Carol. "The Origins of the Beguines." *Sisters and Workers in the Middle Ages*, ed. by J. Bennett et al. (1989), 240–260.

Newman, Barbara. *Sister of Wisdom: St. Hildegard's Theology of the Feminine*. Berkeley, CA, 1987.

Nicholas, David. *The Domestic Life of a Medieval City: Women, Children and the Family in Fourteenth Century Ghent*. Lincoln, NB, and London, 1985.

Noonan, John Thomas, Jr. *Contraception: A History of Its Treatment by the Catholic Theologians and Canonists*. Cambridge, MA, 1965.

_____. "Marriage in the Middle Ages: Power to Choose." *Viator: Medieval and Renaissance Studies* 4 (1973), 419–434.

Norwich, John Julius. *History of Venice*. New York, 1982.

_____. *The Kingdom in the Sun, 1130–1194*. London, 1976.

_____. *The Normans in the South, 1016–1130*. London, 1967.

Nowell, Charles Edward. *History of Portugal*. New York, 1952.

O'Callaghan, Joseph F. *A History of Medieval Spain*. Ithaca, NY, and London, 1975.

O'Faolain, Julia. *Not in God's Image: Women in History from the Greeks to the Victorians*. London, 1973.

Oakley, Stewart. *A Short History of Denmark*. New York and Washington, DC, 1972.

Olmert, Michael. "Points of Origin; The Sporting Chance." *Smithsonian* 12, #1 (February 1982), 32–34.

Origo, Iris. "The Domestic Enemy: The Eastern Slaves in Tuscany in the Fourteenth and Fifteenth Century." *Speculum* 30, #3 (July 1955), 321–366.

_____. *The World of San Bernardino*. New York, 1962.

Orme, Nicholas. *Education in the West of England, 1066–1548*. Exeter, 1976.

_____. *English Schools in the Middle Ages*. London, 1973.

Otis, Leah Lydia. "Municipal Wet Nurses in Fifteenth Century Montpellier." *Women and Work in Pre-Industrial Europe*, ed. by B. Hanawalt (1986), 83–93.

_____. "Prostitution and Repentance in Late Medieval Perpignan." *Women of the Medieval World*, ed. by J. Kirshner and S. Wemple (1985), 137–160.

_____. *Prostitution in Medieval Society: The History of an Urban Institution in Languedoc*. Chicago and London, 1985.

Owen, Dorothy M. "White Annays and Others." *Medieval Women*, ed. by Derek Baker (1978), 331–346.

Oxford Book of Late Medieval Verse and Prose. Ed. by Douglas Gray. Oxford, 1985.

Paris, Matthew. *Chronicles of Matthew Paris: Monastic Life in the Thirteenth Century*. Ed. by Richard Vaughan. New York, 1986.

Parker, Rozsika, and Griselda Pollack. *Old Mistresses: Women, Art, and Ideology*. New York, 1981.

Payer, Pierre J. "Early Medieval Regulations Concerning Marital Sexual Relations." *Journal of Medieval History* 6 (1980), 353–376.

Payne, Robert. *The Dream and the Tomb: A History of the Crusades*. New York, 1984.

Pernoud, Régine. *La Femme au temps des cathédrales*. Paris, 1984.

_____. *Joan of Arc, by Herself and Her Witnesses*. Trans. by Edward Hyams. London, 1964.

_____. *The Retrial of Joan of Arc; The Evidence at the Trial for Her Rehabilitation, 1450–1456*. Trans. by J.M. Cohen. London, 1955.

Petersen, Karen, and J. J. Wilson. *Women Artists: Recognition and Reappraisal from the Early Middle Ages to the Twentieth Century*. New York, 1976.

Petroff, Elizabeth A. *Medieval Women's Visionary Literature*. New York and Oxford, 1986.

Phillips, Dayton. *Beguines in Medieval Strasbourg: A Study of the Social Aspect of Beguine Life*. Ann Arbor, MI, 1941.

Phillips, Tom, trans. and illus. *Dante's Inferno: The First Part of the Divine Comedy of Dante Alighieri*. London, 1985.

Pisan (Pizan), Christine de. *The Book of the City of Ladies*. Trans. by Jeffrey Richards. New York, 1982.

Porète, Marguerite. *Le Miroir des simples âmes*, ed. by R. Guarnieri. Rome, 1961.

Post, John. "The King's Peace." *The Making of Britain*, ed. by L. Smith (1985), 149–162.

Power, Eileen. *Medieval English Nunneries*. Cambridge, England, 1922.

_____. *Medieval Women*. Cambridge, 1975.

_____. "The Position of Women." *The Legacy of the Middle Ages*, ed. by C. G. Crump and E. F. Jacob (1962), 401–435.

_____, and M. M. Postan. *Studies in English Trade in the Fifteenth Century*. London, 1933.

Powicke, Sir Frederick M. *The Christian Life in the Middle Ages and Other Essays*. Oxford, 1935.

Prescott, Orville. *Princes of the Renaissance*. New York, 1969.

Previte-Orton, C.W. *Outlines of Medieval History*. New York, 1965.

_____. *The Shorter Medieval History*, vol. I. Cambridge, England, 1952.

Provost, William. "The English Religious Enthusiast: Margery Kempe." *Medieval Women Writers*, ed. by K. Wilson (1984), 297–319.

Radice, Betty. "The French Scholar-Lover: Heloise." *Medieval Women Writers*, ed. by K. Wilson (1989), 90–108.

Ragg, Laura M. *The Women Artists of Bologna*. London, 1907.

Ranke-Heinemann, Uta. *Eunuchs for Heaven: The Catholic Church and Sexuality*. Trans. by John Brownjohn. London, 1990.

Rashdall, Hastings. *The Universities of Europe in the Middle Ages*. Oxford, 1936.

Razi, Zvi. "Family, Land, and the Village Community in Later Medieval England." *Past and Present* #93 (Nov. 1981), 3–36.

Reeves, Marjorie. *The Influence of Prophecy in the Later Middle Ages: A Study in Joachimism*. Oxford, 1969.

Revelations of Mechtild de Magdeburg ("*The Flowing Light of the Godhead*.") Trans. by Lucy Menzies. New York and London, 1953.

Reyerson, Kathryn L. "Women in Business in Medieval Montpellier." *Women and Work in Pre-Industrial Europe*, ed. by Barbara Hanawalt (1986), 117–144.

Reynolds, Susan. *Kingdoms and Communities in Western Europe, 900–1300*. Oxford, 1984.

Richards, Jeffrey. *Sex, Dissidence, and Damnation: Minority Groups in the Middle Ages*. London and New York, 1991.

Riddle, John M. "Theory and Practice in Medieval Medicine." *Viator: Medieval and Renaissance Studies* 5 (1974), 157–184.

Riemer, Eleonor S. "Women, Dowries and Capital Investment in Thirteenth Century Siena." *The Marriage Bargain: Women and Dowries in*

European History. Women and History 10, ed. by Marion Kaplan (NY, 1985), 59–79.

Robbins, Rossell Hope. *Encyclopedia of Witchcraft and Demonology*. New York, 1959.

Robertson, D. W. Jr. *Chaucer's London*. New York, 1968.

Robinson, James Hardy. *Readings in European History*, vol. I. Boston, 1904.

Rokseth, Yvonne. "Les Femmes musiciennes du XII au XIV siècle." *Romania* 61 (October 1935), 464–480.

Rolle, Richard. *The Fire of Love and the Mending of Life or the Rule of Loving*, ed. by Rev. Ralph Harvey. Early English Text Society. London, 1896.

Roncière, Charles de la. "Tuscan Notables on the Eve of the Renaissance." *A History of Private Life*, vol. 2, ed. by G. Duby (1988), 157–309.

Rose, Mary Beth. *Women in the Middle Ages and Renaissance*. Syracuse, NY, 1986.

Rosenthal, Joel T. *Nobles and the Noble Life, 1295–1500*. London, 1976.

_____. *The Purchase of Paradise: Gift Giving and the Aristocracy, 1307–1485*. London, 1972.

Ross, Alan S. C. "The Assize of Bread." *Economic History Review*, 2nd series, vol. IX, #1 (1956), 332–342.

Ross, James B., and Mary Martin McLaughlin, eds. *The Portable Medieval Reader*. New York, 1949.

Rossiaud, Jacques. *Medieval Prostitution*. Trans. by Lydia G. Cochrane. New York, 1988.

Rowland, Beryl., ed. and trans. *Medieval Woman's Guide to Health: The First English Gynaecological Handbook*. London, 1981.

Rowling, Marjorie. *Everyday Life in Medieval Times*. London, 1968.

Rubin, Stanley. *Medieval English Medicine*. London, 1974.

Ruether, Rosemary, and Eleanor McLaughlin, eds. *Women of Spirit: Female Leadership in the Jewish and Christian Traditions*. New York, 1979.

Russell, Jeffrey B. *Witchcraft in the Middle Ages*. Ithaca, NY, and London, 1972.

Sabine, Ernest L. "Butchering in Mediaeval London." *Speculum* 8 (1933), 335–353.

Sacchetti. "Fashions in Italy." *The Portable Medieval Reader*, ed. by J. Ross and M. McLaughlin (1949), 167–169.

Saenger, Paul. "Silent Reading: Its Impact on Late Medieval Script and Society." *Viator: Medieval and Renaissance Studies* 13 (1982), 367–414.

Salzman, L. F. *English Industries of the Middle Ages*. Oxford, 1923.

_____. *English Life in the Middle Ages*. London, 1966.

Sass, Lorna. *To the King's Taste: Richard II's Book of Feasts and Recipes Adapted for Modern Cooking*. New York, 1975.

Savage, Henry L. "Hunting in the Middle Ages." *Speculum* 8 (1933), 30–41.

Schimmelpfennig, Bernhard. "Ex Fornicatione Nati: Studies on the Position of Priests' Sons from the Twelfth to the Fourteenth Century." *Studies in Medieval and Renaissance History* n.s. 2 (1979), 1–50.

Schulenburg, Jane Tibbetts. "Female Sanctity: Public and Private Roles, ca. 500–1100." *Women and Power in the Middle Ages*, ed. by M. Erler and M. Kowalewski (1988), 102–125.

_____. "Sexism and the Celestial Gynaeceum." *Journal of Medieval History* 4, #2 (June 1978), 117–134.

_____. "Women's Monastic Communities, 500–1100: Patterns of Expansion and Decline." *Sisters and Workers in the Middle Ages*, ed. by J. Bennett et al. (1989), 208–239.

Scofield, Cora L. *The Life and Reign of Edward the Fourth*. 2 vols. London, 1923.

Searle, Eleanor. "Seigneurial Control of Women's Marriage: The Antecedents and Function of Merchet in England." *Past and Present* #82 (February 1979), 3–43.

Select Cases in the Court of King's Bench under Edward I, vol. I. Ed. by G. O. Sayles. Selden Society, vol. 55. London, 1936.

Shahar, Shulamith. *The Fourth Estate: A History of Women in the Middle Ages*. London and New York, 1983.

Shank, Michael H. "A Female University Student in Late Medieval Krakow." *Signs: Journal of Women in Culture and Society* 12, #2 (1987), 373–380.

Sheehan, Michael M. "The Influence of Canon Law on the Property Rights of Married Women in England." *Mediaeval Studies* 25 (1963), 109–124.

Sherman, Claire Richter. "The Queen in Charles V's Coronation Book: Jeanne de Bourbon and the Ordo ad reginam benedicendam." *Viator: Medieval and Renaissance Studies* 8 (1977), 255–298.

Sizeranne, Robert de la. *Beatrice d'Este and Her Court*. Trans. by N. Fleming. London and New York, 1926.

Smith, Lesley M., ed. *The Making of Britain: The Middle Ages*. New York, 1985.

Smith, Rhea Marsh. *Spain: A Modern History*. Ann Arbor, MI, 1965.

Snow, Joseph. "The Spanish Love Poet: Florencia Pinar." *Medieval Women Writers*, ed. by K. Wilson (1984), 320–332.

Somerset, Anne. *Ladies-in-Waiting*. New York, 1984.

Sommerville, C. John. *The Rise and Fall of Childhood*. London, 1982.

Southern, R. N. *The Making of the Middle Ages*. London, 1967.

Spence, Keith. *Cathedrals and Abbeys of England and Wales*. New York, 1984.

St. Aubyn, Giles. *Year of Three Kings: 1483*. New York, 1983.

St. Catherine of Siena as Seen in Her Letters (*Letters of Catherine Benincasa*). Trans. and ed. by Vida D. Scudder. New York and London, 1906.

Strayer, Joseph R. *The Albigensian Crusades*. New York, 1971.

Stuard, Susan M. "Fashion's Captives: Medieval Women in French Historiography." *Women in Medieval History and Historiography*, ed. by S. M. Stuard (1987), 59–80.

_____. "A New Dimension? American Scholars Contribute Their Perspective." *Women in Medieval History and Historiography*, ed. by S. M. Stuard (1987), 81–99.

_____, ed. *Women in Medieval History and Historiography*. Philadelphia, 1987.

_____, ed. *Women in Medieval Society*. Philadelphia, 1976.

Summers, Montague. *The Geography of Witchcraft*. New York, 1970.

Szarmach, Paul E., ed. *An Introduction to the Medieval Mystics of Europe*. Albany, NY, 1984.

Talbot, C. H., and E. A. Hammond. *The Medical Practitioners in Medieval England: A Biographical Register*. London, 1965.

Tannahill, Reay. *Food in History*. New York, 1973.

_____. *Sex in History*. New York, 1980.

Tanner, Norman P., ed. *Heresy Trials in the Diocese of Norwich*. London, 1977.

Thièbaux, Marcelle, trans. and ed. *The Writings of Medieval Women*. New York and London, 1987.

Thompson, James Westfall. *The Literacy of the Laity in the Middle Ages*. New York, 1960.

Thompson, Sally. "The Problem of the Cistercian Nuns in the Twelfth and Early Thirteenth Centuries." *Women in Medieval Society*, ed. by S. M. Stuard (1976), 227–252.

Thrupp, Sylvia. *The Merchant Class of Medieval London*. Chicago, 1948.

Trexler, Richard C. "Infanticide in Florence: New Sources and First Results." *History of Childhood Quarterly* 1, #1 (1973), 98–116.

_____. "Measures against Water Pollution in Fifteenth-Century Florence." *Viator: Medieval and Renaissance Studies* 5 (1974), 455–467.

_____, ed. *Persons in Groups: Social Behavior as Identity Formation in Medieval and Renaissance Europe*. Binghamton, NY, 1985.

Trotula. *The Diseases of Women*. Trans. by Elizabeth Mason-Hohl. Los Angeles, 1940.

Tuchman, Barbara W. *A Distant Mirror: The Calamitous Fourteenth Century*. New York, 1978.

Two Fifteenth Century Cookbooks. Ed. by Thomas Austin. London, 1888.

Tyerman, Christopher. *England and the Crusades, 1095–1588.* Chicago and London, 1988.

Uitz, Erika. *Women in the Medieval Towns and Cities: The Legend of Good Women.* Mount Kisco, NY, 1990.

Underhill, Evelyn. *The Mystics of the Church.* New York, 1964.

Valous, Guy de. *Le Patriciat Lyonnais aux XIII et XIV siècles.* Paris, 1973.

Verdier, Philippe. "Woman in the Marginalia of Gothic Manuscripts and Related Works." *The Role of Women in the Middle Ages,* ed. by R. T. Morewedge (1975), 121–187.

Vernadsky, George. *Kievan Russia.* Vol. II of *History of Russia.* New Haven, CT, 1948.

_____. *The Mongols and Russia.* Vol. III of *History of Russia.* New Haven, CT, 1953.

_____. *Russia at the Dawn of the Modern Age.* Vol. IV of *History of Russia.* New Haven, CT, 1959.

Vinogradoff, Paul. "Customary Law." *The Legacy of the Middle Ages,* ed. by C. G. Crump and E. F. Jacob (1962), 287–320.

Vitalis, Orderic. *The Ecclesiastical History of Orderic Vitalis,* vols. I–IV. Trans. and ed. by M. Chibnall. Oxford, 1969.

Wakefield, Walter L., and Austin P. Evans. *Heresies of the High Middle Ages.* New York, 1969.

Walker, Sue Sheridan. "Proof of Age of Feudal Heirs in Medieval England." *Mediaeval Studies* 35 (1973), 306–323.

Warren, Ann K. *Anchorites and Their Patrons in Medieval England.* Berkeley, CA, 1985.

Warren, W. L. *Henry II.* Berkeley and Los Angeles, 1973.

Wason, Betty. *Cooks, Gluttons and Gourmets: A History of Cookery.* New York, 1962.

Weiss, Michael. "The Castellan: The Early Career of Hubert de Burgh." *Viator: Medieval and Renaissance Studies* 5 (1974), 235–252.

Wemple, Suzanne. *Women in Frankish Society: Marriage and the Cloister, 500–800.* Philadelphia, 1981.

Wensky, Margret. "Women's Guilds in Cologne in the Later Middle Ages." *Journal of European Economic History* 11, #3 (1982), 631–650.

Wentersdorf, Karl P. "The Clandestine Marriages of the Fair Maid of Kent." *Journal of Medieval History* 5 (1979), 203–231.

Werveke, H. Van. "Industrial Growth in the Middle Ages: The Cloth Industry in Flanders." *Economic History Review,* 2nd series, vol. VI, #3 (1954), 237–245.

Wessley, Stephen. "Female Imagery: A Clue to the Role of Joachim's Order of Fiore." *Women of the Medieval World,* ed. by J. Kirshner and S. Wemple (1985), 161–178.

Wickham, Glynne. *The Medieval Theatre.* 3rd ed. Cambridge, England, 1987.

Wiesner, Merry E. *Working Women in Renaissance Germany.* New Brunswick, NJ, 1986.

Willard, Charity Cannon. "A Fifteenth Century View of Women's Role in Medieval Society: Christine de Pizan's 'Livre des Trois Vertus'." *The Role of Women in the Middle Ages,* ed. by R. T. Morewedge (1975), 90–120.

_____. "The Franco-Italian Professional Writer: Christine de Pizan." *Medieval Women Writers,* ed. by K. Wilson (1984), 333–363.

Wilson, Katharina M., ed. *Medieval Women Writers.* Athens, GA, 1984.

_____. "The Saxon Canoness: Hrotsvit of Gandersheim." *Medieval Women Writers,* ed. by K. Wilson (1984), 30–63.

Wolf, Leonard. *Bluebeard; The Life and Crimes of Gilles de Rais.* New York, 1980.

Wood, Charles T. *The Age of Chivalry: Manners and Morals, 1000–1450.* New York, 1970.

_____. "The Doctors' Dilemma: Sin, Salvation and the Menstrual Cycle in Medieval Thought." *Speculum* 56 (1981), 710–727.

_____. "Queens, Queans and Kingship: An Inquiry into Theories of Royal Legitimacy in Late Medieval England and France." *Order and Innovation in the Middle Ages,* ed. by W. Jordan et al. (1976), 385–400.

Wrightman, W. E. *The Lacy Family in England and Normandy, 1066–1194.* Oxford, 1966.

Wylie, James Hamilton. *History of England under Henry the Fourth.* London, 1969.

Zarnecki, George. "The Contributions of the Orders." *The Flowering of the Middle Ages,* ed. by Joan Evans (1976), 41–80.

INDEX

INDEX

Only some of the most important subjects and people, and those mentioned more than once within the text, are listed below.